# Praise for *Beyond Performance 2.0*

"*Beyond Performance 2.0* is the change management manifesto for the modern-day organization. Keller and Schaninger pair evidence-based support, case studies, and insights into human behavior with a clear roadmap to creating sustainable change in any company. This is a must-read for CEOs and any leader that aspires to be a catalyst for change in their organization."

**—Alain Bejjani, Chief Executive Officer,
Majid Al Futtaim Holding**

"Even if you have great momentum, you can't stay ahead without acceleration. This is where Keller and Schaninger's *Beyond Performance 2.0* comes in—it combines left-brained and right-brained approaches to provide a reliable methodology for accelerating the delivery of results at scale. This isn't just a play book, it's a game changer."

**—Greg Case, CEO, Aon**

"At a time where management books are plentiful yet largely vacuous, *Beyond Performance 2.0* truly stands out from the pack. Keller and Schaninger have created a user-friendly roadmap to organizational change that is evidence based, profoundly insightful, and practical. I have learned so many of these lessons the hard way! You don't have to, because it is all here."

**—Hussain Dawood, Chairman, Engro Corporation**

"A must-read for senior leaders. Even the most skeptical will be won over by the pragmatic, data and research driven approach to improving performance by also giving equal weight to improving organizational health. From my experience, the application of the Five Frames methodology described in this book will give your organization a tailor-made prescription for executing successful large-scale change."

**—Lynn Elsenhans, former CEO, Sunoco**

"Scott and Bill's new book provides the framework and proof that investing in and integrating the people, processes, and cultural elements of organizational transformation are essential to achieve enduring and inspiring impact."

**—Michael Fisher, CEO, Cincinnati Children's
Hospital Medical Center**

"In our experience, the approach described in *Beyond Performance 2.0* is the best one to follow if you want to thrive as a business and as an agent of change for your people and the community around you"

**—Carlos Labarthe, Chairman, former CEO,
and Co-founder, Gentera**

"Keller and Schaninger offer leaders a clear, effective framework for optimizing organizational performance and health. This work of "where do we want to go" to "how do we continue to improve" is never finished. But the journey is made easier with this insightful guide."

**—Satya Nadella, CEO, Microsoft**

"The approach and methods of *Beyond Performance 2.0* apply well beyond the business world. Leaders of any large or growing organization will benefit from this thoroughly researched update, and its clear and direct lessons will have near-immediate impact. Scott Keller and Bill Schaninger have crafted a powerful guidebook that ought to be read and implemented on a grand scale. It is for the bold, engaged and tenacious leader, and for those who aspire to be one."

**—Admiral Eric Olson, 8th Commander,**
**U.S. Special Operations Command (Retired)**

"In *Beyond Performance 2.0*, Keller and Schaninger combine rigorous data analysis and their own extensive experience to provide a step-by-step method for creating major change in any organization. If you're hoping to build a workplace that can nimbly adapt to changing times, this is the ultimate how-to guide."

**—Daniel H. Pink, author of *When*, *To Sell Is Human*, and *Drive***

"Many companies fail to truly change, even when it's essential both to survive and thrive. Keller and Schaninger treat the culture topic with same degree of rigor and discipline as strategic and operational elements. My view: if you're looking for radical change, to make bold moves, and to mobilize leadership and the entire workforce in doing so, *Beyond Performance 2.0* is a must-read."

**—Frans van Houten, CEO, Philips**

"Both organizational health AND performance need to be measured and managed rigorously. In the VUCA world, enterprises need the continuous reshaping of both business portfolio AND organization transformation. *Beyond Performance 2.0* provides inspiring insights and practical guidance to make it happen!"

**—Liang Yu, Chairman, China Vanke**

# Beyond Performance 2.0

# Beyond Performance 2.0

## A Proven Approach to Leading Large-Scale Change

**SCOTT KELLER**
**BILL SCHANINGER**

**WILEY**

Published by John Wiley & Sons, Inc., Hoboken, New Jersey.
Published simultaneously in Canada.

***Library of Congress Cataloging-in-Publication Data:***

ISBN 978-1-119-59665-3 (Hardcover)
ISBN 978-1-119-59668-4 (ePDF)
ISBN 978-1-119-59666-0 (ePub)

Printed in the United States of America
V10016607_122619

# Contents

# Foreword

In my 35 years of observing top companies, CEOs, and boards, there's one challenge that I've seen consistently vex leaders: how to make large-scale change happen successfully and sustainably. In far too many cases, what started with bold aspirations ended up delivering little in terms of results. This mattered less in a time when industry structures, physical assets, and privileged relationships enabled leaders to win by being good at "running the company." In today's volatile, fast-paced, and ever-increasingly competitive marketplace, however, few if any leaders will succeed unless they also know how to "change the company."

In *Beyond Performance 2.0: A Proven Approach to Leading Large-Scale Change*, Scott Keller and Bill Schaninger tackle that critical challenge head-on—and do so with great energy and deep insight. I look for three things, in particular, in my reading and my own writing. First, I want to see something different than all the advice already out there, advice that too often hasn't helped leaders improve their odds of success. Second, I want to see ideas that leaders can put into practice on Monday morning. Finally, I look for concepts founded on a deep fact base.

Not surprisingly, given that the authors are senior partners and leading practitioners at McKinsey & Company, *Beyond Performance 2.0* is packed with data and richly researched, and to that extent truly delivers on the word "proven" in its title. But as I read Scott and Bill's book, I was delighted to find even more. For one thing, there is a simplicity to their prescription that I find appealing—and in no way simplistic. The core notion is that successful change happens when leaders put as much emphasis on boosting the health of the organization as they do on improving its financial performance. This big idea resonates extremely well with my experience advising CEOs in times of corporate transformation.

What I wasn't necessarily expecting from McKinsey & Company senior partners was to see such full and profound treatment of the human side of the change equation. As Scott and Bill put it in their introduction, "At the end of the day, organizations don't change, people do. Take the people away and the life-blood of the organization is gone." In their five-stage roadmap showing how to put equal emphasis on performance and health, they draw on the best of behavioral psychology and speak to how to capture hearts and minds in practical terms.

This combination of hard science, practical experience, and insight into the human factor is rare and hugely valuable. I can say with confidence that, if you are facing a large-scale change challenge, *Beyond Performance 2.0* is an essential read.

Ram Charan
January 2019

**Ram Charan** *is a world-renowned business adviser, author, and speaker. He has authored over 25 books that have sold more than 2 million copies, including numerous* Wall Street Journal *and* New York Times *best-sellers.*

# Introduction

# Excellence Found

What is the greatest invention of all time? In our view, it isn't the wheel, it is the organization: people working together toward a common goal. Organizations can achieve feats that go far beyond anything that individuals can accomplish alone. As each successive generation finds better ways of working together, it performs at levels that could barely have been imagined a few decades earlier. And when there are improvements in the effectiveness of our organizations—whether they be private enterprises, governments, public agencies, charities, community groups, political parties, or religious bodies—these gains translate into benefits for society as a whole. Innovations such as mass production, public transport, space travel, the internet, and the mapping of the human genome are all products of human organizations.

When we wrote the first edition of *Beyond Performance* almost a decade ago, we emphasized what it takes to lead and manage an effective organization (a "healthy organization"). We then outlined the change management needed to get there (the "Five Frames of Performance and Health"). In this, the second edition, we've chosen to flip the emphasis. Why? Well, quite frankly, because you—our readers who lead organizations—told us to! We've received countless e-mails, phone calls, and personal outreaches indicating that struggling change programs had been unlocked by applying the Five Frames of Performance and Health. Further, new change programs that employed the Five Frames of Performance and Health as their change methodology from the outset were delivering results far beyond expectations.

The feedback seemed almost too good to be true, based on the history of the field of change management. As many readers will no doubt be aware, in 1996, Harvard Business School professor John Kotter published one of the best-selling books on the topic, *Leading Change*. In it, he reported that only 30 percent of all change programs succeed and offered an eight-step process for managing change. The popularity of his work triggered an explosion of

1

thinking on the topic. In the 15 years that followed, over 25,000 books were published, hundreds of business schools built change management into their curricula, and many organizations created change management functions. By 2011, when the first version of *Beyond Performance* was published, one would have expected success rates to be much higher. The facts, however, were clear: multiple studies, including our own, had shown that the odds of leading a successful change program remained unchanged: just 30 percent.[1] The field of change management, despite its prolific output, hadn't changed success rates.

Before we go on, we want to be clear that we are not intending to say that all of the work done by many brilliant people wasn't good and helpful. In fact, it's possible that maintaining 30 percent success rates in a rapidly changing external environment is proof that the state of the art has been continually advanced, and it's also possible—and even likely—that the two variables are intrinsically linked (the more change programs succeed, the more the overall pace of change in the world at large increases). Our goal wasn't to unravel these complex dynamics at play, however, it was simply to offer a better way. Why? Well, put it this way: If we needed to get to London from New York for an important meeting and upon boarding the plane the pilot said, "Welcome aboard, there's a 30 percent chance we'll make it as far as London today…," we certainly wouldn't stay in our seats and discuss why—we'd disembark and catch a different flight with better odds!

## Flipping the Odds of Success

Almost five years after *Beyond Performance* was written, we felt enough time had passed that we could test whether the positive messages we were hearing reflected a broader reality. We conducted a global survey of 1,713 executives who had been part of at least one large-scale change program in the past five years. The sample represented a full range of regions, industries, company sizes, functional specialties, and tenures. The results spoke for themselves: 79 percent of those organizations who fully implemented the recommended Five Frames of Performance and Health methodology reported change success.[2]

We were obviously thrilled to see these results. First and foremost, however, we credit them to the determined leaders of the change programs in question—having a process and tools laid out is one thing; getting the job done is entirely another. As London Business School professor and influential management thinker Gary Hamel said, "Changing things at scale is never easy: the endeavor is always complex, perilous, and gut-wrenching."[3] William C. Taylor, the co-founder of *Fast Company*, agrees: "The truth is, the work of making deep-seated change in long-established organizations is the hardest work there is."[4]

We also attribute the results to the many members of McKinsey's Global Leadership and Organization Practice, whose work and insights shaped our methodology. We also add to our acknowledgments the experience and research of innumerable leaders around the world and throughout history whose thinking has informed our methodology—within the Five Frames there are numerous tools and approaches that we in no way claim to be our own. We have endeavored to be students of all that has come before us, and as such, the results are also a validation of what in many ways is our life's work. Both of us have been part of the group that has directed the research that led to this book since its inception almost 20 years ago, and have spent our careers applying the approaches as consultants to organizations around the world. True to Malcolm Gladwell's perspective on what it takes to become an expert, by this time in our careers we've both done our 10,000 hours of practice![5]

If you are a leader who wants to beat the dismal odds and successfully make change happen at scale, this book is for you. If you also want to improve how your organization is managed and led so that it has the capability to *continuously change* to stay ahead of the competition, this book is also for you. What's more, the concepts, approaches, and tools apply to any human system, whether a public company, family-owned business, professional services firm (we at McKinsey & Company take our own medicine!), public sector body, activist group, nongovernment organization, or social enterprise. They also apply to virtually every type of change program, whether related to a company-wide transformation, marketing, sales, technology, operations, finance, risk, culture, talent, and so on.

How can it apply so broadly? Simple: At the end of the day, organizations don't change, people do. Take the people away and the life-blood of the organization is gone, leaving only the skeleton of infrastructure: buildings, systems, inventory. If a change program requires *people* to think and behave differently, the Five Frames of Performance and Health is proven to be the best approach available to leaders.

## What Sets This Book Apart

The central premise of our work is that leaders should put equal emphasis on the health elements of making change happen as they do the performance elements. While these will be described fully in the chapters to come, a simple analogy to a manufacturing company helps explain in brief. The performance elements of a change program relate to the changes that need to be made to improve how the company "buys, makes, and sells": how will it *buy* its raw materials, *make* them into products, and *sell* them into the market more efficiently and effectively? The health elements, on the other hand, relate to the changes that need to be made to how it "aligns, executes, and renews": How does it *align* the full organization on a shared direction, *execute* the work that needs to be done with minimum internal friction (e.g., from politics, bureaucracy, silos, and so on), and rapidly adapt and *renew* itself in response to an ever-changing environment?

In answering these questions, there are at least five things that set this book apart.

1. **Research and rigor behind the recommendations.** The world of management is rife with opinion and conjecture. In writing this book, we don't just draw on our own experience as management consultants, but ensure that our arguments are as objective and fact-based as possible. That isn't to say that there aren't plenty of other business books out there that do have a strong research base. One of the best-selling and most influential business books of all time, Tom Peters and Robert Waterman's *In Search of Excellence: Lessons from America's Best-Run Companies,* was based on a study of 43 of the Fortune 500 list of top-performing companies in the United States. Another highly influential bestseller, Jim Collins and Jerry Porras's 1994 book *Built to Last,* analyzed patterns among 18 successful companies. This book, however, draws on a far broader array of evidence. The first edition of *Beyond Performance* already represented the most extensive research effort ever undertaken in the field of organizational effectiveness and change management, and this edition has been fully updated with almost another decade's worth of data including:

   - Data from over five million Organizational Health Index survey respondents from more than 2,000 organizations across the globe.

   - Data from five biennial *McKinsey Quarterly* Five Frames of Performance and Health–related surveys sent to our 32,000-member Global Survey Panel.

   - Data and learning from more than 1,000 clients served by McKinsey on engagements specifically related to performance and health.

   - In-depth reviews of more than 900 top-tier management books and articles from academic journals.

   - Data from McKinsey's "Wave" implementation tracking software solution that has been used by over 600 clients globally.

   - More than 150 change leaders' seminars, each bringing together 20 to 40 leaders from different industries for two days to share their experiences and insights.

- In-depth, one-on-one interviews with over 30 CEOs and other senior executives who shared their personal experiences of leading change and driving performance

- Close working relationships with five eminent scholars who helped to challenge and augment our findings

2. **Comprehensiveness and pragmatism of the tools.** Many leaders have told us this is what they value most. It allows them to bring the same degree of rigor, discipline, and measurement to managing the "soft" side of change as they have for the "hard" aspects. Whereas in our first edition, we provided a mix of concepts and practical steps, here you'll find a clear and specific roadmap for putting equal emphasis on performance and health. We walk you step-by-step through how to set your change aspirations, assess how ready your organization is to change, develop a powerful plan to move your organization from where it is today to where you want it to be, master what it takes to implement this plan successfully, and transition from being in change-program mode to a state of continuous improvement. Every aspect of leading change is covered in depth, with specific tools, methodologies, and real-life examples that make it easy to quickly distill what the most important and practical implications are for your organization. We've also incorporated learnings from various advances in the field of management from the past 10 years, for example, agile, big data and analytics, and digital transformations.

3. **Uniqueness of the solutions.** Many companies have analyzed how Southwest Airlines delivers low-cost air travel, the Ritz-Carlton sets standards in customer service, Apple drives continuous innovation, or Netflix creates a culture of empowerment. And yet, few, if any, are able to replicate their success based on these analyses. Instead of suggesting you copy what other organizations do, we provide a robust process by which you can find the right answer for your organization given its context: its history, the capabilities and passions of its people, its external environment, and its aspirations. The answer will be unique to your situation and one your competitors can't copy (or attempt to copy at their peril). In short, we help you create the "ultimate competitive advantage."

4. **Proof that the approach works in practice as promised.** We've already shared the data that shows using the Five Frames of Performance

and Health methodology flips your odds of change success, moving them from 30 to 79 percent. The facts also indicate that you'll deliver on average 1.8 times higher impact from your change efforts than otherwise.[6] Furthermore, companies who use the methodology, not just to deliver a successful change program but to become top quartile in their overall organizational health, deliver on average 3 times higher total returns to shareholders (TRS), 2.2 times EBITDA margin, 1.5 times growth in net income/sales, and on that order of magnitude, higher results on every comparable measure we've been able to test across industries (a total of 15 so far).[7] As Sir William Castell, former chairman of the Wellcome Trust, puts it, "Healthy organizations get things done quicker, better, and with more impact than unhealthy ones."[8]

5. **Increases an organization's ongoing capacity for change.** This is much more than a book about change management. By applying the Five Frames of Performance and Health in your change program, you are not just increasing your odds of success, but also fundamentally increasing your organization's capability and capacity to continuously improve after your change program objectives have been achieved. Gary Hamel put it well in his foreword to our first edition, "*Beyond Performance* is far more than a guide to leading a successful change program. It's a manifesto for a new way of thinking about [how] organizations … become, fundamentally, pro-change."[9] It's not just about getting ahead; it's about staying ahead.

## Why It Matters

That the pace of change in business is on an ever-increasing trajectory isn't new, but it is most certainly true. Consider how long an average company from the S&P 500 stays in the index. In 1958, it was estimated to be 61 years; in 1980, 25 years; and in 2011, 17 years.[10] A S&P 500 company in this decade is being replaced once every two weeks, which translates to roughly 75 percent of today's firms being superseded by newcomers in the index in the next 10 years.[11] There are only 60 companies today that appear on the original list of 500 when it was first compiled just over 60 years ago. Sixty years from now it's unlikely any of the companies that exist today will remain in prominence. Yes, we are saying the likes of Amazon, ExxonMobil, Berkshire Hathaway, and so on are all at risk. Seem hard to believe? No doubt the employees and customers of companies such as Blockbuster, Compaq, Kodak, Circuit City, Enron, General Foods, Pan Am, WorldCom, Digital Equipment Corporation, Lehman

Brothers, Arthur Andersen, and British Leyland, during their prime, felt just as invincible.

Need more convincing? Let's go back to Peters and Waterman's *In Search of Excellence* and Collins and Porras's *Built to Last*. It's revealing to look at what has become of these "excellent" companies. Ten years after the latter was published, 20 percent of the companies featured in these books no longer existed, 46 percent were struggling, and only 33 percent remained high performers.[12] Not all of these changes in standing can be attributed to the companies themselves, of course. As Chris Bradley, Martin Hirt, and Sven Smit point out in their book, *Strategy Beyond the Hockey Stick*, a portion of business results are driven by macroeconomic forces, industry attractiveness, and sheer luck.[13] But they are also driven by what leaders choose to do and not do (in particular, what Bradley, Hirt, and Smit refer to as "big moves," all of which require exceptional change management to deliver the desired impact) and the way they lead, which are things under every leader's control. While the homage to Charles Darwin's findings that says, "The fittest win out at the expense of their rivals because they succeed in adapting themselves best to their environment" (i.e., they make change happen), may have become something of a cliché in management literature, that's only because of how right it is when it comes to success in the business world.

If we look beyond the world of commerce to society at large, the ability to make change happen at scale has never been more important. In the political process, for instance, leaders committed to change continue to attract unprecedented levels of public engagement. When we wrote the introduction to our first edition, we noted how leaders around the world had run on platforms such as "Change we need," promising massive overhauls of public sector practices and outcomes. Almost a decade later, little has changed. In the United States, the winning election narrative promised to "make America great again" in as sharp and acerbic a tone as the country had ever seen.[14] In France, Sarkozy's successors, François Hollande in 2012, and Emmanuel Macron in 2017, both focused on large-scale change in their respective campaigns: "le changement," or *the change* and "en marche" or *moving forward*.[15] In Malaysia, the new prime minister Mahathir Mohammed vowed to make changes that will fight corruption and unite the country.[16] Virtually everywhere you turn, you'll see similar messages. In Canada, Prime Minister Justin Trudeau ran on the promise of bringing "real change" to the country.[17] In New Zealand, Jacinda Arden promised "a government of change."[18] In Mexico, President Andrés Manuel López Obrador won in a landslide victory with promises of great reform.[19]

Outside politics, nongovernmental and not-for-profit organizations continue to tackle key cross-border challenges such as sustaining the environment and helping the developing world break the cycles of poverty, corruption, and inadequate education. Meanwhile, numerous factors continue to drive widespread change globally: the historic shift in economic and labor force growth from the developed to the developing world, the rise of global energy demands with an uncertain supply source, the rapid expansion of the global consumer class, changes in global demographics with an aging world population, the rise of new networks of hitherto unimaginable complexity for communication and trade, the increasingly urgent challenge to balance economic growth with environmental sustainability, and the race to increase productivity through accelerated technology and the knowledge economy.[20]

The way we respond to these business and societal challenges will have a profound effect on all our futures. What are the odds of their being successful? And what will be the consequences if they aren't? What will be the social costs? And who will bear them?

## Our Greatest Hope

If this book helps you lead a more successful change program, our writing it has been worth it. If it goes further, and helps you create an organization whose capacity to continuously change enables it to thrive long into the future, we'll be delighted. If this book helps people make faster progress in tackling the major social and political issues of our time, it will have achieved more than we could have hoped for.

The reason why we wrote it, however, goes much deeper. According to Gallup, roughly 1.3 billion people work for a full-time employer (i.e., they are part of an organization of some sort).[21] These people spend half or more of their waking hours at work. In their remaining time outside of work, they are spending fewer and fewer hours pursuing traditional activities involving family, community, or religious institutions than ever before (in political scientist Robert Putnam's parlance, they are "Bowling Alone").[22] Taken together, this means the workplace is taking on an increasing role as a source of identity, belonging, and meaning for us as a human race.

Workplaces that are characterized by any or all of competing agendas and conflict (no alignment on direction), politics and bureaucracy (low quality of execution), and where work is "just a job" (low sense of renewal), aren't just unhealthy for sustainably delivering bottom-line results—they are unhealthy for the human soul. As the Japanese proverb goes, "Vision without action is a daydream. Action without vision is a nightmare."

Healthy organizations, however, unleash human potential and uplift the human spirit. They inspire (aligning on a big, important goal), they create a sense of belonging (executing as one team), and they foster creativity and innovation (through a sense of renewal). Paraphrasing motivational speaker

Joel Barker's riff on the aforementioned Japanese proverb, healthy organizations "connect vision with action to change the world."

If this book's contents make their way into management practice at a scale that meaningfully reduces the frictional cost of human progress—that'd be our dream come true!

We don't claim to have all the answers, but at this point in our research efforts, we're more confident than ever that we do have insightful (beyond common sense) and pragmatic (readily applicable) advice, methodologies, and tools that work. They are battle tested and proven in practice. They will help you lead more successful change programs and simultaneously create a healthy organization that is able to continuously adapt and therefore thrive long into the future. With the benefit of another decade of research and practice under our belts, we have observed so many successes in so many industries and from so many different starting points that we have no question change program success and sustained excellence are within reach for virtually any organization.

# PART I

# The Big Idea

# CHAPTER 1

# Performance and Health

When Neville Isdell took over as CEO of the Coca-Cola Company (TCCC), it was during troubled times. In his words, "These were dark days. Coke was losing market share. Nothing, it seemed—even thousands of layoffs—had been enough to get the company back on track."[1] TCCC's total return to shareholders stood at negative 26 percent, while its great rival PepsiCo delivered a handsome 46 percent return.

Isdell was the former vice chairman of the Coca-Cola Hellenic Bottling Company, then the world's second-largest bottler, and had enjoyed a long and successful career in the industry. Since retiring from that role, he had been living in Barbados, doing consulting work, and heading his own investment company. However, the opportunity to lead the transformation of one of the world's most iconic companies was a powerful lure. Isdell was clear-eyed about the challenge ahead as he recognized, "There were so many problems at Coke, a turnaround was risky, at best."[2] For the former rugby player, however, the game was on. He was soon installed in the executive suite at headquarters in Atlanta.

Isdell had a clear sense of what needed to be done. The company had to capture the full potential of the trademark Coca-Cola brand, grow other core brands in the noncarbonated soft drinks market, develop wellness platforms, and create adjacent businesses. These weren't particularly new ideas, however, and each of his predecessors had failed to make change happen at scale. Why would his tenure be any different?

Experience told him that focusing solely on "what" needed to get done—the new strategy and initiatives to support it—wouldn't get TCCC where it needed to be. Regardless of what direction he set, progress couldn't be made while morale was down, capabilities were lacking, partnerships with bottlers were strained, politics were rampant, and its once-strong performance culture was flagging.

Just a hundred days into his new role and having got his head around the current state of the organization, Isdell announced that TCCC would fall short of its meager third- and fourth-quarter target of 3 percent earnings growth. "The last time I checked, there was no silver bullet. That's not the way this business works," Isdell told analysts.[3] Later that year, TCCC announced that its third-quarter earnings had fallen by 24 percent, one of the worst quarterly drops in its history.

Having acknowledged the shortfall in performance, Isdell ploughed onward, launching what he called TCCC's "Manifesto for Growth" process. The goal was to outline a path to growth showing not just where the company aimed to go—its strategy—but what it would do to get there, and how people would work together differently along the way. And then, of course, to deliver on it. A number of working teams were set up to tackle performance-related issues such as what the company's targets and objectives would be and what capabilities it would require to achieve them. Another set of teams tackled organizational effectiveness-related issues: how to work better as a global team, how to improve planning, metrics, rewards, and people development to enable peak performance, and how to go back to "living our values." The whole effort was designed through a collaborative process that ensured all of the work being done remained integrated, and that the leaders of the organization would feel deep ownership and authorship of the answer. As Isdell explained, "The magic of the manifesto is that it was written in detail by the top 150 managers and had input from the top 400. Therefore, it was their program for implementation."[4]

It wasn't long before the benefit of Isdell's approach to making change happen became apparent. Within three years of having taken the role, shareholder value jumped from a negative return to a 20 percent positive return. Volume growth in units sold increased almost 10 percent to 21.4 billion, roughly equivalent to sales of an extra 105 million bottles of Coca-Cola per day. TCCC had amassed 13 billion-dollar brands, 30 percent more than Pepsi. Of the 16 market analysts following the company, 13 rated it as outperforming, and the other 3 as in line with expectations.

These impressive performance gains were matched by quantifiable improvements in people-related measures. Staff turnover at U.S. operations fell by almost 25 percent. Employee engagement scores saw a jump that researchers at the external survey firm hailed as an "unprecedented improvement" compared with scores at similar organizations. Other measures showed equally compelling gains: employees' views of leadership improved by 19 percent, and communication and awareness of goals increased from 17 percent to 76 percent. According to Isdell, however, the biggest change was a more qualitative one that could only be felt in the company's halls. Three years into the role, Isdell noted, "When I first arrived, about 80 percent of the people would cast their eyes to the ground. Now, I would say it's about 10 percent. Employees are engaged."[5]

When Isdell retired as CEO, he was handing over a healthy company that was performing well.

■ ■ ■

To what does Isdell credit the success of the turnaround? In his words, "Having taken the 'how' as seriously as the 'what.'"[6] Another way to put it would be that he put as much effort into the "soft stuff" as he did the "hard stuff." Others may prefer terminology such as talking about the balance between the "business and behavioral," "adaptive and technical," or "right brain and left brain." We believe the most helpful juxtaposition is to say that he put equal emphasis on performance as he did on health. But what specifically do we mean by this when it comes to leading large-scale change?

*Performance* is what an enterprise does to deliver improved results for its stakeholders in financial and operational terms. It's evaluated through measures such as net operating profit, return on capital employed, total returns to shareholders, net operating costs, and stock turn (and the relevant analogues to these in not-for-profit and service industries). As we shared in our introduction, a more memorable way to think about this is through the lens of a manufacturing company in which performance-oriented actions are those that improve how the organization *buys* raw materials, *makes* them into products, and *sells* them into the market to drive financial and operational results.

*Health* is how effectively an organization works together in pursuit of a common goal. It is evaluated in levels of accountability, motivation, innovation, coordination, external orientation, and so on. A more memorable way to think about health-related actions is that they are those that improve how an organization internally *aligns* itself, *executes* with excellence, and *renews* itself to sustainably achieve performance aspirations in its ever-changing external environment.

Make no mistake, leaders have a choice when it comes to where they put their time and energy in making change happen. *The big idea in delivering successful change at scale is that leaders should put equal emphasis on performance- and health-related efforts,* as illustrated in Exhibit 1.1.

Some reject this, as they aren't convinced there is a proven return on investment in the people-oriented aspects of driving change. Those who think this way have their heads well and truly in the sand as the facts to the contrary are incontrovertible, which we'll share in the next section. Other leaders accept and are even intuitively drawn to the concept, but simply have no idea how they'd fill 50 percent of their time taking action related to the soft stuff. Rest assured, they won't lack for answers once they understand the Five Frames of Performance and Health that will be introduced at the end of this chapter and expanded on throughout this book.

Exhibit 1.1

## The Big Idea

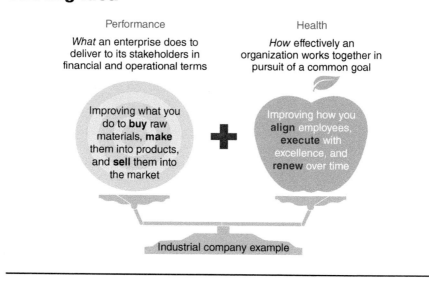

Performance

*What* an enterprise does to deliver to its stakeholders in financial and operational terms

Health

*How* effectively an organization works together in pursuit of a common goal

Improving what you do to **buy** raw materials, **make** them into products, and **sell** them into the market

**+**

Improving how you **align** employees, **execute** with excellence, and **renew** over time

Industrial company example

## The Value of Health

That organizational health matters is repeatedly borne out by the testimonies of successful leaders. Larry Bossidy, former chairman and CEO of Honeywell and Allied Signal, comments, "The soft stuff—people's beliefs and behaviors—is at least as important as the hard stuff. Making changes in strategy or structure by itself takes a company only so far."[7] Don Argus, retired chairman of BHP, suggests the key to success is to "mobilize and develop our people to unleash their competencies, creativity, and commitment to get things moving forward."[8] Sheikh Mohammed bin Essa Al-Khalifa, chief executive of Bahrain's Economic Development Board, concurs, "I always worried that we were going to have to spend millions to fix the educational system. But it turned out the solution wasn't the money. It was the soft things—which were usually harder."[9]

We could fill a chapter with similar quotes from virtually every successful leader we have spoken to. Such wisdom, however, is too often dismissed by leaders staring a big change challenge in the face: "Maybe that worked for them, but it won't work here" or "I'm sure that mattered later in the change program, but right now I have to get performance runs on the board" is the all-too-common reaction.

One of the goals of our research, therefore, has been to answer the question, once and for all with hard facts, as to how much value organizational health creates. With millions of data points across thousands of organizations, we have the data required to do so. In Chapter 2, we'll describe the specifics of how we define and measure organizational health in detail, but to cut to the chase: when we tested for correlations between performance and health on a broad range of business measures, we found a strong positive correlation in every case. When we wrote the first edition of *Beyond Performance*, companies in the top quartile of organizational health were 2.2 times more likely than lower-quartile companies to have an above-median EBITDA (earnings before interest, taxes, depreciation, and amortization) margin, 2 times more likely to have above-median growth in enterprise value to book value, and 1.5 times more likely to have above-median growth in net income to sales. Now, almost 10 years later and having increased the data points more than eightfold, the analytics tell the same story. As Exhibit 1.2 shows, companies in the top quartile of organizational health have a 3 times greater total return to shareholders (TRS) than bottom quartile companies over an eight-year period.

Exhibit 1.2

## Healthy Companies Perform Better

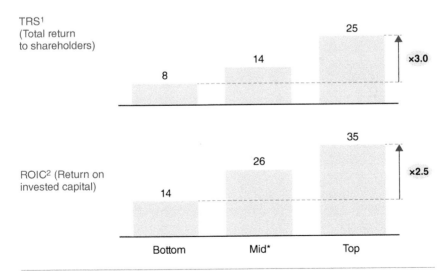

* Comprised of second and third quartiles
1 8 year average used to exclude volatility from 2007/2008 global financial crisis
2 Average 3 year financial indicators of companies in respective quartile

They also have 2 times higher return on invested capital (ROIC). Further, whereas bottom-quartile health companies don't see any growth in sales, top-quartile companies average 24 percent sales growth.[10]

Savvy readers will know that a correlation between health and performance does not mean that there is a causal relationship (higher health leads to higher performance). We'd be the first to admit that correlations need to be treated with caution. Take an example: education and income are highly correlated, but that doesn't mean that one causes the other. It's just as logical to argue that a higher income creates opportunities for higher education as it is to argue that higher education creates opportunities for a higher income (and even if it does, we can't infer that everyone who gains more education will have a higher income).

We haven't been content to rest our case on correlations; we've also invested heavily in testing for the relationship over time. To start with, we've looked at regression coefficients between comparable units within organizations. For example, we've compared the performance and health of branches within bank networks, of hospitals in healthcare networks, stores within retail networks, oil refineries in oil companies, and so on. In every case, we've found statistically significant relationships between health and performance that indicates health explains over 50 percent of the variance in performance across locations. Exhibit 1.3 shows an example of a linear regression analysis across 16 refineries at a large multinational oil company.

We've gone even further than regressions to test causality, as well, by conducting extensive research that compares experimental and control groups over a period of approximately two years. One group would embark on making change happen in a traditional, relatively performance-heavy fashion, and the other would use the Five Frames approach, which puts equal emphasis on performance and health. In viewing performance and measuring health regularly over this fairly long period, we sought to remove any distortions that might derive from the Hawthorne effect, whereby subjects alter their behavior simply because they are being studied, not because of the interventions being tested. After running five of these longitudinal tests in industries as diverse as telecommunications, mining, banking, and retail and finding that, on average, the experimental groups who applied the balanced performance and health approach delivered on average 1.8 times higher impact, we felt the case for causation was well and truly closed, as shown in Exhibit 1.4.

At a large financial services institution, for example, we selected two experimental groups and a control group that were comparable and representative of the wider organization across a range of criteria, including net profit before taxes (in terms of overall growth and average over the longest coherent period of data available), customer economics (average income

## Exhibit 1.3

# Impact of Health on Performance at Business-Unit Level

**Example: Refineries at an oil company**
US$ per unit produced

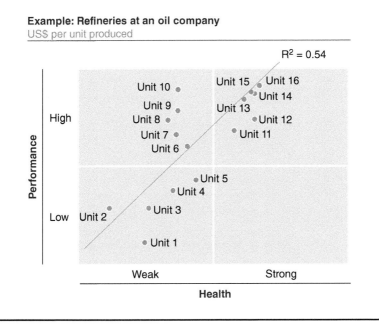

## Exhibit 1.3

# Impact of Health on Performance at Business-Unit Level

**Example: Refineries at an oil company**
US$ per unit produced

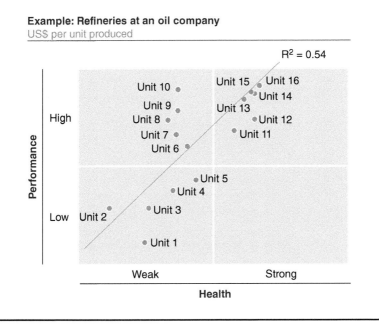

per customer in retail banking; industry composition in business banking), and branch staff characteristics (performance rating and tenure). Each of the experimental groups then pursued a sales stimulation program over an 18-month period, one using a more traditional, performance-heavy approach and the other the balanced performance and health approach. During the study, we took care to minimize any distortions during the trial—operational restructuring, changes in leadership, significant staff turnover, or other corporate initiatives—that might have a disproportionate effect on one group.

The results of the study were compelling. In business banking, the traditional approach yielded improvements in value of 8 percent versus the control group, whereas adopting our new "performance and health" approach delivered improvements of 19 percent. In retail banking, the traditional approach delivered a 7 percent improvement, compared with 12 percent for our new approach.

To shed more light on this causal link, here's an anecdote from our own experience. At McKinsey, we have an internal competition called the New

## Exhibit 1.4

# Testing the Power of Performance and Health Interventions

Comparison of traditional and experimental change efforts over an 18- to 24-month period

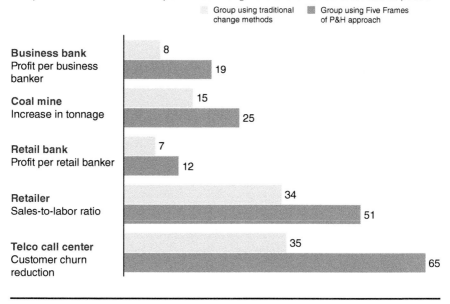

|  | Group using traditional change methods | Group using Five Frames of P&H approach |

**Business bank**
Profit per business banker
8
19

**Coal mine**
Increase in tonnage
15
25

**Retail bank**
Profit per retail banker
7
12

**Retailer**
Sales-to-labor ratio
34
51

**Telco call center**
Customer churn reduction
35
65

Ventures Competition to develop new knowledge and service offerings. In the New Ventures Competition, teams of consultants compete to develop new management ideas and present them to a panel of judges at local, regional, and organization-wide heats. In the 2006 version of the event, our topic of organizational health made it through to the last round.

A few days before their final presentation, the organizational health team decided to add in an extra ingredient. Rather than drawing conclusions from a retrospective view of performance and health at various organizations, they asked themselves, "If we look at the health of today's high-performing companies, what does it tell us about their prognosis for performance in the future?" After reviewing publicly available information about many companies, the team singled out Toyota.

In 2005, Toyota had set an aspiration to become the world's largest carmaker. Renowned for its manufacturing expertise, the company had developed unusually close collaborations with suppliers during decades of shared experience. But this new aspiration would force it to expand so rapidly that it was hard to see how its supply-chain management capability could keep up. The company would have to become increasingly dependent on new relationships with suppliers outside Japan, yet it didn't have enough senior engineers in place to monitor how these suppliers were fitting into the Toyota system. And the engineers it did have wouldn't be able to give new suppliers a thorough grounding in how to do things the Toyota way in the limited time available.

In front of the judges at the finals of the 2006 New Ventures Competition, the team put their stake into the ground. Toyota, with its proud reputation for building quality into its products at every step, was likely to have health issues that would affect its medium-term performance. Having sat through a day of novel ideas, the panel of judges reacted with outright disbelief. Toyota had just posted a 39 percent increase in net profit largely driven by sales, and appeared to be on a roll. One of the judges remarked that the team's prediction was "provocative, but completely ridiculous."

Fast forward to 2010, and Toyota was in the throes of recalling a number of models on safety grounds. So serious was the situation that its president Akio Toyoda was called before the U.S. Congress to offer an explanation and an apology for the defects. The general consensus was that one of the primary reasons for the quality breakdown was the turn of events the team had foreseen four years earlier.

We see the proof that health is a significant causal driver of performance as great news for leaders. Unlike many of the other factors that influence performance—changes in customer behavior, competitive moves, government actions—your organization's health is something that *you* can control. It's a bit like our personal lives. We may not be able to avoid being hit by a car speeding around a bend, but by eating properly and exercising regularly, we are far more likely to live a longer, fuller life.

## The Perils of Performance

Putting equal emphasis on performance and health is not easy. When your back is up against the wall and large-scale change is required to reverse downward trends, it often feels counterintuitive to spend time on health. Indeed, short-term gains can be made without tending to health, but they are unlikely to last.

Perhaps the starkest example of the perils of pursuing performance at the expense of health is the story of Albert J. Dunlap, famous for taking over struggling companies, ruthlessly downsizing them, and selling them at a profit. Dunlap's mantra was, "If you're in business, it's for one thing—to make money." When he took over U.S. appliance maker Sunbeam Products, true to his "Chainsaw Al" nickname, he sold two-thirds of its plants and fired half of its 12,000 employees. Ironically, at this point, Sunbeam's stock price proceeded to rise so high that it wrecked his plans to sell the company. Having compromised Sunbeam's health, Dunlap now found he needed to sustain its performance for the coming years. But the damage was too great. Just two years later, Sunbeam was facing quarterly losses as high as US$60 million, and Dunlap was fired.

Compare Dunlap's tactics to those of Lou Gerstner when he took the helm at IBM. Despite pressure from Wall Street to engineer a rapid turnaround at the ailing technology giant, Gerstner decided not to focus exclusively on improving its performance, but to put considerable effort and resources into improving its health, as well. Under Gerstner's stewardship, the company worked on collaborating as "one IBM" across businesses. It became more externally oriented, reduced bureaucracy, and moved from an arrogant to a continuous-learning mindset. By the time Gerstner retired nine years later, the stock had increased in value by 800 percent, and IBM had regained its leadership in multiple areas of the computer, technology, and IT consulting industry.

Perversely, the worst enemy of putting an appropriate emphasis on health isn't the presence of an urgent performance imperative, but the lack of one. When an organization is doing great financially, it's easy for a degree of complacency to set in that allows for health to decline, which in turn leads, in the best case, to a slow performance decline and in the worst case, an existential crisis.

Here the history of Atari provides a cautionary tale. The company was founded in 1972 to exploit what was then no more than a figment of a designer's imagination: the electronic game. In 1973, Atari sold US$40 million worth of these games (remember Pong?) and earned US$3 million in profits. Not long after, it was bought by deep-pocketed owners who invested heavily in R&D. By 1980, it was on top of the world, posting record revenues of US$415 million and being hailed as the fastest-growing company in U.S. history. Two years later, it was saluted by Thomas Peters and Robert Waterman in their book *In Search of Excellence.*

But even as the book's readers were discovering how Atari excelled, the company was crumbling. Teamwork began to decline, communication broke down, a culture of risk avoidance set in, investment in R&D was cut, and product quality was sacrificed to the cause of faster time-to-market.

The result was some of the biggest duds in video-gaming history. The shoddy visuals and poor playing characteristics of the game console versions of Pac-Man and E.T. alienated hitherto devoted customers. Fed-up engineers left in droves, many to set up or join rival companies whose innovative products would soon woo away Atari's fan base. By 1983, the rot had set in. The company lost US$536 million and resorted to massive layoffs.

Atari never recovered to the glory of its heyday. The shell of the company, by then little more than a brand name, was sold in 1998 for a paltry

US$5 million. Although Atari may have been consigned to history, the gaming market to which it belonged has gone from strength to strength. Worth US$138 billion globally, it is still growing at a tremendous pace.

Two questions arise from this sorry story. Where did Atari go wrong? And how did Peters and Waterman miss it? A single answer will suffice. Both the company and its chroniclers were so intently focused on performance that they were oblivious to the symptoms of deteriorating organizational health.

By way of contrast, consider the case of Pixar. Fifteen of the CGI animation studio's films are among the 50 highest-grossing animated films of all time. The studio has also earned 19 Academy Awards, 8 Golden Globes, and 11 Grammys—all the more impressive given that its president, Ed Catmull, had no business experience before he co-founded the company. In a talk about Pixar's creative process, he noted that the company's development process differs from that at most Hollywood studios: "Our development team doesn't look for stories. Their job is to create teams of people that work well together."[11] While an average Hollywood studio produces between 6 and 12 films in a year, Pixar produces just one, a risky bet given that an animated film costs approximately US$180 million to make. "We have realized that having lower standards for something is bad for your soul," Catmull explained. Taking the right risks and accepting that bold, innovative ideas require a tolerance for uncertainty are central to the whole culture. As Catmull says, "Talent is rare. Management's job is not to prevent risk but to build the capability to recover when failures occur."[12]

In the first edition of *Beyond Performance,* we profiled numerous examples of the catastrophic impact an overemphasis on performance versus health can have. We discussed how Enron's obsessive short-term return culture caused it to develop increasingly complex off-balance sheet financing systems that drove it to Chapter 11 bankruptcy and left some of its leadership serving jail sentences. We also described how, in spite of lawmakers having in place significant financial and accounting reforms to prevent such behavior, a similar fate was met by Lehman Brothers seven years later as it became intoxicated with short-term returns at the expense of maintaining its health. Further, we profiled BP's 2010 Deepwater Horizon catastrophe, the worst environmental disaster the United States had ever seen, which was driven by health issues related to its safety and risk culture.[13]

We noted that the temptation to put performance before health isn't just a private-sector failing. We illustrated this point with the example of the systematic failures of hospital care in England at the Mid-Staffordshire NHS Foundation Trust that left patients, as one newspaper reported, "routinely neglected, humiliated and in pain as the Trust focused on cutting costs and hitting government targets."[14] After an extensive inquiry, the root causes were reported to be short-term target-driven priorities, disengagement of clinicians from management, low staff morale, a lack of openness, acceptance of poor standards of conduct, and denial of criticisms. In other words, the Mid-Staffordshire NHS Foundation Trust was suffering from a breakdown in organizational health.

Sadly, since our first edition, there have been numerous further examples. There was Volkswagen's "dieselgate" scandal in 2015, which caused its stock price to fall by a third, and was attributed to its health—in particular, a "mindset within the company that tolerated rule-breaking."[15] And then, Samsung's 2016 Galaxy Note 7 smartphone recall, which led to an almost 10 percent drop in share price that was attributed to its "deeply entrenched culture of urgency."[16] Meanwhile, an investigation attributed Wells Fargo's sales practices scandal that wiped $9 billion from the bank's market capitalization to an "aggressive sales culture."[17] In 2017, Uber's widely reported "culture that values results above all else"[18] led to multiple employee scandals and illegal operations, ultimately forced the CEO, Travis Kalanick, to resign, and saw the company's first drop in market share for rides.[19] We could fill page after page with further examples. Just as with human health, all these cases illustrate how an organization's health will decline if not regularly tended. They also highlight that when the health declines, it doesn't just affect shareholders, but also hurts employees, customers, and communities.

The flip side is also true, however. Consider the case of General Motors, another company from Peters and Waterman's research on excellence. We discussed in our first edition how organizational health issues had brought the world's most dominant carmaker to its brink. In 2009, it filed for bankruptcy and received a government bailout of US$50 billion to resurrect itself. The company then underwent an 18-month turnaround that enabled it to pay back a significant portion of the bailout money and return to the stock market in 2010. Many observers were suggesting the company was now back on track, but our opinion differed. From our outside-in standpoint, we suggested that while the short-term financial pressures had been dealt with, the company's health issues had not. In turn, we suggested that if left untreated these issues would result in big challenges in the medium-term.

Sure enough, the internal investigation, known as the Valukas Report, into the devastating ignition-switch crisis in 2014 that left at least 124 people dead and 275 injured, was attributed to health factors such as, "No sense of urgency. No accountability or responsibility. A siloed mentality."[20] Mary Barra, who took over as CEO in 2014, vowed not just to deliver performance but also to improve GM's health by "driving accountability, owning each other's problems, a relentless desire to win … having candor and transparency, [and] being customer-focused."[21] Her efforts appear to be paying off now, with three profitable years and a strong balance sheet under her belt. As the GM experience shows, when an organization tends to its health, it improves—and with it, so does performance.

## The Five Frames of Performance and Health

No doubt you already believed performance is important before you picked up this book. We hope that at this point, there is little question in your mind as to the importance of organizational health. With that well established, we bring you back to the big idea that enables leaders to successfully lead large-scale change—putting equal emphasis on performance and health. The most important word in that statement is not performance, or health; it's *and*! By putting equal emphasis on each aspect, change programs improve their odds of success from 30 percent to 79 percent, and on average deliver 1.8 times more impact than if the focus is put disproportionately on one or the other.

Analogies from the sporting world are instructive in illuminating why this is the case. Consider a sports team that is focusing single-mindedly on its performance. If all it thinks about is winning games and titles this season, it will have a rude awakening in years to come. It will have failed to recruit new members, develop the bench, secure stakeholder support, obtain financial backing, build community relationships, and so on.

On the other hand, if the team takes steps to improve its health, it will improve its performance, as well. Recruiting promising new members will help it perform better in the future. In turn, performing better will make it easier to recruit new members and secure financial backing. A team that performs well this year is a product of superior financing, recruitment, and training in the past. In this way, paying attention to performance *and* health creates a virtuous cycle of sustained excellence over time. An important aspect of the "and" concept is that both performance and health require action *today*, even though returns on investments in health may not materialize until later.

So how, in practice, can you, as a change leader, put equal emphasis on both? If you're looking for simple recipes or quick rules of thumb that characterize much of the management literature in the social media era, you won't find them here. Large-scale change requires far more than quick fixes. As Louis Lavelle, in a book review in *Businessweek*, explains: "To hear most authors of business books tell it, there is no management conundrum so great that it can't be solved by the deft application of seven or eight basic principles. The authors are almost always wrong: big public companies have too many moving parts to conform to any set of simple precepts."[22] We agree. At the same time, we've tried not to introduce any complexity that doesn't add value—abiding by Einstein's edict that everything should be made as simple as possible, but no simpler.

We recommend leaders of large-scale change apply what we call the Five Frames of Performance and Health. The first step in understanding the approach is to see how the overall change journey has been divided into a set of smaller, more manageable stages. This is not a new idea. In 1947, German-American psychologist Kurt Lewin developed one of the first models to structure the change process. Lewin's three-stage process consisted of "unfreezing" (dismantling defense mechanisms), "moving" (towards the intended change), and "refreezing" (stabilizing new levels of performance).[23] In the past 70 years, academics, commentators, and practitioners have offered numerous variations. There's the "identify, plan, adopt, maintain, evaluate" model. There's also the "believe, decide, act, achieve, maintain" model. Or, how about the "evaluate, vision, organize, link, vest, embed" model? Wait, what about the "prepare, connect, discover, activate, integrate" model? Or the "define, discover, dream, design, destiny" model? The good news for leaders is that most of these people are saying much of the same thing.

For our purposes, we chose to break the change journey into five stages. We found that less didn't allow for enough practical specificity, and more added unnecessary complexity. We also chose to describe each stage by the basic question that should be answered by the work, to make it simple to know when to move from one stage to the next (if you have the answer, move forward!). Finally, we wanted to keep the five stages as simple and memorable as possible, so we summed each up in a word beginning with the same letter. Taken together, the five stages in the change process that we advocate are collectively known as the "5As." They are:

- *Aspire:* Where do we want to go?
- *Assess:* How ready are we to go there?
- *Architect:* What do we need to do to get there?
- *Act:* How do we manage the journey?
- *Advance:* How do we continue to improve?

What distinguishes our approach is not these 5As. What is unique is the explicit and practical guidance given to tackle the performance and the health aspects in each of the five stages. This is provided in the form of five frameworks for performance (one for each stage of the journey), and five frameworks for health (also one for each stage). Hence the shorthand nomenclature, the Five Frames of Performance and Health.

The five performance frameworks are:

- *Aspire:* **Strategic objectives**. Create a compelling long-term change vision, roll back the future to a mid-term aspiration, and guard against biases in the process.
- *Assess*: **Skillset requirements**. Forecast skill "demand" and understand skill "supply" dynamics, and then identify how any gaps will be closed.

- *Architect*: **Bankable plan.** Define the portfolio of initiatives to deliver on your strategic objectives and fulfill your skill requirements, then programmatically sequence actions and reallocate resources to deliver.

- *Act:* **Ownership model**. Establish strong governance; decide how to scale up your portfolio of initiatives; monitor progress and dynamically adjust as plans are implemented.

- *Advance:* **Learning infrastructure**. Institutionalize processes and expertise to enable knowledge sharing, continuous improvement, and continuous learning to characterize the day-to-day workings of the organization going forward.

The five health frameworks are:

- *Aspire:* **Health goals**. Objectively check your health, choose where to be exceptional, and target any ailing areas in need of immediate improvement.

- *Assess:* **Mindset shifts**. Pinpoint the helping and hindering behaviors related to health priority areas, explore the underlying mindset drivers of these behaviors, and name and reframe the critical few "root-cause" mindsets.

- *Architect:* **Influence levers.** Reshape the work environment to influence needed shifts in mindsets and behaviors by hardwiring health interventions into performance initiatives and interactively cascading the change story.

- *Act:* **Energy generation.** Mobilize influence leaders, make the change personal for a critical mass of leaders, and maintain high impact two-way communications.

- *Advance:* **Leadership placement**. Prioritize roles by value-creation potential based on the go-forward strategy, match the best talent to priority roles, and operationalize the talent match process to ensure it's regularly revisited.

We realize that written out in this fashion the Five Frames of Performance and Health is a lot to take in, and it's hard to visualize how it all comes together. A sporting analogy is helpful. Imagine that you *aspire* to become a marathon runner. You decide the marathon you'd like to compete in, find out when it takes place, work out how long you have to train for it, and set your performance targets accordingly. Perhaps you even have a finishing time in mind. Having decided on your performance aspiration, you can then work out your health aspiration: the level of fitness you'll need to run the marathon in your chosen time.

Next you need to *assess* your current skills and mindsets as a runner. On the performance side of things, how fast can you run? How good is your technique? Do you have the right equipment? Can you get access to the facilities you need? On the health side, do you have the mental toughness to achieve your target fitness level? What dietary changes are you prepared to make to get into better shape? How much time are you willing to dedicate to training? If you have unhealthy habits like smoking or staying up too late, do you have the willpower to give them up?

Armed with this information, you can *architect* a training plan to improve your performance by alternating high- and low-intensity workouts and extending your range gradually over a few months. On the health side, you can plan a diet that will give you the energy you need. You may also want to make adjustments in other aspects of your life: letting go of commitments to free up time, telling your friends you won't be seeing them as often for a while, finding the money to pay for a trainer, and so on.

Then it's time to *act* on the plan. In terms of performance, you start out gradually and then ramp up your training. You manage your schedule to allow for the planned training to occur. You monitor and review your results and adjust your approaches as you go to ensure you're hitting the required milestones in terms of timing and distance. In terms of health, you take personal accountability for the changes to your diet and your life in general rather than procrastinating and find ways to keep your energy levels and motivation high—writing a blog, having a running partner, and celebrating small victories along the way.

Once you've successfully completed your first marathon, you consider how to make this more than a one-off event—how you can *advance* your running after the event. On the performance side, what marathons will you train for next, or will you branch out into triathlons or other Ironman competitions? Will you take a break after the marathon before resuming a fitness regime and, if so, for how long? What will that baseline training program look like before you ramp up again for your next marathon? If you get injured, what is your backup plan? On the health side, you ensure you've got the right people in the right roles to support you in the journey ahead. Who is the best trainer at this point in your running journey, now that you have more experience and different objectives? Who's the best running partner? What friends and family should you gravitate toward and away from to maintain healthy habits? Do you need a nutritionist, and if so who is the best for you? And so on.

Many readers will no doubt sense in reading the above that the Advance stage sounds a lot like it's setting the stage for another cycle of the Five Frames, starting with Aspire. They'd be right. The approach is tailor-made for an organization to drive multiple "S-curves" of change (ramping up into an intensive period of activity and radical improvement followed by a period of restoration while still improving incrementally, giving way to another ramp-up in intensity, and so on). If both performance and health are improved during each cycle, over time the organization "learns to learn" and becomes characterized by continuous change. The old adage applies: give a person a fish and he will eat today; teach a person to fish and he will eat every day. To extend the metaphor, teach a person to learn and he or she will be able to hunt and gather and farm as well as fish!

Having now described each element of the Five Frames, it's important to emphasize how they work together "horizontally" and "vertically." Let's start with the horizontal elements. In practice, the performance and health elements in each stage are far more integrated with one another than the lists above imply. Exhibit 1.5 illustrates their relationship more clearly.

## Exhibit 1.5
## The Five Frames of Performance and Health

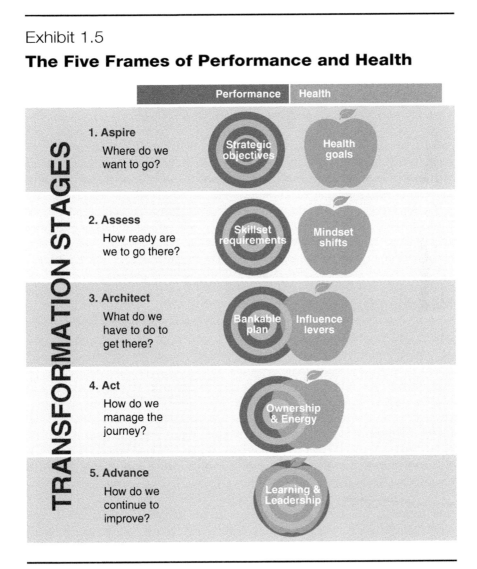

In the initial stages of the journey, the work related to each of the performance and health elements is more self-contained than not (though not completely: in the Aspire stage the health goals chosen will be those that enable the performance aspiration, as we'll cover in Chapter 3). As the change journey progresses, however, working on performance increasingly reinforces health, and vice versa. By the Act stage, in which the initial implementation of the plan takes place, there is one integrated change program that employees experience—the distinction between performance and health is really just semantics at this point.

We have seen some cases of leaders grasping the concept of performance and health, but not understanding this need for integration, and therefore saying to their business heads, "do the performance stuff" and to their HR department, "do the health stuff." Unfortunately for all involved, any approach that runs two programs in parallel is doomed to failure.

Now let's move to what we mean by the "vertical" relationship between the elements of performance and health. While we lay out the 5As change process in a linear fashion (start with Aspire, then move to Assess, then Architect, and so on), in practice its application is far more dynamic and iterative. If we go back to the marathon analogy, as the event approaches an injury or personal circumstances may require the aspirations and the plan to be reassessed. Similarly, an organization may find out in the Assess stage that its change readiness is such that the aspiration set in the Aspire stage just isn't realistic, and so the next step is to move backwards in the process. Or, new learnings or unexpected events in the Act stage may mean assumptions that went into the Architect stage no longer hold, requiring it to return to previous stages in the process.

## Mastering Irrationality

Nobel Prize–winning physicist and co-founder of the Santa Fe Institute Murray Gell-Mann once said, "Think how hard physics would be if particles could think."[24] His sentiment captures the importance and complexity of dealing with the human side of the change equation. This is precisely why having a rigorous and disciplined approach to the health aspects of change management is so refreshing for leaders. As one of our Aerospace and Defense clients enthused, "This is an approach that we engineers can get our heads around and deliver against!"[25] Or, as one investment banker put it, "I finally believe that the soft stuff drives value. More importantly I actually know what to do about it—and believe it makes good sense."[26]

Once understood, it's all quite logical, rational, and sensible. There is one problem, however. The "particles" in the physics of change management (employees) aren't just able to think—they very often do so seemingly *irrationally*. This dynamic accounts for why smart, hard-working leaders often find themselves increasingly frustrated as a change journey unfolds by a raft of unintended consequences stemming from their well-intentioned actions. "We've told them what we need them do, why don't they get it?"; "We've changed their incentives, why hasn't their behavior changed?"; and "Don't they understand that if we don't make money then no one has a job?" are the kind of comments we hear behind closed doors from many a change leader.

Leaders who master the art of leading change take into account the lessons from the social sciences that relate to what has become known as "predictable irrationality." To bring the concept of predictable irrationality to life, consider some common day-to-day experiences that many of us can relate to. When we're in a hurry, how many of us circle around a parking lot looking for the most convenient space when we'd have been much quicker walking from the first one we saw? Why might we think nothing of spending US$3,000 to upgrade to leather seats for our new US$25,000 car, but consider it extravagant to spend it on a leather sofa that all the family will use every day? Why are we happy to spend a small fortune during sales, but reluctant to spend so much on full-price goods? How come we'd take home a pencil from the office for our kids without a thought, but be shocked at the idea of raiding the petty cash to buy them one? As these examples show, in certain situations, we are all susceptible to irrationality in our decision-making.

Dan Ariely, author of *Predictably Irrational*, drives this point home by showing his audiences an optical illusion.[27] It's a powerful way to demonstrate that knowing something to be true doesn't necessarily make people believe it—a prime example of irrationality. Have a look at the two tables in Exhibit 1.6. Which is longer? Easy: the one on the left. Now take out a ruler and measure them.

Lo and behold, they are exactly the same length. Now look at the picture again. Which table is longer? Still the left! It's as if you've not learned anything in the past few seconds.

How do we know which table you see as longer? Because there are certain predictable ways in which our eyes deceive us, and this is one of them. What's most striking about optical illusions like the "two tables" (a.k.a. the Shepard illusion) is that processing visual information is one of the things human beings do best: the visual cortex is the biggest part of the brain. So, if we make mistakes in vision—something that by and large we are very, very good at—what are the odds we'll make mistakes in something that we aren't so good at, like change management?

The social, cognitive, and emotional biases that lead to seemingly irrational decisions are already well understood and incorporated into the field of economics. The same is not true of the field of change management and organizational leadership, however. It should be, and with that in mind, in each of the 5As we call out the most important lesson from human irrationality that should be considered and how to constructively work with it—something we

Exhibit 1.6

**Two Table Illusion**

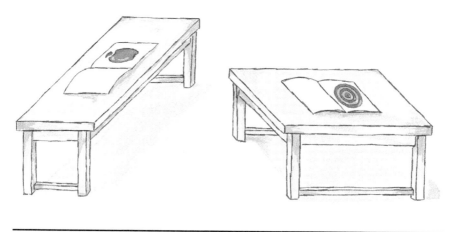

call the change leader "Master Stroke." These enable you to foresee other-wise counterintuitive and unpredictable barriers to change and masterfully use them to accelerate progress and maximize impact instead.

■ ■ ■

At this point, we hope that if someone saw this book on your desk and asked you what it's about, you'd respond with, "How to successfully lead large-scale change programs." When pressed for more, you'd be able to expand on the central thesis by saying, "It says the key is to put equal em-phasis on actions related to performance (e.g., the *buy, make, sell* stuff) and health (e.g., the *align, execute, renew* stuff)." If you were then asked the logical follow-up question about how to do that, we hope you'd respond with, "There's a five-stage methodology called the Five Frames of Perfor-mance and Health, which is covered in detail in chapters to come."

We also hope you'd answer the questions with a deeper understanding and conviction that what is often referred to as the "hard stuff" turns out to be the easier part of making change happen. As Roger Enrico, former chairman and CEO of PepsiCo, put it, "The soft stuff is always harder than the hard stuff."[28] In this spirit, the next chapter will be dedicated to diving deeper into organizational health, its components, and the full research base behind it. We'll then get into the practical specifics of how to apply each of the Five Frames of Performance and Health to ensure your change program is a resounding success.

# Chapter 2

# The Science of Change

In 1996, Harvard Business School professor John Kotter reported to the world the results of his 10-year study of more than 100 companies that attempted large-scale organizational change. In his book, *Leading Change*, he wrote, "I estimate today more than 70 percent of needed change either fails to be launched, even though some people clearly see the need, fails to be completed even though some people exhaust themselves trying, or finishes over budget, late and with initial aspirations unmet."[1] His thinking resonated with findings published three years earlier by Michael Hammer and James Champy in *Reengineering the Corporation,* who estimated that "50 percent to 70 percent of the organizations that undertake a reengineering effort do not achieve the dramatic results they intended."[2]

Truth be told, all of this research happened before our time playing leadership roles in the workplace. In fact, it wasn't until the early 2000s, when we read Dr. Martin E. Smith's *Success Rates for Different Types of Organizational Change,* that reality sunk in for us. Smith's article reviewed 49 studies that in total encompassed a sample size of over 40,000 respondents. Each of the studies he analyzed had already been published in various business and professional publications (e.g., by the Conference Board, the Academy of Management, *Harvard Business Review, The Economist,* the *Wall Street Journal,* and so on). His conclusion? Thirty-three percent of large-scale change programs succeed.[3]

To use a football (soccer for our readers in the United States) analogy, the weight of the evidence was such that if the success rates were a "yellow card" on leaders, it was a "red card" on their advisers. Especially for us, we felt, given we were young leaders of the Organization Practice of McKinsey & Company, the preeminent consulting firm to whom clients bring their hardest, biggest, and most important change challenges. We felt compelled to provide better answers to our clients, so they can beat the odds. Since then, each of us has spent nearly 20 years in this pursuit.

Our journey is not a hero's journey, however. We have been fortunate to be in the right organization at the right time, conducting research on a scale previously unimaginable. McKinsey & Company has an incredible global reach: a presence in 129 cities in 65 countries, clients that represent 80 percent of the Fortune 500, and unrivaled access to CEOs and senior teams. Our work has also been conducted at the front end of the digital age—with the advantage of instant, global 24/7 connectivity and computing power to store and analyze data in ways that would have seemed like science fiction back when management classics such as *In Search of Excellence* were written.

## The Quest Begins

With a vast pool of potential data sources at our fingertips, our first challenge was to decide what to ask. How could we investigate the difference between change success and failure in a way that would yield robust new insights? Finding out the companies that had been successful and the ones that had failed would be relatively easy. So would probing what had happened to them. But how should we investigate the central question of *why*?

We began by invoking Isaac Newton's notion of standing on the shoulders of giants. Before we started to gather data at scale, we wanted to consult three groups of giants in particular: our colleagues, a small group of senior executives, and a select group of leading thinkers from the academic world. If we could draw on the help of these three sources to develop an integrated view of what makes organizations successful in making change happen, we could then use McKinsey's global reach to test and refine it at scale.

Our first group of giants was by far the hardest to tame. We began by interviewing our colleagues who had deep experience in leading major change programs, and colleagues whose clients had sustained high performance over long periods. We then brought our sources together for a series of working sessions. Discussions about the real drivers of success soon turned into heated debates. One camp contended, "The right incentives are 80 percent of the answer," while another countered with "The real secret is to engage hearts and minds." Yet another insisted, "You start with strategy, then get the structure right, then produce a strong implementation plan and you're there," only to be contradicted with, "Top-down solutions don't work in large, complex global organizations—what you need is shared vision and values, then you kick off change from the bottom up." These debates went on late into the night and were continued via e-mail for months after the formal sessions were over.

Our second group of giants—the senior executives—were better behaved, but equally diverse in their recipes for success.[4] We heard, "It's all about your vision," as well as, "A vision was the last thing on my agenda."

Some said, "Make a clear plan and pursue it consistently," while others asserted, "You have to adapt as you go and pray for all the things you can't control." One set emphasized, "Trust and collaboration are the key," and others focused on, "Individual accountability and incentives are what matter." To say that no clear consensus emerged would be putting it mildly.

The third group—the academic giants we spoke to, and those authorities whose work we reviewed—also offered a vast array of contrasting advice. Some suggested that long-term competitive advantage is determined largely by the nature of the industry a company competes in; others placed the emphasis on the top team and decision-making patterns within the organization. Still others argued that luck plays as big a role as any other factor. We were also struck by the many different angles they used to approach the topic, which ranged from the technical (we learned much about "meta-analytic path estimates," "empirical tests of relative inertia," and "efficacy-performance spirals") to the playful (as found in *Who Moved My Cheese?*, *The Complete Idiot's Guide to Change Management*, and *Fish! A Remarkable Way to Boost Morale and Improve Results*, among others), with seemingly every other approach in between.

None of the groups converged on an answer—that would have been too easy—but when we stepped back to look for patterns across everything we had heard and read, we saw three themes emerging.

There was no doubt that long-term success required some sort of internal *alignment* on direction—a compelling vision and well-articulated strategy that are meaningful to individual employees and supported by the culture and climate of the organization.

A high quality of *execution* was also key: this meant having the right capabilities, effective management processes, and high motivation.

The final common thread was a capacity for *renewal*: an organization's ability to understand, interact with, shape, and adapt to changes in its situation and the external environment.

With these three themes in mind, we put together a first draft of a framework to describe the essential components of successful and sustainable change.

## The Road Less Traveled

At this point, although we had done a lot of work, we didn't have an answer. All we had was a starting point and a route. We also knew that there would be many roadblocks, detours, and dead ends along the way. So, we set off on the next phase of our work.

First, we started to gather data from hundreds of organizations and thousands of senior leaders around the world, using both surveys and workshop-based approaches. Second, we tested our hypotheses in the field by applying them in large organizations and monitoring their impact over long periods of time—not weeks or months, but years. Third, we embarked on a deeper dive into the relevant literature to pressure-test our emerging model.

On the survey front, our first step was to create a tool to measure the themes of alignment, execution, and renewal that had emerged from our earlier work. In putting it together, we used a combination of our own experience and psychometric best practices to judge what to include, what to leave out, and how to group the various elements. We had an initial version of the survey completed by the end of 2002. As we gathered more data, we continued to develop and refine it. Over the next few years, it evolved rapidly, and by 2005, it had become a robust tool for measuring organizational health, known as the Organizational Health Index (OHI).

By that time, we had a sizeable database that we could mine to validate the link between self-reported health data and objective financial performance. That gave us confidence that we were on the right road to what promised to be an exciting destination. The OHI had enabled us to identify and measure the heretofore largely opaque "soft" characteristics that enabled change success and sustainability of that success over time. However, it didn't give us much insight into what the organization could do to *improve* its health.

Imagine you go to a doctor with a bad cold, and the doctor tells you, "You have a cold. It means your nose is running, your head feels stuffed up, your eyes are watering, you sneeze and cough, your temperature is all over the place, and you probably aren't sleeping well. When I look at the data on others with your condition, I can say with a high degree of certainty that you won't be able to achieve much in this state. Were you to not have a cold you'd both feel better and be able to do a lot more." So you ask, "Okay, what can I do to get better?" The doctor replies, "Good question. I'm not really sure." Chances are that's not a doctor you'll be visiting again. Therefore, the next step in our journey was to gather data related to our emerging hypotheses about how organizations could become—and stay—healthy.

We started with a simple three-step model that we referred to as the 3D approach: first, *diagnose* your current state; second, *design* an intervention program; and third, *deliver* against the plan. Over time we came to believe that the diagnostic step should have two elements: first, setting a performance aspiration; second, assessing the organization's readiness for change. We also found it was helpful to separate the delivery step into two: first, delivering against the plan; second, making the transition from being in a "change program" mode to a steady-state characterized by continuous improvement. As we learned these lessons, the 3D approach became the 5As (Aspire, Assess, Architect, Act, Advance).

In order to understand the work required on performance and health at each stage of a transformation, we looked to the 32,000-member Global Executive Survey Panel, a portion of the *McKinsey Quarterly's* million-plus reader base. This group, with its broad geographic reach and representatives from the full spectrum of industries, functions, and ownership models, was an ideal sounding board for testing our approach as it developed.[5]

As well as conducting surveys, we also gathered input through a series of multi-day workshops that we call the Change Leaders Forum (CLF). CLFs are peer-learning events involving executives from a cross-section of leading organizations throughout the world. Through 2010, we held 18 forums in a variety of locations including the United States, the United Kingdom, France, Dubai, and South Africa. As participants shared best practices at these events, we took the opportunity to refine our thinking about how to make change happen at scale during what were often heated debates. We then drew further insights from staying in touch with the network of more than 1,000 participants from these sessions, gathering further feedback from them on what was and wasn't working in the field.

Although surveys and focus groups gave us huge amounts of data to work with, they ultimately rely on perceptions: we ask people a set of questions, and they tell us what they think. We wanted to go further and test our emerging hypotheses in the crucible of real large-scale change efforts. To do that, we set out to compare experimental and control groups over long periods of time—typically two years. One group would embark on making change happen in a fairly traditional fashion, and the other would use the new approach we were starting to develop—one that gave equal weight to performance and health and employed our embryonic Five Frames approach. We conducted such trials in industries as diverse as financial services, retail, mining, and telco, and in every case, the very positive results compelled us to continue to push our research forward (these results are shared in Exhibit 1.3).

Survey data, workshops, and field tests still weren't enough, however. We were getting a good sense of what worked in practice, but why did it work in theory? For this we went back to academia. We had a strict screening criterion for credible sources. Studies needed to have applied tests of statistical significance at 95 percent certainty levels; the impact reported had to include "hard" financial, economic, commercial, technical, or social metrics; and articles had to have been published in top-tier peer-reviewed journals.[6] Further, we asked four eminent scholars to challenge and extend our findings.

By 2010, we had conducted a body of research that we were confident was more exhaustive than anything previously undertaken in the field. We had also seen success in so many varied contexts that we were confident our findings were broadly applicable for any leader whose change efforts required people to adjust their behaviors to be successful. Meanwhile, we had regularly confirmed that in the broader world of management practice, the success rates of large-scale change programs had remained unchanged. Our 2006 survey of 1,536 global business executives who had experienced a large-scale change program in the last five years found that 30 percent were "mostly" or "completely" successful in both delivering the desired performance and equipping the organization to sustain it over the long-term.[7] In our 2008 survey of 3,199 and 2010 survey of 2,314 executives we found a similar result: one in three programs were considered successful.[8] Given this, we put pen to paper and wrote the first version of *Beyond Performance*.

Since then, our research has continued and our experience in applying the findings has expanded exponentially. A big part of our focus has been on upskilling leaders and our McKinsey colleagues on the Five Frames of Performance and Health approach to change. To do so, we made our CLFs into two-day events where senior McKinsey colleagues and senior client executives attend in pairs, with overall group sizes ranging from 20 to 40 participants. During a typical CLF, 20 percent of the time is spent learning the methodology, and 80 percent is spent discussing how it applies to their organizations. At the time of this writing, we have done over 150 of these McKinsey-client training sessions.

With the increased use of the OHI during change programs, the amount of data in our OHI database has exploded. As such, we've been able to continually refine our findings both in terms of the business impact that a focus on health delivers and, more predictively, how to help organizations choose the aspects of health to focus on—something that we'll cover in depth with our most recent data in Chapter 3. We've also taken our own medicine in McKinsey & Company, discarding our previous employee satisfaction and engagement surveys in favor of the OHI. Further, we've reframed all of our internal impact reviews as "Performance and Health Dialogues."

One thing that worried us, however, was the length of the OHI survey. To get an objective view on the matter, we hired Stanford PhD and Duke University professor, Dr. Sunshine Hillygus, an expert in survey methods, to challenge and pressure-test the instrument. She helped us streamline the survey, cutting its length by over a third, in ways that maintained scale reliability and construct validity (we'll talk more about these shortly for those inclined to want to dive into such things—if you know what Cronbach's coefficient alphas, P-values, and factor analyses are, the next section will be for you!).

We've also developed a number of additional tools to support large-scale change programs, including the McKinsey "WAVE" implementation tracking software solution that allows activities and impact to be rigorously managed during the Act stage. WAVE has now been used by over 600 clients globally, and by analyzing the data in the tool at the aggregate level we can now answer questions such as: What proportion of initiatives typically don't deliver their forecasted impact? What do these initiatives have in common? What portion of milestones in change programs will likely get delayed, by how long, and why? These findings have enabled us to further sharpen our views on what it really takes to make, and execute against, robust plans.

In the Introduction, we shared the full list of statistics regarding the research base that supports everything we cover in this revised edition. As we mentioned, if a more comprehensive effort has ever been undertaken, we aren't aware of it. It'd be hard to overstate just how fortunate we feel to have been able to tap into such a massive pool of data, experience, and expertise to help us develop and refine the thinking you hold in your hands. When we look at the academic world, even those who have been conducting research in the field for over 20-plus years at most can claim to have "worked with hundreds of companies"—nothing on the order of the thousands we've had privileged access to learn from. When we look at the business world, there are few if any firms that have the global reach and top management access that McKinsey has, and the nature of turnover in the consulting industry is such that it's hard to find anyone who has had the luxury of spending 20-plus years in one field.

In our first edition, we closed this section by saying, "We're convinced that many more new and valuable insights will emerge as our sample continues to grow from 500 today to—who knows?—maybe 5,000 organizations one day." Now, with over 2,000, we're well on our way. Even so, we remain humble and excited about learning more between this and the publishing of *Beyond Performance 3.0*. Perhaps by then we can bring you insights gleaned from well beyond a 5,000-organization sample! Stay tuned …

## Organizational Health Defined

Enough about the journey, let's talk about the destination. You'll remember that we identified three key attributes of good health: internal *alignment*, quality of *execution*, and capacity for *renewal*. We had also identified nine aspects of organizational life that were empirically proven to drive performance. We put these two bodies of thinking together to develop our definition of organizational health as shown in Exhibit 2.1.

Let's take a look at each of the nine elements.

1. **Direction:** A clear sense of where the organization is heading and how it will get there that is meaningful to all employees.
2. **Leadership:** The extent to which leaders inspire actions by others.
3. **Work environment:** The shared beliefs and quality of interactions within and across organizational units.
4. **Accountability:** The extent to which individuals understand what is expected of them, have sufficient authority to act, and take responsibility for delivering results.

5. **Coordination and control:** The ability to evaluate organizational performance and risk, and to address issues and opportunities when they arise.

6. **Capabilities:** The presence of the institutional skills and talent required to execute strategy and create competitive advantage.

7. **Motivation:** The presence of enthusiasm that drives employees to put in extraordinary effort to deliver results.

8. **External orientation:** The quality of engagement with customers, suppliers, partners, and other external stakeholders to drive value.

9. **Innovation and learning:** The quality and flow of new ideas and the organization's ability to adapt and shape itself as needed.

These elements are an organization's health "outcomes." Every organization has within it a certain, measurable amount of each (motivation, capability, external orientation, and so on). Knowing how much you have of each of these is important in the same way that when you go to the doctor for a health check-up, the first part of the appointment is assessing your health outcomes: pulse, blood pressure, oxygenation, cholesterol, weight, and so on. All are vital indicators of health.

## Exhibit 2.1

## Nine Elements of Organizational Health

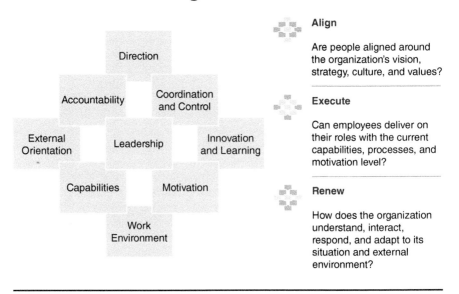

Direction

Accountability

Coordination and Control

External Orientation

Leadership

Innovation and Learning

Capabilities

Motivation

Work Environment

**Align**

Are people aligned around the organization's vision, strategy, culture, and values?

**Execute**

Can employees deliver on their roles with the current capabilities, processes, and motivation level?

**Renew**

How does the organization understand, interact, respond, and adapt to its situation and external environment?

Our definition and measurement of health doesn't stop here, however; it goes one step further to also look at health "practices." To continue the analogy with human health, by the end of your appointment a good doctor won't just talk about your outcomes, she'll also inquire about your practices—the things you do that give you the results you have. If you have high blood pressure and are overweight, she'll want to know about diet, exercise, stress at work, and so on.

Organizational health is similar. If, for example, accountability is low, we wouldn't just say you need to get more of it. Instead, we'd want to discuss your management practices—the things you do—that create accountability. We'd talk about the extent to which *performance contracts* create clear objectives and measurable targets, the extent to which there is *role clarity*, how *consequence management* is used, and how more intrinsically driven *personal ownership* is fostered. For each of the nine health outcomes, there is a set of management practices that drive them. In total, we've identified 37 management practices (listed in Exhibit 2.2) that drive the nine health outcomes. These management practices take health from the conceptual to the exceedingly tangible, observable, and above all, actionable—not qualities that are always associated with models of organizational effectiveness and change management.

## Exhibit 2.2
## The Practices Underpinning Organizational Health

| Element | Practice | Description |
|---|---|---|
| Direction | 1. Shared Vision | • Sharing a clear and compelling vision of the future with everyone |
| | 2. Strategic Clarity | • Creating a plan with specific goals, targets, and milestones that is tied to the vision |
| | 3. Employee Involvement | • Involving co-workers in shaping and translating the vision and strategy into what it means for them |
| Leadership | 4. Authoritative Leadership | • Using authority and pressure to get things done |
| | 5. Consultative Leadership | • Involving and empowering employees through communication and delegation |
| | 6. Supportive Leadership | • Caring about the welfare of co-workers when making decisions and creating a positive team environment |
| | 7. Challenging Leadership | • Encouraging employees to take on big challenges and consistently raising the bar |
| Work environment | 8. Open and Trusting | • Ensuring honesty, transparency, and candid dialogue |
| | 9. Performance Transparency | • Making results visible to enable best practice sharing and foster a healthy sense of competition |
| | 10. Operationally Disciplined | • Setting and communicating clear work standards to improve productivity |
| | 11. Creative and Entrepreneurial | • Protecting time to support creativity and encourage initiative-taking |
| Accountability | 12. Role Clarity | • Getting clear on what everyone is responsible for, has authority over, and who to work with |
| | 13. Performance Contracts | • Setting clear and measurable performance targets |
| | 14. Consequence Management | • Creating a direct link between performance and consequences |
| | 15. Personal Ownership | • Feeling personally obligated and invested in achieving performance objectives |

*(continued)*

## Exhibit 2.2 *continued*

| Element | Practice | Description |
|---|---|---|
| Coordination and control | 16. People Performance Review | • Using formal performance feedback and assessments to evaluate, develop, and deploy people |
| | 17. Operational Management | • Focusing on a clearly defined set of operational metrics to manage performance |
| | 18. Financial Management | • Focusing on a clearly defined set of financial metrics to manage performance |
| | 19. Professional Standards | • Using clear standards and policies to set expectations and reinforce compliance |
| | 20. Risk Management | • Identifying and mitigating anticipated risks and responding rapidly to unexpected problems |
| Capabilities | 21. Talent Acquisition | • Hiring the best outside talent when and where needed |
| | 22. Talent Development | • Improving employee skills through defined learning journeys |
| | 23. Process-based Capabilities | • Regularly documenting and updating procedures and training guides |
| | 24. Outsourced Expertise | • Outsourcing activities that external partners can do better |
| Motivation | 25. Meaningful Values | • Sharing and living a meaningful set of values day-to-day |
| | 26. Inspirational Leaders | • Exemplifying what's valued, providing praise and generating meaning for employees |
| | 27. Career Opportunities | • Providing merit-based promotions and other career opportunities to motivate employees |
| | 28. Financial Incentives | • Providing attractive financial incentives to motivate employees |
| | 29. Rewards and Recognition | • Acknowledging performance with public recognition and non-financial rewards/opportunities |

| Element | Practice | Description |
|---|---|---|
| Innovation and learning | 30. Top-down Innovation | • Driving innovation through large-scale initiatives sponsored by senior leaders |
| | 31. Bottom-up Innovation | • Encouraging and enabling co-workers to solve problems that directly impact what they do |
| | 32. Knowledge Sharing | • Proactively asking for and sharing knowledge with others |
| | 33. Capturing External Ideas | • Identifying and using best practices from outside the company |
| External orientation | 34. Customer Focus | • Putting customer impact at the forefront of the decision-making process |
| | 35. Competitive Insights | • Systematically reflecting on competitors' strengths and weakness during decision making |
| | 36. Business Partnerships | • Building and maintaining effective relationships with external business partners |
| | 37. Government and Community Relations | • Investing resources to build relationships with government, community, regulatory, and consumer groups |

# A *Far* Better Measure than Employee Engagement

The OHI survey, a tool for measuring health in a rigorous and comprehensive manner, is based on these nine outcomes of organizational health and their related 37 practices. We are often asked how it differs from other surveys, in particular those used to assess employee satisfaction and engagement. The differences are legion, including among them:

- **Breadth:** The OHI asks about the full set of topics related to how effectively the company is run that are proven to drive business performance (including external orientation, capabilities, innovation, risk controls, and so on), not just whether employees are engaged or satisfied.

- **Depth:** The OHI measures both outcomes and practices, not one or the other, so that leaders have specific guidance regarding what they need to do to get the results that they want to see.

- **Benchmarks:** The results are benchmarked against global, industry-specific, and geography-specific benchmarks, not simple scales of good to bad.

- **Systemic perspective:** The questions are by and large about the company ("we") versus about the individual ("I"), which enables results to speak to patterns in how the organization is managed and led and reduce optimism biases.

- **Action orientation:** The questions are more objective and action-oriented ("how often …") than subjective and emotion-oriented ("how do you feel about …").

- **Focus:** The data is used by senior leaders to pick a few things that will make the biggest difference for the whole organization to focus on from the top to the bottom, not trying to be great at everything or asking local areas to set their own direction (which creates fragmentation).

- **Sophistication:** It offers company-specific predictive analytics to inform business strategy-specific solutions, not generic best practices that apply across all companies (more of this in Chapter 3).

To be honest, we worry about companies who are still using traditional engagement or satisfaction surveys. A staggering number of companies in poor health have been using them for years. Leaders of these companies were no doubt sold on these tools by vendors sharing some empirical data suggesting what they measure is correlated to business performance, and appealed to the leaders' intuitive sense that they needed a "people measure." It's not that the vendors were lying, of course; in fact, no doubt they were very well-intentioned. The problem is that this is like someone selling you a scale by saying, "If you maintain a healthy weight, you'll both never get sick and be able to perform at your peak!" Sure, one's weight is correlated to health and one's health is correlated to performance, but it's certainly not the only thing. As anyone whose life has been enhanced or even saved by early detection of cancer or other issues will attest, getting a good all-points physical is absolutely worth the extra effort.

We could fill pages with similar analogies—would you drive a car that only had a mileage counter on the dashboard (no speedometer, fuel gauge, temperature gauge, tachometer, voltmeter, oil pressure gauge, warning lights, and so on) simply because total miles driven by a vehicle are correlated to its safety and soundness? Would you invest in a stock having only knowledge about its dividends (nothing on earnings growth, stability, industry comparisons, debt-to-equity ratios, price-to-earnings ratios, and so on)? We suspect not, so why would you use an engagement survey that typically covers less than 20 percent of the topics assessed by the OHI, the latter of which was built to measure *all* of the organization-related elements proven to drive value creation? And it's not just engagement surveys that are anemic in this way—typical employee satisfaction surveys fare little better, covering about 25 percent of topics included in the OHI.

## A New Management Accounting?

As indicated above, one of the most attractive elements of the OHI is that an organization's health can be benchmarked at multiple levels, be it overall, by industry or geography (or both). Our database spans all major industries included in the Datastream global index, which represents the 15 sectors shown in Exhibit 2.3.

In developing the OHI so comprehensively and robustly, our aspiration was to establish for organizational health what the accountancy profession has long had for financial health: a consistent method of measurement that allows "apples to apples" comparisons to be made both within and between organizations. We were convinced that if organizations had at their disposal a reliable evidence-based tool for measuring organizational health, the results it reported would be just as important as this quarter's profits or last year's operating performance as far as shareholders, customers, employees, regulators, governments, and other stakeholders were concerned.

Alas, this did not happen in the wake of the first edition of *Beyond Performance*. Some interesting trends have appeared, however, such as the application of the OHI to entire industries and countries. In South Korea, for example, the Korean Chamber of Commerce & Industry (KCCI) sponsored the survey in over 100 companies simultaneously. In Brazil, over 70 companies operating in 18 industries participated in the survey at the same time. These national benchmarks are changing the discourse about

## Exhibit 2.3

# Industries Represented in the OHI Sample

| Sector | Percent of sample |
|---|---|
| Global Energy and Materials | 27 |
| Banking | 13 |
| TMT (High Tech-Media-Telecom) | 10 |
| Consumer | 9 |
| Advanced Industries | 7 |
| Public Sector | 5 |
| Asset Management and Institutional Investors | 5 |
| Insurance | 4 |
| Healthcare Systems and Services | 4 |
| Travel, Transport, and Logistics | 4 |
| Pharmaceuticals and Medical Products | 4 |
| Infrastructure | 4 |
| Professional, Scientific, and Technical Services | 2 |
| Social Sector | 1 |
| Multisector Conglomerate | 1 |

how to run successful businesses in these countries. In South Korea, moves are being made to address issues related to the work environment outcome that drive habitual overwork and gender equality issues, as well as the coordination and control outcome that drives inefficient meetings and reporting. In Brazil, work is underway to address the cultural overreliance on the "challenging leadership" practice, while also improving practices related to the accountability outcome. In the current state, leaders tend to be very challenging of employees, yet employees generally aren't clear as to what their performance (and health) expectations are.

It's too early to know what impact this elevated attention to health will create in these countries but suffice to say all involved have found the effort invaluable. Sponsoring organizations have been thrilled with the level of insight provided that enables them to act and provide services to their member organizations on a broader scale. The companies who have taken the survey have been thrilled to see their results vis-à-vis fresh data from their peers as well as global benchmarks, helping them pinpoint the health improvements that will lead to performance improvements. Finally, employees and society at large have weighed in by commenting on the news reporting of the findings, indicating, "At last, we are getting to the real issues that hold us back."

This broad-based embracing of organizational health gives us hope that there may still come a day when organizational health becomes a public standard. The case for such, we believe, is stronger now than ever. Our guess is that if you're deciding whether to expand internationally, you would find it extremely helpful to have not only economic, sociodemographic, and market data at your fingertips, but also information on the general heath of management practices in your target country. If you're contemplating a merger, having a window into how well (or badly) your management practices will dovetail with the other company's practices could give you a head start. If you're making strategic decisions, knowing how healthy your industry is compared with others could have a bearing on your future direction. And if you're voting for elected officials, imagine the difference it would make if you could understand the health of the institutions your taxes pay for, and see the direct results of any changes as they happen over time.

Here's another "human" example to clarify. Let's say you've signed an athlete to a five-year contract to play on the team that you own and coach. If, through regular health check-ins, you find out the player is drinking, smoking, staying up late, and letting her diet go, that's vital information to have and to act on, even if today she is performing at world-class levels (she won't be for long!). The more time it takes you to detect the brewing health issues and intervene, the more likely it costs your team some games and the harder and longer the road will be back to the top for the player in question. The same is true for organizations, and if you're an owner or investor, we're hard-pressed to think of any reason why you wouldn't demand to know the health of the organizations you're investing in.

In spite of our optimism, some have advised us to give up our hopes in this area. Health will never be a concept regularly encountered in annual reports, analyst reports, or in the business press, they tell us. Why? Because analysts and traders are forever fixated on the next quarter's earnings, and therefore, so are boards and management teams. We believe this is selling those in the business community short. In spite of a noisy segment of short-term focused analysts and investors, the evidence suggests that capital markets do value those things that drive long-term performance.

As a former managing director of McKinsey and current chairman of Rolls-Royce, Ian Davis, observes, "An examination of share prices demonstrates that expectations of future performance are the main driver of shareholder returns. In almost all industry sectors and almost all stock exchanges, up to 80 percent of a share's market value can be explained only by cashflow expectations beyond the next three years. These longer-term expectations are in turn driven by judgments on growth and on long-term profitability."[9]

This makes us believe that those leaders who are first movers in reporting their organization's health will be rewarded. If there's a more robust, concrete, and measurable current indicator of future success than organizational health, we have yet to see it.

## Healthy Change Programs

With the importance of organizational health and its link to performance now fully established, let's return to why it is essential to making change happen at scale. A review of the significant amount of research that exists into why change programs fail tells us all we need to know. What we might think of as the usual suspects—inadequate resources, poor planning, bad ideas, unpredictable external events—turn out to account for less than a third of change program failures. In fact, more than 70 percent of failures are driven by what we would categorize as poor organizational health, as manifested in such symptoms as negative employee attitudes and unproductive management behavior (Exhibit 2.4).[10]

Given that organizational health-related issues are the predominant stumbling blocks to change success, it comes as little surprise that when executives

Exhibit 2.4

## Barriers to Organizational Change

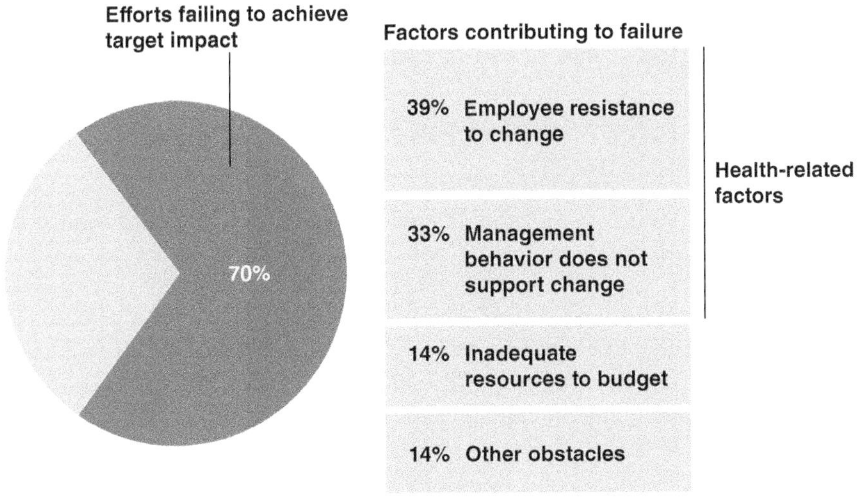

**Efforts failing to achieve target impact**

**Factors contributing to failure**

70%

39% Employee resistance to change

33% Management behavior does not support change

14% Inadequate resources to budget

14% Other obstacles

Health-related factors

are asked to nominate the areas where they need better information to help them design and lead large-scale change programs, only 16 percent chose "determining what needs to be done to generate near-term performance." On the other hand, more than 65 percent chose "determining what needs to be done to strengthen the company's health for the longer term."[11]

The magnitude of people-related challenges in making change happen also accounts for why the data suggests that, while the best answer in leading change is putting equal emphasis on performance and health, it also reveals that if you're going to err on one side or the other, your odds of success are higher if you overemphasize health than if you overemphasize performance.[12]

In light of the above, while we'll be talking about both the performance and health-related aspects of managing change extensively throughout the rest of this book, you'll find the content skewed toward insights, methods, and tools to get the health side of the equation right.

## More on Our Methodology

By this point, we hope we've persuaded you that we've done our homework, and that the advice and guidance you'll find throughout this book have a solid foundation in evidence. We're tempted to dive straight into the "How to" of the Five Frames of Performance and Health. But we suspect there may be a few statisticians, academics, or skeptics out there who'd like to know more about our survey methods or analyses that underpin our definition of organizational health. If you're one of these, please continue reading. If you aren't, we strongly suggest you skip to the next chapter, unless you happen to be reading in bed and need help falling asleep. You have been warned!

### What Research Underpins the Nine Elements of Organizational Health?

Here is a brief summary of the primary and secondary research that contributed to our identification of the nine elements of organizational health.

1. **Direction.** Our analysis of the data gathered in our OHI survey shows that the EBITDA (earnings before interest, taxes, depreciation, and amortization) margin is 1.9 times more likely to be above the median when people feel clear about and excited by where their organization is heading. External research by Bart, Bontis, and Taggar working with data from 83 of the largest organizations in the United States also found there was a strong correlation between a clear

direction (where the company mission is aligned with performance management systems), employee behavior ($r=0.51$), and return on assets ($r=0.32$).[13] Research by Collins and Porras drawing on a survey of 1,000 CEOs confirms that visionary companies outperform their peers financially.[14]

2. **Leadership.** As long ago as 1972, Lieberson and O'Conner, in their review of data for 167 companies over 20 years, found that performance is correlated with leadership across all industries (between 6.5 percent and 14.5 percent of the variance in company profit margin performance could be explained by a proxy for leadership, after considering year, industry, and other company characteristics).[15] In 2016, Hartnell and colleagues found a positive and significant relationship ($r=0.20$) between CEO relational leadership rated by the top management team and return on assets nine months later.[16] McKinsey research provides confirmation: companies with top-quartile scores in leadership have a 59 percent likelihood of having above-median EBITDA.

3. **Work environment.** An analysis of the OHI data reveals that companies that are top quartile in their work environment are 1.8 times more likely to have above-median EBITDA. A landmark 1992 study by Kotter and Heskett that tracked 207 large U.S. companies in 22 different industries over an 11-year period yielded similar results.[17] Companies with strong cultures had a cumulative annual growth rate that far outpaced that of companies with weak cultures: 21 percent compared with 9 percent in revenue, 23 percent compared with 5 percent in stock price, and 22 percent compared with 0 percent in net income. Meanwhile in 2002, Stanford University professor Jasper Sørensen found a strong correlation between culture strength, ROI ($r=0.30$), and operating cash flow ($r=0.29$).[18]

4. **Accountability.** Our research shows that the likelihood of demonstrating an above-median EBITDA margin for companies with an accountability score in the top quartile was 65 percent, 1.9 times more likely than for companies with a bottom-quartile score. A 2003 study by Wagner, Parker, and Christiansen demonstrated that employees who feel psychological ownership work harder at making their company more profitable because they feel ownership of the organizational outcomes. The study showed a strong relationship between psychological ownership beliefs and ownership behaviors ($\beta=0.79$) and between ownership behaviors and financial performance ($\beta=0.35$).[19] In 2014, Brown, Pierce, and Crossley linked psychological ownership with sales performance ($r=0.12$) among over 400 U.S.-based salespeople.[20]

5. **Coordination and control.** Our data shows that this is among the most critical of the nine elements of health: a high score on coordination and control gives an organization a 73 percent chance of an above-average EBITDA. We also know that balancing five measures of performance (financial, operational, people, professional, and risk) produces significant benefits. A study by Davis and Albright in 2004 showed that banks that introduce balanced scorecard systems outperform those that implement only financial metrics for at least 18 months after introduction in terms of non-interest income, percentage loan yield, and non-income deposit volume.[21] Another study by Gittel in 2002, in a hospital setting, showed that "relational" coordination (work routines, cross-functional liaisons, and team meetings) improves organizational performance by facilitating interaction among employees in the work process, and is positively associated with quality of care ($r=0.23$) and reduced length of stay ($r=-0.34$).[22]

6. **Capabilities.** The likelihood that a company with top-quartile capabilities has above-median EBITDA margin is 67 percent, suggesting it is a key contributor to financial performance. A study by McGahan and Porter (1997) indicated that 36 percent of the difference in performance between specific businesses can be attributed to institutional capabilities residing in organizations, with variations by industry ranging from 27 percent in agriculture and mining to 46 percent in retail.[23] A 2011 quantitative review of 66 studies by Crook and colleagues indicated a positive and significant relationship ($p=0.21$) between human capital (defined as the knowledge, skills, and abilities embodied by individuals within an organization) and firm performance.[24]

7. **Motivation.** The likelihood of a company with top-quartile motivation also having above-median EBITDA margin was found to be 73 percent: 1.8 times the likelihood for comparable bottom-quartile companies. Companies showed a 42 percent chance of beating the median no matter whether they were bottom-quartile scorers or in the middle half, indicating that only truly distinctive motivation provides real financial benefit. Research by Gallup in 2005 confirms the importance of employee motivation, indicating that unhappy, demotivated, and disengaged employees cost the U.S. economy up to US$350 billion a year in lost productivity from absence, illness, and other problems.[25] In 2014, Cerasoli, Nicklin, and Ford found a significant correlation ($p=0.26$) between motivation and individual effectiveness based on correlations derived from 154 published and unpublished studies.[26]

8. **External orientation.** Our research shows that the likelihood that a company with top-quartile external orientation has above-median

EBITDA margin is 59 percent, and that the additional benefit gained from being in the top rather than middle quartiles is limited. This means most companies need not be concerned with excelling on this measure, although they should take care not to lag behind. In their seminal 1994 paper, Stanley Slater and John Narver found that a market orientation was significantly related to ROA ($\beta=0.63$), sales growth ($\beta=0.91$), and new product success ($\beta=0.52$).[27] In a 2004 meta-analytic review of 58 studies conducted in 23 countries spanning five continents, Cano, Carrillat, and Jaramillo determined that market orientation is significantly correlated to business performance ($p=0.35$) and is even more salient to service providers than manufacturers.[28]

9. **Innovation and learning.** Our research shows that the likelihood that a company with top-quartile innovation has an above-median EBITDA margin is 66 percent, suggesting that it is a key contributor to performance. Further, we found that the relationship between innovation and performance was relatively linear, with improvements in innovation showing roughly commensurate improvements in financial outcomes. A 1994 study by Zahra and Covin showed that product innovation was positively linked to net profit margin ($r=0.31$), sales growth ($r=0.29$), and return on sales ($r=0.27$).[29] In 2007, Paladino sampled 249 senior executives from top-performing companies in a range of industries and found a correlation ($r=0.2$) between innovation and product quality, itself an important driver of performance.[30]

Phew! Don't say we didn't warn you that this section is only for the statisticians, academics, or hardcore skeptics! That said, in truth the preceding data provided is but a brief, representative summary of our primary and secondary research. Our hope is that it gives you the same confidence we have that our model of organizational health is robust. The rest of this chapter is somewhat more engaging, but we still encourage those looking for practical examples versus theory and statistics to head to the next one!

## How Is the OHI Survey Organized?

Completing the survey involves answering a number of questions about the nine health outcomes and their respective management practices.

**OUTCOMES**   In the "outcomes" part of the survey, we make statements describing a positive, healthy attribute of an organization and ask respondents to what extent the statement applies to their company or organization.

For instance, under the outcomes relating to "direction," we include the following statement: "The vision for the company's future is widely understood by its employees," and ask respondents the extent to which they agree. The possible responses are: 1 Strongly disagree; 2 Disagree; 3 Neutral; 4 Agree; 5 Strongly agree.

Each respondent is asked up to three questions of this nature on each of the nine outcomes. We combine the answers to these questions to determine an overall score for each outcome. This is reported in two ways: as an average between 1 and 5, and as an overall "agreement" score (defined as the percentage of respondents who answer 4 or 5). We typically report the latter since many people find it easier to understand.

**PRACTICES**   In the "practices" part of the survey, we make statements describing the actions that an organization and its leaders can take to drive the associated outcome and ask respondents how often these practices are demonstrated at their organization.

For instance, in the section on the practice of "shared vision" (which is one of the drivers of the "direction" outcome), we include the statement: "Management articulates a vision for the future of the company that resonates with my personal values." Respondents are asked the extent to which this is true of their organization. The possible responses are: 1 Never; 2 Seldom; 3 Sometimes; 4 Often; 5 Always.

Each respondent is asked one or two questions of this nature for each of the 37 practices. As with the questions on outcomes, the responses to all questions on a given practice are combined to arrive at an overall score for that practice.

For a list of the 37 practices covered in the survey, see Exhibit 2.2.

## What Is the Reliability and Validity of the OHI Survey?

As we mentioned earlier, the OHI was built using a rigorous process and a strong research foundation. But some people may still be wondering, is this survey any good? The best way to assess whether a survey is high quality is to measure its *reliability* and *validity*.

The reliability of a survey refers to its consistency and stability. When a survey has high reliability, it generally produces consistent results over time. Take a bathroom scale used to weigh oneself. If every time you step on the scale, it reports the same weight (assuming your weight has not changed), it can be considered reliable. That is no guarantee that the number the scale is reporting is your actual weight, however, which is where validity comes into play. Validity refers to the accuracy of an assessment. The goal of any survey or assessment is to have high reliability and high validity, so you can feel confident in the inferences you're able to draw from it.

The most widely used assessment of reliability is the Cronbach's coefficient alpha, which measures an intercorrelation of the individual items in the survey, so as to evaluate its internal consistency. Alpha scores range from 0.0 (not reliable) to 1.0 (perfectly reliable—items are all measuring the exact same thing). Ideally, you want to fall at least roughly within 0.70–0.99.[31] Reliability is important for each characteristic you are measuring, and not for the *entire* assessment—unless that assessment is only measuring one characteristic. For example, in the OHI, you wouldn't expect that items relating to leadership will be consistent with items measuring accountability or external orientation. As can be seen in Exhibit 2.5, the reliability of each dimension on the OHI is strong and falls within the desired window we mentioned earlier.

For validity, there are several different types of evidence that can be gathered. One is *face validity*. This tests whether, to a lay person, the survey seems to measure what it's intended to measure. The second is *content validity*, which tests whether subject-matter experts think the questions cover each of the facets and dimensions within a given construct (i.e.,

---

Exhibit 2.5

## Scale Reliabilities

| | $\alpha$ |
|---|---|
| Direction | 0.97 |
| Leadership | 0.99 |
| Work environment | 0.94 |
| Accountability | 0.86 |
| Coordination and control | 0.97 |
| Capabilities | 0.94 |
| Motivation | 0.94 |
| External orientation | 0.98 |
| Innovation and learning | 0.94 |

accountability). This ensures that the conclusions drawn can be considered accurate. The third is *criterion-related validity*, where it is statistically demonstrated that the variables of interest are related to important outcomes, which in our case is company performance. On all three of these fronts, we've already established that the OHI is on very safe ground.

A fourth validity test is *construct validity*, which uses multivariate statistical procedures to determine whether a test measures the intended construct. In order to test for construct validity, we ran two types of factor analyses: an exploratory factor analysis (EFA) and a confirmatory factor analysis (CFA).

An EFA is used to reduce data into a smaller set of summary variables. Results of an EFA show the number of overall factors (i.e., the number of concepts you're measuring in the survey) and the individual item factor loadings, which map onto a larger concept to show that the items are measuring what they're supposed to. In the case of the OHI, for example, for it to be valid the EFA would need to say that nine factors would emerge (our nine outcomes) and that each of the items relating to the factors would "load" onto that factor. As can be seen in Exhibit 2.6, we found support for the overall structure of the OHI with minimal cross-loadings and relatively strong factor loadings—suggesting that the internal structure of the assessment has validity.

Whereas the EFA is conducted to *discover* the summary variables from a data set, the CFA is used to test *hypotheses* about the summary variables one expects to find. With a CFA, there are an assortment of fit indices to look at, and we chose to focus on two that are relatively robust to issues like sample size and model complexity: the Comparative Fit Index (CFI) and the Standardized Root Mean Square Residual (SRMR). The CFI is a "goodness of fit" measure and the goal is to have a CFI over 0.85. On the other hand, the SRMR is a "badness of fit" measure, where the desired index is 0.05 or lower. Exhibit 2.7 shows the results from the CFA, and as can be seen through the fit indices and paths, the data is a good fit for the structure, and there is further validity evidence for the OHI.

We did warn you we'd be nerding-out in this section!

## What Data Is Used in Analyzing the Correlation between Health and Financial Performance?

The data gathered during the OHI survey is pulled in accordance with strict criteria. For inclusion in the analysis, surveys have to be completed in full, not in short or customized versions; they have to come from a broad cross-section of the organization in question, not just top team members; and a large enough group must be involved to be representative of the organization concerned.

Exhibit 2.6

# Exploratory Factor Analysis (EFA)

| Outcome | Outcome items | Mean | Standard Deviation | Factor 1 | Factor 2 | Factor 3 | Factor 4 | Factor 5 | Factor 6 | Factor 7 | Factor 8 | Factor 9 |
|---|---|---|---|---|---|---|---|---|---|---|---|---|
| Direction | Direction Item 1 | 3.73 | 0.39 | 0.76 | | | | | | | | |
| | Direction Item 2 | 3.69 | 0.39 | 0.66 | | | | | | | | |
| | Direction Item 3 | 3.45 | 0.37 | 0.57 | | | | | | | | |
| Leadership | Leadership Item 1 | 3.78 | 0.31 | | 0.62 | | | | | | | |
| | Leadership Item 2 | 3.69 | 0.32 | | 0.57 | | | | | | | |
| | Leadership Item 3 | 3.86 | 0.32 | | 0.53 | | | | | | | |
| Work environment | Work environment Item 1 | 3.58 | 0.4 | | | 0.61 | | | | | | |
| | Work environment Item 2 | 3.58 | 0.39 | | | 0.55 | | | | | | |
| Accountability | Accountability Item 1 | 3.88 | 0.28 | | | | 0.71 | | | | | |
| | Accountability Item 2 | 3.84 | 0.25 | | | | 0.63 | | | | | |
| | Accountability Item 3 | 3.24 | 0.34 | | | | 0.48 | | | | | |
| Coordination & control | Coordination & control Item 1 | 3.65 | 0.34 | | | | | 0.56 | | | | |
| | Coordination & control Item 2 | 3.59 | 0.34 | | | | | 0.52 | | | | |
| | Coordination & control Item 3 | 3.42 | 0.36 | | | | | 0.37 | | 0.58 | 0.60 | |
| Capabilities | Capabilities Item 1 | 3.91 | 0.28 | | | | | | 0.69 | | | |
| | Capabilities Item 2 | 4.04 | 0.3 | | | | | | 0.57 | | | |
| Motivation | Motivation Item 1 | 3.33 | 0.43 | | | | | | | 0.87 | | |
| | Motivation Item 2 | 3.46 | 0.37 | | | | | | | 0.83 | | |
| Innovation & learning | Innovation & learning Item 1 | 3.54 | 0.38 | | | | | | | | 0.77 | |
| | Innovation & learning Item 2 | 3.44 | 0.38 | | | | | | | | 0.73 | |
| | Innovation & learning Item 3 | 3.53 | 0.37 | | | | | | | | 0.73 | |
| External orientation | External orientation Item 1 | 3.70 | 0.38 | | | | | | | | 0.67 | 0.86 |
| | External orientation Item 2 | 3.71 | 0.32 | | | | | | | | | 0.72 |
| | External orientation Item 3 | 3.58 | 0.37 | | | | | | | | | 0.56 |

Exhibit 2.7

# Confirmatory Factor Analysis (CFA)

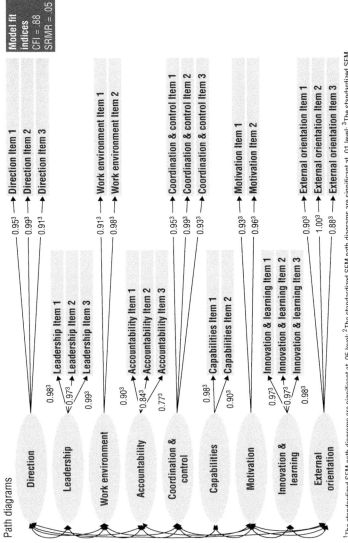

Path diagrams

Model fit indices
CFI = .88
SRMR = .05

[1] The standardized SEM path diagrams are significant at .05 level; [2] The standardized SEM path diagrams are significant at .01 level; [3] The standardized SEM path diagrams are significant at .001 level.

Note: The CFA path diagram are similar to but not the same as partial correlations. They range from −1 to +1. The closer the number is to −1/+1 the stronger the relationships.

Surveys also have to meet one further requirement: that robust, publicly available data on financial results is available either for the organization concerned or for the broader corporation to which it belongs. Nonprofits, government entities, and private companies are excluded for analytical purposes if financial performance data is unavailable or inadequate.

The data from our survey is assumed to reflect the state of the organization's health at the time the survey is administered and for a period of roughly six months prior to that. Separate surveys for the same company are aggregated and matched to financial data for the appropriate fiscal year. In the analysis of the external data on financial results, scores are again aggregated at the company level.

We use Bloomberg and Compustat as sources for raw data on metrics such as sales, pretax income, EBITDA, net income, employee numbers, book value, shareholder equity, and net debt. We convert this data into ratios (such as return on sales and EBITDA to sales) and percentages (such as sales growth).

We normalize our data on financial results by constructing industry benchmarks for each of the industry sectors for which we have OHI data. We select at least 100 publicly traded global companies for each industry sector and create percentile benchmarks for selected ratios and growth numbers. We then allocate, to each company in the survey, a percentile ranking for each financial metric on the basis of benchmarks for the year in which the survey was conducted or the year following. Companies are categorized as to whether they were performing at, above, or below the industry median on the metric in question. We use this as the critical criterion or dependent variable for further analysis. The companies surveyed have shown a wide range of performance relative to industry peers, suggesting that our sample is robust and representative.

■ ■ ■

Albert Einstein reputedly had a poster in his office that declared, "Not everything that counts can be counted, and not everything than can be counted counts." The people-related aspects of leading successful change at scale have long been grouped into the realm of those things that cannot be counted. In the exhaustive research underpinning our definition of organizational health and the OHI measurement tool that we've developed, we believe this is no longer the case. We also believe the evidence that's been amassed demands only one verdict: organizational health counts!

# PART II

# The Five Frames

# Chapter 3

# Aspire

## *Where Do We Want to Go?*

When Alejandro Baillères, the son of Mexican billionaire Don Alberto Baillères, took the reins of Mexico's largest national insurance company, Grupo Nacional Provincial (GNP), it was facing challenges on many fronts. Founded in 1901, it had a proud heritage as the nation's first life insurance company. In 1969, it became a universal insurer, and in 1972, it was purchased by the family-owned Grupo Bal, one of the largest entrepreneurial conglomerates in the country. The company prospered for many years, enjoying a privileged position as the largest Mexican-owned insurer in a regulatory environment that favored domestic players.

But as the twenty-first century dawned, the industry began to experience a dramatic increase in competitive intensity. In the wake of sweeping government reforms, a host of new players piled into the market: multinational insurers, mono-line attackers specializing in particular products, and global banks looking to extend their reach into insurance. With them came a push toward doing business through direct channels, along with a number of product offerings that were not natural strengths for GNP.

Prior to Baillères' appointment, GNP had lost money for two years running. Its market share was eroding fast, its cost structure was high for the industry, and employee satisfaction was on a downward trajectory. His mandate was to restore GNP to its former glory and then take it to the next level of performance and health.

The first step for the company was to understand where the performance opportunities were. In personal insurance, the affluent client segment served by the sales force was a big driver of revenue. Unfortunately, many products that were being sold to this segment were not profitable. The mass market segment created significant value when served through alternative channels, though this rarely happened due to the misalign-ment of internal incentives. In commercial insurance, a shortlist of clients created the most value, yet GNP didn't approach those clients as one company, and competitively disadvantaged itself by not underwriting busi-ness considering the value of the overall relationship. Customer retention challenges were also pinpointed to specific issues in the claims and servicing areas.

GNP also wanted to get an objective read on how effectively the organi-zation was being managed and led—its health. The employee satisfaction survey that had been in place for a number of years hadn't helped the com-pany avoid its decline and didn't answer the full range of organizational ef-fectiveness questions for which they wanted data. After a wide-ranging look at various measurement tools available, the OHI was chosen. The results told some hard truths about what had become a complacent culture, with low- to mid-quartile scores on most health elements.

Having gathered the data from across the organization, the company's leaders rolled up their sleeves and got to work on setting new perfor-mance objectives. In a series of working sessions involving as many as 300 leaders at a time, GNP developed and agreed on a set of strategic objec-tives. They looked at where there were opportunities (e.g., selling direct to the mass market, approaching commercial clients as one firm), where they had distinctive capabilities (e.g., agency management, 100 percent Mexican ownership, strong government relationships), and where they were col-lectively passionate about winning (e.g., staying Mexico-focused, creating a superior customer experience). At the highest level, the goal was to be "1 on 3 in 5": to be number one in the industry on three dimensions—profitability, client service, and employer of choice—within a five-year time frame. This goal was then broken down into three "500-day" phases, to make progress more manageable. Clear medium-term goals were set for what was aspired to be achieved in each phase.

While there was genuine excitement about the new strategic direction, GNP leaders realized that the probability of success was low given GNP's current state of health. After all, the OHI was unambiguous in its message. The organization wasn't effective at aligning itself on a shared direction. Ex-ecution was slowed by vertical (between levels of hierarchy) and horizontal (between functions and businesses) friction. Renewal was sorely lacking, as most employees were internally focused and going through the motions versus looking for ways to improve the business. Assisted by predictive ana-lytics from the OHI database, GNP's leaders set a health aspiration to enable delivery against its strategic objectives. Overall, the goal was to move from its lower third-quartile health standing in its industry to become top quar-tile. More specifically, it would do so by creating step change improvement in four management practices: strategic clarity, performance transparency, employee involvement, and consequence management.

Once GNP's leadership team felt confident they had a robust performance and health aspiration, they asked a group from its holding company, Grupo Bal, to do a "red-team" review of the strategy to test it for biases—testing every assumption and purposefully building as strong a case as possible for why GNP would fail to achieve its goals. Overall, the performance and health aspiration stood up well to Grupo Bal's scrutiny, though the process did raise important points regarding potential channel conflicts and how to deal with certain large government accounts. After making adjustments to mitigate these risks, GNP finalized its aspiration and was ready to move to the Assess stage and answer, "How ready are we to go there?"

■ ■ ■

Whether applying the Five Frames approach or not, GNP would likely have started their journey by setting an aspiration. The importance of doing so is hardly newsworthy: management literature is virtually unanimous in extolling the virtue of setting clear aspirations. Yet, when a McKinsey survey of almost 3,000 executives asked, "If your company undertook the change program again, what, if anything, would you do differently?" nearly half (48 percent) picked "set clearer targets" as their top choice from a set of 16 potential responses.[1]

Clearly, there's still a gap between what senior managers *should* do (and probably *know* they should do) and what they *actually* do. To help leaders get it right from the start, we now offer our best guidance on how to go about setting performance and health aspirations for your organization. When both are defined clearly, change programs are 1.8 times more likely to succeed than when only one of the dimensions is defined clearly, and 3 times more likely to succeed than when neither is well defined.[2]

## Performance: Strategic Objectives

The aspirations your organization chooses will depend to a great extent on your starting point. They will also depend on your industry or sector: a bank's performance aspirations will be quite different from those of a mining company, a hospital, or a government agency. All the same, there are three steps that almost any organization can and should apply when setting its performance targets: create a compelling long-term vision, roll back the future to mid-term aspirations, and guard against biases in the process. Let's explain each one.

## Create a Compelling Long-Term Vision

A McKinsey survey of 2,724 change leaders asked the question, "Choosing from 10 options given, what is the most important leadership behavior during a change program?" The answer? Communicating a compelling vision to motivate and inspire (ranked first by 62 percent of respondents). It was also ranked as the number one hardest leadership behavior to build (ranked first by 42 percent of respondents).[3]

Certainly, in the vast majority of successful large-scale change programs that we have witnessed, there is a compelling long-term aspiration at play. Take, for example, the U.K.-based supermarket chain Tesco, whose turn-around focused on, in the words of former CEO Sir Terry Leahy, "A plan to build Tesco around its customers, to make it number one in the U.K., and to find new long-term growth in nonfood, in services, and in international expansion." During Leahy's tenure, Tesco quadrupled in size, to the point of taking £1 in every £7 that consumers spend in Britain. It also became the first British supermarket to transform itself into a global brand.[4]

Other examples abound. On taking over Microsoft, Satya Nadella and his team reset the company's direction to focus on, "Building best-in-class platforms and productivity services for a mobile-first, cloud-first world."[5] When Howard Schultz retook the CEO role at Starbucks, he focused first on creating the aspiration, "To become an enduring, great company with one of the most recognized and respected brands in the world, known for inspiring and nurturing the human spirit."[6] Looking back in time, Stanford University's 1940s vision to become the "Harvard of the west" and Sony's 1950s drive to overturn the reputation of Japanese electronic goods for poor quality provide iconic examples of compelling long-term change visions.

We acknowledge that the term *vision* can invoke for some a sense of an airy-fairy statement that amounts to little more than eye-roll-inducing sloganeering. Lou Gerstner, for example, early in his tenure as CEO of a beleaguered IBM, boldly stated, "The last thing IBM needs right now is a vision."[7] Make no mistake, we're talking about something more concrete. In fact, Gerstner did have a long-term vision—keep IBM one company, fix its underlying problems, and then become a broad-based technology integrator. In situations where a vision is essentially nothing more than a feel-good slogan or an impossible stretch, the role of a new leader may be to ramp back aspirations. As Alan G. Lafley explains, when he first became Procter & Gamble's CEO, "The first thing I did was to set lower, more realistic goals."[8]

So how do you set a compelling long-term vision that isn't pie in the sky and yet still inspires and guides the organization to bring its A-game in its pursuit? We advocate that the best vision for any change effort lies at the intersection of three areas: opportunity, capability, and passion, as illustrated in Exhibit 3.1.

Exhibit 3.1

## Setting a Compelling Vision

Example analytics

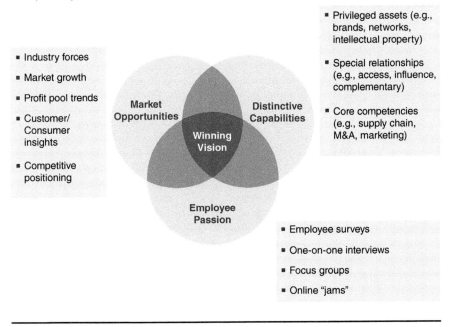

- Industry forces
- Market growth
- Profit pool trends
- Customer/ Consumer insights
- Competitive positioning

- Privileged assets (e.g., brands, networks, intellectual property)
- Special relationships (e.g., access, influence, complementary)
- Core competencies (e.g., supply chain, M&A, marketing)

- Employee surveys
- One-on-one interviews
- Focus groups
- Online "jams"

Having a strong fact base in each of these areas is vital to decision-making. Our research shows that those programs that do so are 2.4 times more likely to succeed.[9] Facts you want to gather related to opportunities include understanding the industry forces at work, which areas of the market are growing, where the profit pools are and how they are migrating, how customer preferences and needs are evolving, what your current competitive positioning is and scenarios for how it is likely to evolve, and so on. Facts related to your capabilities include determining what your privileged assets are (e.g., brands, networks, intellectual property), what special relationships you have (e.g., partnerships or affiliations that give you access, influence, or enable complementary offerings), and where it is you've built distinctive competencies (e.g., supply-chain excellence, M&A, brand leadership).

The final, and most often neglected, element of deciding on the right long-term vision is understanding what the leaders and employees are passionate about driving forward. Done well, this can ensure the vision taps into the internal motivation of leaders and employees (making execution less dependent on external drivers such as incentives). We'll talk about various techniques to understand where leader and employee passions lie when we talk at the end of this chapter about the "Master Stroke" for setting an aspiration, but suffice to say here that asking the question of what employees' passion and purpose are—what winning means for them—is an important input to setting the long-term vision.

To illustrate the power of tapping into employee passions, consider the experience of the head of sales at a retail company who shared with us that he kept telling his team the direction they needed to go in, but progress was slow and he (and they) became increasingly frustrated. At the end of his rope, he asked them what *they* wanted to do. He didn't believe their strategy was as good as his plan, but there was nothing particularly wrong with it and they were passionate about making it happen, so he gave them the green light and his full support. The approach paid off: his division moved from lower-quartile to top-quartile sales in a matter of months.

The preceding example, no doubt, sounds fairly straightforward. So why, as reported at the start of this section, do so many leaders report they regret that they didn't do it well? In our experience, the hardest part of creating a vision is finding the balance between what is bold and transformational and what is realistic and achievable. The phrase many use for this is landing on a vision that is "tough but doable." If the vision feels too incremental, cautious, or overly tailored to existing capabilities, it will fail to create momentum or pressure for an organization to push the limits of what is possible and therefore won't lead to breakthroughs. At the same time, if people see goals as simply "pie in the sky" and beyond reach, they will become disillusioned and give up.

Often, examining the "art of the possible" can help find the sweet spot. For example, ask what performance would look like if every area operated at the level of the current best practice within the company? What if all of our processes and systems were operating at the top of their technical limits? What if we achieved best practice in the industry on not one, but all key measures? In the financial services sector, for example, a bank that is in the lowest performance quartile of its industry could manage a six-fold increase in its ratio of operating profits to total revenue if it were able to move to the top quartile. Even a top-quartile bank could boost its performance by 50 percent if it combined the sector's peak level for income per employee with top-tier labor-cost efficiency. By considering the art of the possible in this way, leaders can aim high without the goal feeling untethered to reality.

Going beyond this type of thinking risks not only "pie in the sky" reactions to your goals, but also unintended consequences. Consider healthcare start-up Theranos. The company promised to create a medical device that could run 70 blood tests on only a 25- to 30-microliter blood sample—a feat that had never been done before. When it turned out that their technology was not producing accurate results, Theranos proceeded to show fake proficiency tests while using commercial machines to complete the blood tests and present false and misleading information to investors, patients, and the media. Within fifteen years of being founded, Theranos closed down and the leaders were facing many lawsuits. Theranos isn't alone, unfortunately. Consider also the automaker that aspired to create a new model that weighed less than 2,000 pounds, sold for less than US$2,000, and would be in showrooms within two years. The resulting vehicle was rushed out so quickly that safety issues abounded, leaving the bold aspiration's legacy to be only one of tragedy and lawsuits. Or the retailer who set goals for its auto repair staff that were so high they motivated employees to both overcharge and to complete unnecessary repairs—unethical behaviors for which the company paid a hefty price in the end.[10]

The final aspect of setting a long-term vision that we haven't covered is what we mean by "long-term." We've remained purposefully vague on this point given that the answer is highly context-dependent. For CEOs of public companies, we advocate they think somewhere between 5 and 10 years out. For leaders of businesses or functions, we typically find 3–5 years to be a helpful range. Lower down in an organization, a vision for 2–3 years out may make the most sense. And all of this depends, of course, on the context of whether the change is a turnaround scenario, a good to great effort, or a great to greater-still journey.

## Roll Back the Future to Mid-Term Aspirations

While a long-term performance vision is important, our research and experience suggest a vital next step is to "roll back the future" by defining concrete medium-term objectives for the change program. Why is that? Because it makes the aim nearer and clearer. Having this immediacy and tangibility greatly aids in setting a rapid pace for change, creating an action-oriented attitude, and provides more "beginnings, middles, and ends" in the course of the journey to help generate energy and motivation along the way.

When Ravi Kant became managing director of Tata Motors, an India-based vehicle manufacturer, the company was in crisis. After a decade of strong revenue and margin growth, it had been suddenly hit by the collapse of demand for its trucks. At the same time, there were growing threats from overseas competitors, as well as cost pressures resulting from Tata's entry into the passenger car business and investment in complying with new emissions standards. In a turn of events that shocked the markets, Tata Motors reported a 5-billion-rupee (US$110 million) loss for the fiscal year.

Under the circumstances, Tata might have been expected to devote all its energies to tackling the immediate problems that beset it. But that's not what happened. Instead, Kant worked closely with his senior leaders to create a bold long-term vision for the company. They planned not merely to restore it to its former glory as India's leading truck manufacturer, but to turn it into a diversified automobile giant with global ambitions. Exciting though this vision was, Kant and his team knew that it wasn't enough. They would be unlikely to mobilize people's energies unless it was broken down into actionable pieces, as illustrated in Exhibit 3.2.

As Kant explains, "We decided on a recovery strategy that had three distinct phases, each of which was intended to last for around two years. Phase one was intended to stem the bleeding, since we just couldn't ignore the fact that our sales volumes were still falling with the shrinkage of the overall market. Costs had to be reduced in a big way, and that was going to be a huge challenge for a company that was not only the market leader but had been used to operating in a seller's market and employing a cost-plus approach to pricing. Phase two was about consolidating our position in India, and phase three was to go outside India and expand our operations internationally."[11]

The plan proved remarkably successful. Having slashed 8 billion rupees (US$176 million) from its cost base in the first phase, Tata then made a successful entry into passenger cars in the compact, midsize, and sports-utility vehicle markets. It was able to capture opportunities presented by

## Exhibit 3.2
## Example Mid-term Aspirations

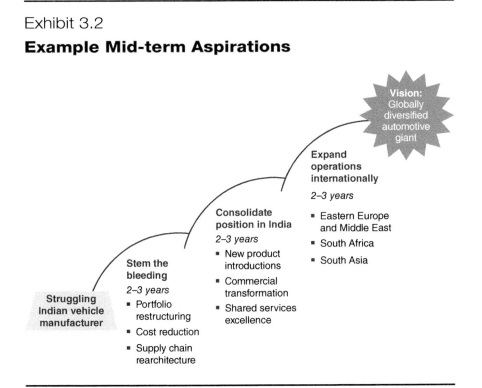

favorable social and economic trends such as the new affluence and desire for mobility among young Indians and the government's substantial road-building program. Eight years later, the company had become India's largest carmaker, and the winner of the coveted title of India's most valuable brand.[12]

Outside its home market, Tata built a significant presence both through its sales efforts in markets such as the former Soviet republics, Turkey, South Africa, countries in the Middle East and South Asia, and through its acquisitions in the United Kingdom, South Korea, Thailand, and Spain. It had successfully become the world's fourth-largest truck manufacturer and second-largest bus manufacturer, and it employed 24,000 workers.

Would Tata have been able to achieve its aspirations without breaking down its long-term vision into a series of medium-term aspirations? It's hard to say, but there is little doubt that the immediacy of medium-term goals makes them more actionable. When managers are planning two or three years ahead, that period is close enough in time to allow them to choose relevant goals and identify specific initiatives to reach them.

On the other hand, what if Tata had simply set objectives in the form of year-on-year targets, without having a longer-term view? Again, we have no way of knowing, but certainly there are advantages in having objectives distant enough to reduce any temptation to rob tomorrow to pay for today—a constant battle for public companies under pressure to achieve quarterly results.

Similar stories can be told for virtually all iconic company-wide change programs. At IBM under Lou Gerstner, the initial phase of performance-related change efforts was similar to that of Tata under Kant: fix the basics. The next focused on growing the IT services and PC businesses. The third enabled its corporate customers to move into a brave new networked world by providing guidance on their technology strategies, helping them build and run their systems, and acting as the architect and repository for their computing.

At Starbucks, when Howard Schultz stepped back into the CEO role to restore the company to a growth trajectory, the first phase of performance-related efforts involved becoming the undisputed coffee authority. Among many actions taken, this involved upgrading coffee-making equipment, creating a customer loyalty program, targeting the at-home coffee market, and extensive barista training. At one point, more than 7,000 stores were closed for 3 hours for "Espresso Excellence Training," where 135,000 baristas learned how to pour a perfect espresso shot and steam milk properly. The second phase focused on expanding Starbucks' global presence, which included redesigning store formats, offering culturally reflective products, and supporting local causes. The third targeted becoming a leader in ethical sourcing and environmental impact through partnerships with fair-trade organizations and recycling programs—enabling the company to differentiate itself as being "Responsibly Grown. Ethically Traded. Proudly Served."[13]

In our view, the idea of defining your desired medium-term aspirations gets less attention than it deserves in management literature. A long-term performance vision isn't enough; it needs to be rolled back to a desired set of medium-term performance milestones that are granular and actionable, but also ambitious about the scale and pace of change.

## Guard Against Biases

Consider a cautionary tale. When former CEO Antonio Perez took over an ailing Eastman Kodak Company whose film revenues were nose-diving, he knew it would need to reinvent itself. Perez quickly redirected the strategy and set a long-term vision to win in the digital printer market. Five years later, Kodak shares were worth less than a dollar. With the company filing for bankruptcy, Perez earned the dubious honor of being named one of the worst CEOs of the year by CNBC.

What happened? The answer, at least in part, lies in what psychologists refer to as the *confirmation bias*. Perez's career prior to becoming CEO included 25 years working primarily in the inkjet printing and imaging areas of Hewlett-Packard. As he looked at the information available, he put more weight on those that confirmed his beliefs and less on those that refuted them (including the fact that the company had already experimented in the space several times without success and lacked manufacturing expertise or scale to achieve attractive returns in such a commoditized industry).[14]

Confirmation bias is just one of a multitude of cognitive biases (check Wikipedia and you'll find over 120 listed) that cause our decisions to deviate from good judgement. In our experience, however, this and two others—groupthink and the optimism bias—are the most prevalent and dangerous.

*Groupthink* refers to a phenomenon whereby the desire for consensus and harmony within a group leads to dysfunctional decision-making processes, including self-censorship (not speaking out) and pressuring. Dr. Jerry B. Harvey provides a wonderful example of this bias at work in his landmark book on organizational behavior, *The Abilene Paradox, and Other Meditations on Management*. He describes the Harvey family sitting around a porch in Coleman, Texas. It's 104 degrees out, but the porch is shaded, so everyone is reasonably comfortable. Jerry Harvey's father-in-law says, "Hey, why don't we drive to Abilene and have dinner at the cafeteria." Jerry thinks to himself, "This is crazy; I don't want to drive 53 miles in the heat of summer in a 1958 Buick to have dinner in a lousy cafeteria." Before he can speak up, his wife interjects, "Sure, that sounds like a good idea." Jerry then hedges, "Okay, I guess … assuming your mother wants to go." Jerry's mother-in-law affirms, "Of course I want to go."

Four hours and 106 miles later, they return to the porch, covered in sweat and dust from driving in the brutal heat with the windows down (there is no air conditioning in a 1958 Buick!). The food, as per Jerry's prediction, had been almost unpalatable. As they sit down, Jerry says sarcastically, "Well, that was a great trip, wasn't it?" Nobody speaks. His mother-in-law then finally says, "To tell the truth, I didn't enjoy it. I'd have rather stayed home, but you all pressured me into going." Jerry responds, "I didn't pressure you. I was happy here; I only went to make the rest of you happy." His wife then says, "But I was just going to make you all happy." Jerry's father-in-law then speaks up, "I never wanted to go to Abilene. I just thought you all might be bored sitting at home!"

Surely this doesn't happen in organizations? Unfortunately, there are many examples of where it has had catastrophic effects, including the collapse of Swissair, the follies of many banks that led to the economic crisis of 2008, the Space Shuttle *Challenger* disaster, the stagnation of the U.S. auto industry, the Bay of Pigs invasion, and so on. As a new leader setting an aspiration, be warned that many around you will make themselves more agreeable to an idea, despite not necessarily believing in it. When this becomes the case, not only is the quality of your aspiration in jeopardy, but so is the commitment to deliver against it.

The third bias to be aware of is the *optimism bias:* the expectation that the best possible outcome will emerge. This accounts for why divorce rates in the western world are around 40 percent, yet when you ask newlyweds to rate their likelihood of divorce they are most likely to put it at 0 percent. It's also why 90 percent of capital projects have cost overruns (on average, 45 percent over their business plan). It also explains why, as our colleagues Chris Bradley, Martin Hirt, and Sven Smit describe, "One of the most emblematic outputs of the dreaded strategic-planning process is the 'hockey stick' forecast—the line that sails upwards on the graph after a brief early dip to account for up-front investment. These hockey sticks, confidently presented by executives pitching their new strategy, are easy to draw but they don't score many goals. What tends to happen in reality is that the strategy fails to meet the bold aspirations and is replaced by a new one."[15]

Being aware of such biases doesn't help one avoid them. As Dan Ariely, one of the foremost thinkers in the field, declares, "I am just as bad myself at making decisions as everyone else I write about."[16] Fortunately, however, there are a number of proven and practical tools to minimize biases in decision-making. These include, among others, the following: the "pre-mortem" (generating a list of potential causes for failure of a recommendation and working backward to rectify them before they happen); "red team–blue team" (assigning one person/group to argue for, and one to argue against, a decision); "clean-sheet redesign" (developing a system from only a set of requirements, free from considerations related to current investments or path); and "vanishing options" (taking the preferred option off the table and asking, "What would we do now?"). Importantly, simply ensuring you are engaging a diverse team in decision-making will reap significant rewards—which research reveals can improve decision-making quality by more than 50 percent.[17]

Note that though we advocate leaders use the tools available to them to de-bias decisions, we aren't saying leaders shouldn't also "gut check" their decisions. We agree with T. Gary Rogers, former chairman and CEO of Dreyer's Grand Ice Cream, when he says, "If it doesn't feel right in your gut, don't do it."[18]

# Health: Goals

As we said earlier, when an organization sets aspirations for its health that are as clear and explicit as those for its performance, it significantly increases its chance of achieving change success. Our research reveals that efforts with clearly defined aspirations for both performance *and* health are 1.8 times more likely to be "very" or "extremely" successful than those with clear aspirations for performance alone. If we look just at those programs reported as "extremely" successful, the difference is a whopping 4.4 times more likely.[19] So how do you know what your organization's health goals should be to enable it to deliver on its strategic objectives? By following a proven process that involves checking your health, choosing where to be exceptional, and targeting broken management practices.

## Check Your Health

In Chapter 1, we introduced the idea of organizational health, defining it as how effectively an organization works together in pursuit of a common goal. Health-related actions are those that improve how an organization *aligns* itself, *executes* with excellence, and *renews* itself to achieve its performance aspirations sustainably in its ever-changing external environment. In Chapter 2, we identified the nine elements of organizational health, namely direction, leadership, work environment, accountability, coordination and control, capabilities, motivation, external orientation, and innovation and learning. We also broke down these nine elements into the 37 management practices that feed into them. Then we described how our survey-based tool, the organizational health index (OHI), can provide organizations with a comprehensive and rigorous understanding of their health.

For the purposes of this chapter, we've developed a high-level overview of the OHI to remind readers what organizational health involves. This is illustrated in Exhibit 3.3. You can use it to conduct a rough assessment of how healthy your organization is. Where does it belong in each element—is it *ailing*, *able*, or *elite*? Which elements are most important to you in achieving your medium-term performance aspirations? Where would you like to be on each element? How much faster and better would your change efforts proceed if you were elite?

Exhibit 3.3

## Assessing Organizational Health

| | Ailing | Able | Elite |
|---|---|---|---|
| **Direction** | Creates a strategy that fails to resolve the tough issues | Crafts and communicates a compelling strategy, reinforced by systems and processes... | ...and provides purpose, engaging people around the vision |
| **Leadership** | Provides excessively detailed instructions and monitoring (high control) | Shows care toward subordinates and sensitivity to their needs (high support)... | ...and sets stretch goals and inspires employees to work at their full potential (high challenge) |
| **Work environment** | Lacks a coherent sense of shared values | Creates a baseline of trust within and across organizational units... | ...and creates a strong, adaptable organization-wide performance culture |
| **Accountability** | Creates excessive complexity and ambiguous roles | Creates clear roles and responsibilities, links performance and consequences... | ...and encourages an ownership mindset at all levels |
| **Coordination and control** | Establishes conflicting and unclear control systems and processes | Aligns goals, targets, and metrics managed through efficient and effective processes... | ...and measures and captures the value from working collaboratively across organizational boundaries |
| **Capabilities** | Fails to manage talent pipeline or deal with poor performers | Builds institutional skills required to execute strategy... | ...and builds distinctive capabilities to create long-term competitive advantage |
| **Motivation** | Accepts low engagement as the norm | Motivates through incentives, opportunities, and values... | ...and taps into employees' sense of meaning and identity to harness extraordinary effort |
| **External orientation** | Directs the energy of the organization inward | Makes creating value for customers the primary objective... | ...and focuses on creating value for all stakeholders |
| **Innovation and learning** | Lacks structured approaches to harness employees' ideas | Able to capture ideas and convert them into value incrementally and through special initiatives... | ...and able to leverage internal and external networks to maintain a leadership position |

Most leaders, even when looking at health using this simple assessment, see how health improvements can be a massive change accelerant. A robust health check, however, requires a much more in-depth analysis. It starts with doing the OHI, which we've already described. The OHI is then augmented with a set of analytics to confirm that perceptions reported in the survey reflect reality. If they prove not to do so, the solution may lie in improving transparency and communication rather than fundamentally changing management practices. One financial services organization, for example, discovered that its staff didn't find monetary incentives motivating because they perceived that pay didn't vary with performance. Analysis showed, however, that this was a misapprehension. Instead of recommending a revamp of the compensation system, the firm quickly concluded that what was needed was a communications program to make the link between pay and performance clearer.

The types of analyses that are often helpful include analyzing data that comes from customer loyalty scores (customer focus), hiring rates from target talent pools (talent acquisition), compensation benchmarking (financial incentives), executive calendar analyses (various leadership practices), and linkages between performance scorecards (strategic clarity). In the vast majority of cases, the additional facts reinforce the survey findings and act primarily to inoculate any skeptics who speculate perception may not match reality (often out of defensiveness, because they don't like the health report they are seeing—much like many people's tendency when they get back less than pleasant diagnostic results from a physical health check!).

Taken together, the OHI and related analyses are the most robust way available to measure your organization's health. They are, in many ways, the equivalent of getting a physical at the Mayo Clinic (widely regarded as one of the best hospitals in the world) versus going to your local physician. It's important to note that, like a human being getting a physical, your health will be whatever it is. You may find some wonderful surprises that give you even more optimism about the future and may even make you return to your strategic objectives and be even bolder. You may find some early warnings and, while they are not currently a big concern, by addressing them you ensure they never will become one. Or you may find something more sinister that requires a significant intervention to ensure it doesn't become terminal.

## Choose Where to Be Exceptional

Whatever your health, once you've had it checked, the next step is to determine what your health goals should be to best enable your performance aspiration. For most organizations who get a health check, there will be opportunities to get healthier. The first indicator of this will be how you stack up against peer organizations not only on your health outcomes, but also on the 37 management practices that create those outcomes.

It's worth noting that the 37 management practices that drive organizational health outcomes are all happening in your organization, whether proactively managed or not. Employees have a perception of what the strategy is, they are working toward targets regardless of whether these have been set implicitly or explicitly, budgets are being allocated rightly or wrongly, people are being hired and fired, performance is being monitored in some way, shape, or form, compensation is being provided, risks are managed (well or not well), stakeholders are being interfaced with, and so on.

So, when it comes to health goals, does it then follow that every company should aspire to be exceptional in all management practices? No. Emphatically, no! We've yet to find a company who is top-quartile in all its management practices, and yet we've worked with many companies who have achieved excellent health outcomes.

To revisit the analogy with human health, what it means for individuals to be healthy, beyond the basics, will depend to some extent on their performance aspirations—what they want to do with their lives. A healthy weight for a body-builder is different from that of a jockey; a pilot requires a higher standard of eyesight than an academic; a ballet dancer needs more flexible joints than a lawyer. When we dug more deeply into the 37 practices, we found that healthy companies aren't great at everything—far from it, in fact. More specifically, analysis shows that being top quartile in just six management practices gives you an 80 percent likelihood of being in the top quartile for *overall* health, which, in turn, drives superior business performance (Exhibit 3.4).

This is a liberating finding for leaders. But if an organization only needs to be exceptional at six management practices (if not broken in others) to have a high likelihood of being healthy, can it just choose any six? Unfortunately, it's not that easy. To understand why requires an understanding of the concept of complementarity, defined by John Roberts in his book *The Modern Firm* as: "Two variables are complements when *doing (more of) one of them increases the returns to doing (more of) the other.*"[20]

To see how this works, let's look at the example illustrated in Exhibit 3.5. If a company wants to increase motivation, it has various management practices at its disposal. If it decides to offer incentives to its staff, it has a 48 percent probability of increasing its motivation to the top-quartile level (perhaps surprisingly, the lowest probability for any motivation practice). However, if the company offers incentives *and* modifies its work environment to create performance transparency, the probability goes up to 95 percent. Adopting two complementary management practices instead of relying on just one greatly increases the chance of success—almost doubling it, in this case.

Exhibit 3.4

# Six Is the Magic Number

Likelihood that an organization's overall health will be in the top quartile if the stated number of practices are in the top quartile, %

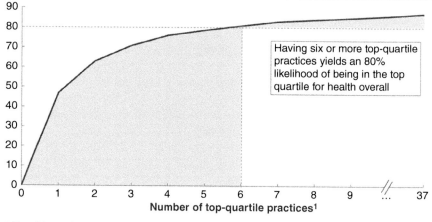

Having six or more top-quartile practices yields an 80% likelihood of being in the top quartile for health overall

Number of top-quartile practices[1]

1 All remaining practices are assumed to be above the bottom quartile

Exhibit 3.5

# Management Practices Work in Combination

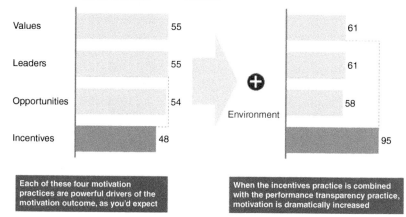

| If an organization is in the top quartile for these individual motivation practices... | ...it has the following % likelihood of being in the top quartile for overall motivation | Adding top-quartile ranking for performance transparency to these scores... | ...results in the following % likelihood of being in the top quartile for overall motivation |
|---|---|---|---|
| Values | 55 | | 61 |
| Leaders | 55 | | 61 |
| Opportunities | 54 | Environment | 58 |
| Incentives | 48 | | 95 |

Each of these four motivation practices are powerful drivers of the motivation outcome, as you'd expect

When the incentives practice is combined with the performance transparency practice, motivation is dramatically increased

The concept of complementarity is easier to grasp if we think about cooking. Flour, yeast, and water are hardly exciting ingredients by themselves, but when they are used in the right proportions and prepared in the right way, they can turn into fresh, hot bread that tastes sensational. Or take peanut butter and jelly: combined in a sandwich, they have a salty-sweet taste that many people far prefer to either filling alone (yes, for our international readers, we realize this last one is a very American analogy!).

The food analogy also illuminates that complementarity has a flipside, as well. Take chocolate cookie dough. Delicious. Take a fresh seafood salad. Wonderful. Now mix the two together, bake, and serve. Yuck! The same is true of management practices. If an organization wants to increase its innovation and learning, for example, it has various practices at its disposal: if it uses top-down innovation as a lever, it has a 58 percent probability of increasing its innovation and learning to the top-quartile level. However, if it emphasizes incentives, performance transparency, and talent-acquisition practices *in addition to* top-down innovation, the likelihood of achieving a top-quartile innovation and learning level drops to 44 percent.

It turns out that large-scale innovation is by nature a collaborative effort. This particular combination of ingredients overemphasizes human capital (people's intellectual contributions and functional skills) at the expense of social capital (networking, collaboration, and information sharing). A far better recipe would combine top-down innovation with a shared vision, knowledge sharing, and customer focus, which yields a 78 percent likelihood of achieving a top-quartile level of innovation and learning.

Having now established the concept of complementarity, the question becomes whether there is a winning recipe—that set of six or so complementary practices that, if exceptional (top-quartile), creates healthy outcomes across the board. Well, we've done the math, and we can tell you that there is no single winning recipe—there are *four!* To be clear, we didn't make these up, they are simply the result of analytically mining our database using cluster-analysis techniques, as visually depicted in Exhibit 3.6.

We have labeled the four clusters based on our interpretation of how the practices in each recipe combine and the nature of the companies that share their attributes, but it's worth emphasizing that the labels shouldn't be the focus; the recipe of six practices should be. To use our cooking analogy, the label is the description on the menu (e.g., a bourbon bread pudding), but the practices are the ingredients that, when combined carefully, make it delicious (eggs, cream, sugar, day-old brioche, raisins, and a splash of the finest Kentucky bourbon). The labels we've chosen are leadership factory, market shaper, execution edge,

Exhibit 3.6

## Visual Representation of Management Practice Cluster Analysis

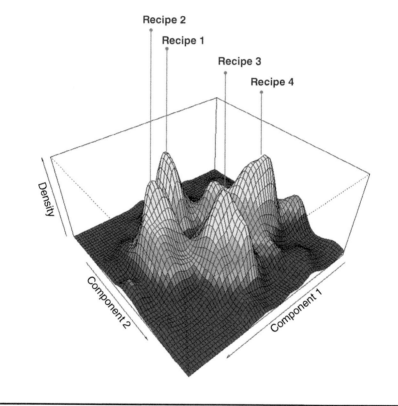

and talent and knowledge core.[21] Exhibit 3.7 shows the ingredients of each recipe—the distinctive management practices that contribute—in order of rank. Let's take a closer look at each recipe in turn.

**Leadership Factory** A leadership factory recipe drives performance by developing and deploying strong leaders, and supporting them through coaching, formal training, and the right growth opportunities. Companies with this recipe are often seen as leadership academy companies, such that other companies actively look to recruit their leaders due to their reputation of being exceptionally well-developed. Leadership factory organizations represent 25 percent of recipe-aligned companies in our database.

Exhibit 3.7

# The Four Recipes and Practices that Drive Them

| | A Leadership Factory | B Market Shaper | C Execution Edge | D Talent and Knowledge Core |
|---|---|---|---|---|
| 1 | Risk management | Capturing external ideas | Performance transparency | Career opportunities |
| 2 | Personal ownership | Business partnerships | Employee involvement | Talent acquisition |
| 3 | Challenging leadership | Role clarity | Creative and entrepreneurial | Rewards and recognition |
| 4 | Career opportunities | Customer focus | Consequence management | Personal ownership |
| 5 | Performance contracts | Top-down innovation | Capturing external ideas | Knowledge sharing |
| 6 | Open and trusting | Competitive insights | Rewards and recognition | Talent development |

If you are a leader in one of these companies, chances are you feel a personal stake in the outcomes you and the company deliver, you trust that career opportunities will be given commensurate with your performance, and you relish that you are always challenged to be better, strive for more, and create more value. For this model to work, it's vital to have an open and trusting environment so that results and feedback can be shared transparently. Perhaps counterintuitively, risk-management practices are also key to ensure that empowered and challenged leaders take calculated risks to achieve sustainable performance, and that no single leader's actions can put the company as a whole in jeopardy.

Leadership factory organizations tend to be structured around business units oriented to grow general managers, with P&L accountability driven lower than usual in the organization. Much of the hiring often happens at or near entry-level positions, with talent developed in-house through clear leadership tracks and early rotation programs. Top leadership time is typically skewed toward grooming the next generation of leaders.

Beverage and convenience foods giant PepsiCo is a good example of a company that embodies the leadership factory recipe. It's renowned for offering its employees excellent opportunities for early responsibility and a culture that encourages initiative and access to decision-makers. Employees are given the freedom to pursue their goals without the burden of excessive structures. Less well known is the rigor of PepsiCo's performance contracts, which tie each individual's objectives to the goals of the business. Performance evaluations are based on delivery against these objectives and on an assessment of a shortlist of leadership competencies that includes weighing both short-term and long-term risks.

**Market Shaper**   Companies that choose this recipe believe that their advantage lies in coming up with products and services that the markets want (or will want) and their competitors will struggle to respond to. As you'd expect given this description, this recipe is characterized by a strong external focus with a significant emphasis on role clarity to ensure products and services are brought to market faster than their peers. Market shaper organizations represent 28 percent of recipe-aligned companies in our database.

In these companies, there generally is no hint of "not invented here" syndrome. Instead, they are keenly aware of the importance of building partnerships and creating and leveraging ecosystems. Further, market shapers aren't content with "let a thousand flowers bloom"-style innovation, and instead are very targeted in where they can fulfill customer needs or outmaneuver competitors from a very strategic and top-down viewpoint. Resources, then, are reallocated accordingly.

Market shapers typically have very strong strategy, finance, and marketing functional capabilities. They also invest heavily in sales and product development functions. These companies are often recognizable for the product and service innovations, or for the "heroes" they hold up as having inspired industry insight and foresight. Therefore, it comes as no surprise that Apple is a good example of the market shaper recipe. As CEO, Steve Jobs' rallying cry to "put romance into computing" gave rise to the sleek and stylish product designs that make customers clamor to get their hands on the latest offerings.[22] Another of the tenets of his leadership was the recognition that "Apple lives in an ecosystem, and it needs help from other partners."[23] Business partnerships are therefore an essential part of Apple's success; in any given year it will have more than 200,000 companies, from software houses to carmakers to newspapers, signed up for partnerships.[24]

**Execution Edge**   Execution edge organizations gain their competitive advantage by involving all employees in driving continuous improvements. The companies that choose this recipe typically find themselves in sectors or markets that are highly competitive or so regulated that real market-shaping opportunities are limited. Execution edge organizations represent 33 percent of recipe-aligned companies in our database.

This recipe emphasizes innovation, but unlike market shaper, the innovation is focused internally on how work gets done. It is driven bottom-up, whereas market shapers drive it top-down. These companies adhere to Al Pacino's philosophy portrayed in the Hollywood movie *Any Given Sunday*, where he describes life as a game of inches, where the margin for error is so small that every inch must be fought for, because, "When we add up all those inches, that's going to make the difference between winning and losing." In these companies, every turn of inventory or point of margin is seen as vital because collectively, they add up to being better than the competition.

Make no mistake, this isn't the sweatshop company trying to squeeze employees for every last ounce of effort. In fact, it's quite the opposite. These are companies where employees are being unleashed from the frontline up to use their skills, entrepreneurship, and creativity to make things better. They promote healthy internal competition by sharing performance transparently, which enables benchmarking and ensures that best practices quickly scale through the system. Rewards, financial and non-financial, and consequences follow accordingly. Within this recipe, the role of the frontline leader is critical. Organizations that do this well spend a disproportionate amount of time selecting, training, and evaluating who gets to lead the frontline.

Walmart is an example of this recipe at work. Its culture of driving out costs and working in partnership across the supply chain means that routine decisions are pushed down to the lowest level of the organization. This enables inventories to move flexibly across the system, and their status is tracked visually so that any problems can quickly be addressed. The entire system is adjusted in real time as numbers are updated from the point of sale, and sales and merchandise inventories in every store are tracked globally via satellite. This data-rich environment enables leaders to know what's working well and what isn't, facilitating best-practice sharing across the organization. Management processes such as these are complemented with Walmart's "grass-roots process"—a way to give every associate a voice in improving the company. The effect is to ensure that all ideas for improvement are captured on a regular basis.

**Talent and Knowledge Core**   The talent and knowledge core recipe creates value by attracting, developing, retaining, and inspiring talent while at the same time accumulating unique and differentiated institutional knowledge so that the collective is far more valuable than the sum of the individuals. As with managing a successful sports team, they need to get the right players (talent acquisition), develop their skills (talent development), get them to work as a team (knowledge sharing), keep them focused (personal ownership), and provide very attractive rewards and recognition and career opportunities so that after they become stars, the players won't be poached by other teams. Talent and knowledge core organizations represent 14 percent of recipe-aligned companies in our database.

These organizations tend to have wider spans and fewer layers to promote more delegation and merit-based promotion. They also typically focus on recruiting the very best, highly skilled, most specialized talent—they have to, as that's their competitive edge. In contrast to organizations who employ the leadership factory recipe (whose value is created through teams directed by a strong leader), talent and knowledge core organizations succeed thanks to highly skilled individual performers working together. As a result, the leaders of these organizations tend to invest significant senior leadership time in talent reviews to ensure talent is being harnessed and developed, and that knowledge is being shared.

One example of this recipe is our own organization. At McKinsey, the talent and knowledge core ethos is embedded in parts of our mission statement: "To build a great firm that attracts, develops, excites, and retains exceptional people." Our core HR resources are small, however. Why? Because it's our partners who are responsible for providing feedback, coaching, and mentoring for junior colleagues. A small number of well-defined roles help to create clear career paths. A merit-based "up or out" model ensures that the talent pool is constantly refreshed and that high performers are able to develop at a rapid pace, opening up career opportunities both inside and outside the firm. Compensation at each level is strategically pitched to reward performance without being at the top of the market, ensuring that people are attracted not just by money but by a sense of personal ownership of McKinsey's values, impact, and development opportunities. A strong culture of collaboration and a state-of-the-art knowledge-sharing system ensure that consultants are continually learning from others and are able to bring the organization's full institutional knowledge to bear on their work for clients no matter where in the world they may be.

While we've emphasized that four recipes aren't something we've theorized or divined—they come from running the numbers—we are struck by how fully these recipes are reflected in organizational life. We saw this recently when a company we were working with indicated they were deeply skeptical that these recipes represented anything more than an academic exercise. By way of response, we asked a few questions on the spot. One of the executives had joined the company just two months earlier, so we asked him, "When was the first time you had any contact with customers?" His answer: on day one as part of his orientation he did a "ride with" in the field (accompanying a sales person to call on clients), and again later that week when he joined a customer dinner with his executive sponsor (another executive charged with helping him in his transition). We then turned to one of our colleagues who had joined our firm recently and asked the same question. Her answer: "I attended three months of business skills training, and then on my first project I did behind-the-scenes work. Only then did I join my first client meeting."

We then asked the executive, "When did your boss first give you feed-back on your performance?" He was mystified. "What do you mean? I've only been on the job for two months. I haven't had any feedback yet." We then turned back to our colleagues and asked, "When did you receive your first formal feedback at McKinsey?" The answer: "Day one, and virtually every day since!"

At this point, the difference between the client's market shaper recipe and our talent and knowledge core recipe couldn't have been clearer. The message is that the practices at the top of the list for each recipe translate directly into the everyday realities of organizational life.

The reality that there are management "recipes" for organizational health and the underlying concept of complementarity sheds light on one of the reasons why management literature has largely been unsuccessful in help-ing leaders drive change and create sustainably excellent organizations. The vast majority of the books and articles we surveyed during our research turned out to have been written from the vantage point of promoting one particular recipe as the answer to all situations.

Pick up *Leadership without Easy Answers* by Ronald Heifetz; John P. Kotter's *On What Leaders Really Do*; *The Captain Class* by Sam Walker; *Superbosses* by Sydney Finkelstein; or *The Power of Servant Leadership* by Robert Greenleaf, and you'll notice that the recommendations they make rely heavily on the leadership factory recipe. Read *Built to Last* by Jim Collins and Jerry Porras; *Doing What Matters* by James M. Kilts; *Execution Excellence* by Sanjiv Anand; or *Execution* by Larry Bossidy and Ram Charan, and you'll find that the execution edge recipe is the implicit model. Should you choose *The Four* by Scott Galloway; *Topple* by Ralph Welborn and Sajan Pillai; *The New Market Leaders* by Fred Wiersema; or *The Innovator's Dilemma* by Clayton Christensen, you'll discover that the discussion hinges on the market shaper recipe. Or, finally, study *Mobilizing Minds* by Lowell Bryan and Claudia Joyce; *Now, Discover Your Strengths* by Marcus Bucking-ham and Donald Clifton; *Work Rules* by Laszlo Bock; or *The War for Talent* by Ed Michaels, Helen Handfield-Jones, and Beth Axelrod, and you'll see that the talent and knowledge core recipe is at the heart of the thinking.

It's not that any of these books are unhelpful or misguided (many are, in fact, exceptional); it's just that their recommendations presuppose a desired recipe that may or may not be right for your organization. What is unhelp-ful and misguided is when a senior executive reads these books and gives the mandate to their teams that, "We want to be the Toyota of lean, ... the Southwest of customer service, ... the Goldman of talent and knowledge, and the Pepsi of leadership development." Unwittingly, in doing so they are asking their teams to create a seafood cookie!

What management recipe is right for your change effort? To decide, we suggest applying three lenses. The first is about *familiarity*: look at the recipe that fits best with your current management practices—it's a lot easier to emphasize or deemphasize a few ingredients in an existing recipe than to change recipes all together. As a neat way to see why this is so, fold your arms. Now try to fold them the opposite way (if you can even figure out how). Difficult, isn't it? What if we asked you to do this not once, but every time you fold your arms from now on? It's not likely the new behavior would last long, regardless of the aspiration. The same is true for management practices—the habitual ways we get things done in our organizations.

The second lens to consider is *fit*: the recipe that fits best with your performance aspiration. Going back to GNP, who we discussed at the beginning of this chapter, their existing health profile was closer to a market shaper recipe. Given the nature of the strategy they were pursuing, however, they felt that an execution edge recipe would be a better fit, and so that's what they chose (essentially ignoring the first lens!).

The third lens to look through is *passion*: what is the senior executive team passionate about driving? Just as passion is an important ingredient in setting the performance aspiration, so too is it important in setting health goals. We often get asked, do you have to have a certain recipe to succeed in a given industry, and the answer is no. In every industry, we see examples of high-health and high-performing companies representative of each of the four recipes. That said, there are some centers of gravity we see, for example, high-performing consumer goods companies are more likely to use the market shaper recipe than not, high-performing industrial companies are more likely to use the execution edge recipe, and in professional services, entertainment, and sports teams, a talent and knowledge core recipe is most common for high performers.

A final question about recipes that often comes up is whether the data suggests an organization has to adopt one of them to be healthy and high performing. The answer is no; only four-fifths of high-performing companies have a clear recipe.[25] So we assert that the recipes and analytics provide good rules of thumb, not a law. That said, organizations that are closely aligned to one of the four recipes are six times more likely to enjoy top-quartile health than companies with weak alignment.[26] This is at least in part because once an effective recipe is chosen and put into place, it is exceedingly difficult to imitate because of the complementarities at work—which takes us back to why organizational health is such a powerful source of competitive advantage.

## Target Broken Management Practices

Knowing where you want to be exceptional is important, but that's not where setting a health aspiration ends. As celebrated sports figure Muhammad Ali said, "It isn't the mountains ahead to climb that wear you out, it's the pebble in your shoe."[27] A good health check won't just help you decide what health recipe to focus on, but it will also give insight into whether any of the 37 management practices are "broken" (fourth quartile). If even one of these is truly broken, it affects the whole system. To draw a human health analogy that many can relate to, consider lower back pain. According to some studies, roughly 80 percent of adults will experience this at some point in their lifetimes. This ailment doesn't just affect one's ability to lift objects; it also makes it harder to concentrate, affects mood, and in the end, causes an overall feeling of not being healthy such that it's the leading contributor to missed work days.[28]

In light of this, an important part of setting a health aspiration is fixing any broken practices. Organizations who have even one broken practice have less than a 25 percent chance of being healthy, regardless of how exceptional they are in other practices. Further, not all practices are created equal. The data science reveals there are four, what we call "Power Practices," that have the greatest impact on organizational health. Companies with even one broken Power Practice have a near-zero chance of attaining top-quartile health. The Power Practices are: personal ownership, role clarity, strategic clarity, and competitive insights.[29]

Knowing this can dramatically alter what a change program focuses on. A financial services company in the Midwest of the United States, for example, undergoing a large-scale customer experience change program, found its efforts stalled. On reading the first edition of *Beyond Performance*, they realized they had only focused on the performance aspects of the change and therefore decided to get their health checked. Even before receiving the results, they had decided they would need to pursue the market shaper recipe. To their surprise, they found the company was broken on all four Power Practices (even though other practices were significantly healthier). Given this, for the next nine months of their change efforts, they didn't worry about recipes and instead focused on "fixing what was broken." Only once they had improved these did they reorient their efforts on achieving distinctiveness in the practices related to the market shaper recipe.

We realize we've covered a lot of ground, and that some of our readers may be wishing that the process for setting a health aspiration was as simple as "Be great at 37 things." We are encouraged by our clients' reactions to doing this work, however, which is that while the analytics behind the curtain are complex, the ultimate answer the process provides is clear, easy to understand, tightly focused, and data-backed. It reflects what psychologist William Schutz described when he said, "Understanding evolves through three phases: simplistic, complex, and profoundly simple."[30]

Ultimately, a robust health aspiration for a change program involves choosing a recipe of practices that will be driven to excellence (sometimes referred to as "signature practices") as well as "fixing what's broken" (to ensure there are no "pebbles in their shoes" on the journey). For example, let's go back to GNP. At the end of the Aspire phase, the answer to, "What are the health goals for our change efforts?" was (profoundly) simple: step-change improvement in *strategic clarity, performance transparency, employee involvement,* and *consequence management.*

## Master Stroke: Involve a Broad Coalition

As we indicated in Chapter 1 (recall judging the length of the two tables illustration!), at the end of each of the Five Frames chapters, we will be sharing the most important lesson from the field of predictable irrationality that should be considered. We call these the change leader "Master Strokes."

The master stroke in the Aspire stage is illustrated by one of Daniel Kahneman's experiments involving a lottery run with a twist. Half the participants were randomly assigned a numbered lottery ticket. The remaining half were given a blank ticket and a pen and asked to choose their own lottery number. Just before drawing the winning number, the researchers offered to buy back all the tickets. They wanted to find out how much they would have to pay people who wrote their own number compared with people who were handed a random number.

The rational expectation would be that there should be no difference. After all, a lottery is pure chance. Every number, whether chosen or assigned, should have the same value. An even more savvy answer would be that you should have to pay the people who write their own number ever so slightly *less,* because of the possibility that there will now be duplicate numbers that, if chosen, would mean the size of the price would be cut in half.

Neither of these turned out to be the right answer. Regardless of nationality or demographic group, people who wrote their own number always demanded at least *five times more* for their ticket. This reveals an important truth about human nature. When we're personally involved in "authoring" an outcome, we are far more committed to it because we feel we own it. The underlying psychology relates to our need for control, which is a deep-rooted survival instinct.

Consider another experiment that examined the importance of a sense of control among elderly people in a nursing home.[31] Some of the residents were given the opportunity to decide how their rooms should be set up, and they were asked to choose a plant to look after. The others had no say in the layout of their rooms, and had a plant chosen and tended for them. After 18 months, the survival rate among residents who had control was 85 percent, but among those who had no control it was just 70 percent. It appears that our desire for control is strong enough to keep us alive.

The lesson for change leaders? If you want to increase the motivation for (and therefore, speed of) the implementation of change, it pays to involve others in creating the aspiration, even when the answer may already be clear in the mind of the leader. Based on the lottery ticket analogy, even if it takes twice as long to do so, the return on investment is five times the motivation to do the work required. Our research confirms that early involvement improves the odds of ultimate success. Change programs whose aspiration phase is characterized by an organization-wide, collaborative effort are 1.6 times more likely to succeed.[32]

Does it mean aspiration setting should become a democratic process? No, absolutely not. Does it create chaos, like a poorly coached children's soccer (*football*, for our international readers) team where all of the players simply move in a swarm versus playing specific roles? Nope. In practice it involves getting broad-based input from the whole organization, bringing together a large group of senior leaders to take on board the input and co-author a solution (most often taking an 80 percent solution created by a smaller working team and refining it), and ensuring that the process of communication enables all employees to spend time self-authoring (writing their own lottery ticket) through a guided process, "What does this mean for me in my role?"

We've seen many different ways the "lottery ticket" lesson has been applied successfully—so many that we could fill a book with just those examples. Here are a few of them, covering a broad spectrum of the methods employed.

Let's start by going back to Neville Isdell's story when he took charge at Coca-Cola. During the Aspire process, he brought together his top 150 people for two-day working sessions once a month for three months in a row so that they could create the company's aspiration and change story together.[33] The work in these sessions drew upon survey and focus group data that had been gathered so employees could provide input and broadly have a sense that their opinions mattered and would be heard. Once the aspiration was set, it and the accompanying change story were rolled out across the organization via one- or two-day sessions, in which small working groups explored the implications (writing their own lottery ticket) for their particular parts of the business. We will describe this process in more depth in Chapter 5.

Some companies leverage technology to enable employees to have their say. IBM's former CEO, Sam Palmisano, spearheaded a change effort to move toward a values-based management system. During the process, more than 50,000 employees were given an opportunity to "write their own lottery ticket" by taking part in a three-day online discussion forum (dubbed ValuesJam) to rewrite the company's century-old values. Out of this effort came a new set of values to guide decision-making and behavior throughout the organization. Following the exercise, more than 200,000 employees— nearly 70 percent of the workforce—downloaded the "values manifesto" that emerged out of the discussion and participated in local-area discussions about its implications on their day-to-day work.

Further examples abound. At 3M, aspiration-setting has moved from a small group exercise to one where a large group of over 1,000 employees from across the company engage in a web-based forum called Innovation-Live over the period of two weeks to provide input. At HCL Technologies, an Indian IT services and software development company, former chairman and CEO Vineet Nayar leveraged a process dubbed "My Blueprint" that opened up the draft strategic aspirations for input from more than 1,000 leaders from across the company via an online platform.[34]

Admittedly, not all transformations allow much time for pursuing co-creative approaches like these, especially when companies need to turn around their performance. When Idris Jala became CEO of the failing Malaysian Airlines in 2005, "We had three and a half months to fix the problem, and if we didn't fix it by then we'd be bankrupt—we'd have no money for salaries, no money for fuel."[35] Yet, despite the burning platform, Jala still found ways to adopt a collaborative approach. After spending time with the P&L to understand where change was most needed (in costs, yield, and network efficiency), Jala assembled groups of 10 to 15 people from various functions and backgrounds—"all people who had a direct stake in a given activity"—and made them accountable for "big results fast."

Executives who adopt the "write your own lottery ticket" approach to aspiration setting are often surprised not only by the sense of ownership and drive for implementation that it creates, but also by the quality of the answers that emerge. At 3M, the company credits the high involvement process with identifying nine future markets worth billions that otherwise wouldn't have been part of the aspiration. At HCL, the process is credited for reframing the aspiration away from an emphasis on commoditized application support toward a handful of new services where HCL had the edge over competitors.

Make no mistake, for decisive leaders who are used to coming up with their own solutions, allowing people to "write their own lottery ticket" is very difficult, even when intellectually, they understand its importance. John Chambers, former chairman and CEO of networking specialist Cisco Systems, observes, "It was hard for me at first to learn to be collaborative. The minute I'd get into a meeting, I'd listen for about 10 minutes while the team discussed a problem. I knew what the answer was, and eventually I'd say, 'All right, here's what we're going to do.' But when I learned to let go and give the team the time to come to the right conclusion, I found they made just as good decisions, or even better—and just as important, they were even more invested in the decision and thus executed it with greater speed and commitment."[36]

The breadth of the leadership coalition that you should involve in setting the aspiration for your change program will very much depend on the context in which you are operating. At the very minimum, your senior leadership team (or if you aren't the most senior leader, the leadership team under whose leadership the change program will be driven) should feel they have written their own lottery ticket regarding the performance and health aspiration. We will discuss specific ideas regarding how to build a strong and committed leadership team in Chapter 8.

■ ■ ■

At the end of the Aspire stage of transformation you'll have answered the question, "Where do we want to go?" for your change program. You'll have a long-term vision and have broken it down into mid-term aspirations so there's a more concrete path to follow. You'll also have tested the strategy for biases, ensuring it's as robust as it can be. You'll also have a health aspiration grounded in a clear understanding of your current health and focused on a shortlist of management practices to make exceptional—your "signature" practices—and those that need to be fixed. Further, you'll have done this in a way that engages a broad coalition so that there are many who feel like they've "written their own lottery ticket" in relation to where the change is headed. This approach will have both created a better answer and generated significant energy and ownership for execution.

Successfully completing the Aspire phase is a great feeling. As GNP's former CEO Alejandro Baillères reflected on his experience of leading change at scale, he recalls, "Setting the aspiration was challenging, but also exhilarating."[37] We liken this point in the journey to how one might feel after poring over a stack of tourist brochures for that once-in-a-lifetime vacation and agreeing with your holiday companions on your dream destination. In spite of the excitement, however, to get from here to your destination there's a lot of work to do to make sure it's realistic. Will you be able to pay for it? Can you find the time to get away? Are your flights and hotels available? Are you willing to put up with the inevitable hassles of getting the right paperwork and then dealing with all the eventualities of a long journey? Questions like these take us to the next phase: assessing "How ready are we to go there?" (Exhibit 3.8).

Exhibit 3.8

# A Proven Approach to Leading Large-Scale Change: The Story So Far

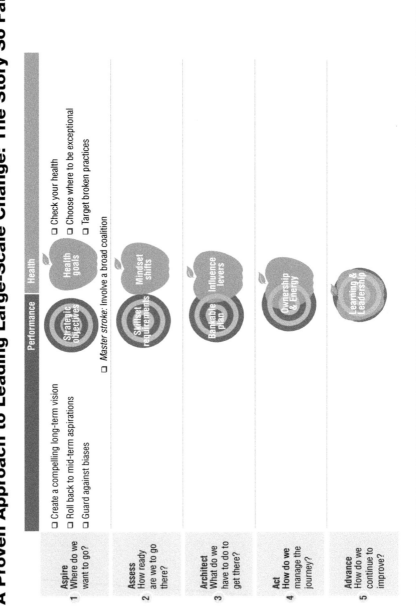

| Performance | Health |
| --- | --- |

**Aspire**
1 Where do we want to go?
- ☐ Create a compelling long-term vision
- ☐ Roll back to mid-term aspirations
- ☐ Guard against biases

Strategic objectives — Health goals
- ☐ Check your health
- ☐ Choose where to be exceptional
- ☐ Target broken practices
- ☐ *Master stroke:* Involve a broad coalition

**Assess**
2 How ready are we to go there?

Skillset requirements — Mindset shifts

**Architect**
3 What do we have to do to get there?

Bankable plan — Influence levers

**Act**
4 How do we manage the journey?

Ownership & Energy

**Advance**
5 How do we continue to improve?

Learning & Leadership

# Chapter 4

# Assess

## *How Ready Are We to Go There?*

When Charles "Chad" O. Holiday Jr. became the 18th CEO of the nearly two-hundred-year-old chemical giant, DuPont, he was the third youngest to have done so and was relatively unknown to the rank and file. His predecessor, John A. Krol, had continued a decade-long strategy to cut back bureaucracy, revitalize its traditional brands, and restructure the company to be more cost-competitive. While this evolution had yielded good results, Holiday felt it was time for a revolution, and set out on a change agenda more profound than any the company had aspired to for a century since it transformed itself from an explosives to a chemicals manufacturing business.

More specifically, Holiday and his team set a long-term vision to expand the company's focus far beyond chemical products to become a science-based products and services company. The strategy to achieve the vision would involve achieving multiple mid-term aspirations such as reshaping the business portfolio, creating more knowledge-intensive value proposition (in Holiday's words, "to get paid for what we know, not just the products we sell"[1]), re-aligning the cost-base to fund growth investments, and improving the company's standing on environmental issues. On the organizational health front, Holiday and his team aspired to move the company from one characterized by "mediocrity" and "malaise"[2] to one characterized by personal ownership, a creative and entrepreneurial work environment, and knowledge sharing.

In the years that followed, many bold actions would need to be taken to deliver against the performance aspirations. Its massive Conoco oil and gas unit, its pharmaceuticals business, and its textiles and nylon business would all be sold. Multiple acquisitions would need to be made to position the company as a major player in the biotechnology space, including the purchases of seed producer Pioneer and the plant-sciences company Verdia, among others. A consulting unit (led by future CEO Ellen Kullman) would need to be created to advise customers on safety and protection. Lean and Six Sigma efforts would be used to ultimately usher in a new, more efficient DuPont Production System (DPS). Environmental goals such as reducing greenhouse emissions by 15 percent, growing revenues by at least US$2 billion from products that create energy efficiencies for its customers, and doubling its annual revenue from nondepletable resources, would be pursued.

Succeeding in these efforts wouldn't be easy—and leadership knew a number of skillsets would be required that weren't historically strong at DuPont. From an industry sector standpoint, the company needed more expertise in the automotive (to drive accelerated growth in its colors and coatings technologies platform) and human health markets (to drive growth in its new acquired agriculture and nutrition businesses). From a geography standpoint, it needed a better understanding of how to work in the faster growing markets of South America, Eastern Europe, and Asia. Further, improved pricing skills would be vital to capturing the full value for the innovation that it would be providing its customers in delivering on its performance aspiration. Finally, lean manufacturing and Six Sigma skills to remove waste and reduce variation in operations would also need to be bolstered.

As important as identifying the priority skillsets that needed to be built was determining how to build them. In some cases, as with pricing and Lean Six Sigma skillsets, multi-year company-wide capability-building initiatives were sponsored by senior executives and supported by external consultants. In other cases, partnerships were formed to augment and build on internal skillsets. In the areas of automotive and human health, for example, partnerships were formed with other companies such as Ford, Merck, and General Mills. A third way skillsets were acquired was through recruiting expertise to join the company and acquiring smaller companies primarily for the purpose of acquiring their talent, as was done to build out geographic skillsets.

Holiday and his team understood that skillsets were only part of the equation. Equally important were the underlying mindset shifts required to enable the skillsets to be fully applied. The vision itself meant the very identity of the company would have to shift from chemicals to sciences, else it would never have had the courage to sell businesses once the core of the company, such as textiles and nylon. "Not invented here" mindsets would have to give way to "the more we learn from others, the better we are" if partnerships were to be successful. Salespeople would need to move beyond "my job is to sell products" to "my job is to articulate and get fair compensation for value-added." Living into environmental aspirations would require a shift from believing "what's good for the environment can be good for business" to "what's good for business must also be good for the environment." And so on.

At a more fundamental level, mindsets related to how to run the organization would have to shift if the company's health was to improve. A deeply ingrained compliance-culture had expanded far beyond the appropriate realms of regulatory and safety to stifle risk-taking of all sorts. A shift in employee mindsets from "my job is to follow the rules" to "my job is to improve what we do, and how we do it" would be required to unlock the creativity and entrepreneurship needed. The traditional command and control structure had also ingrained a mindset of "trust your leader," which had unintendedly created an environment where information was tightly controlled within organizational silos. Shifting this mindset to "trust each other" would prompt relevant knowledge to be shared more freely and transparently across the company. At the heart of increasing personal ownership was a shift from "I own what I control, and others hold me accountable" to "I own the full, positive impact I can have on others, and the business broadly."

■ ■ ■

During Holiday's tenure, multiple actions would be taken to influence both the broad and more fundamental mindset shifts. To describe these further at this point would be getting ahead of ourselves, however! We all too often see leaders wanting to jump straight from having their aspiration into creating the plan to get there (the Architect stage)—this is always a mistake. Care should first be taken to fully assess the required skillsets and underlying mindset shifts so that action planning can take into account an organization's change readiness. Read on to find out exactly how!

## Performance: Skillset Requirements

In Scott's book *Leading Organizations: Ten Timeless Truths,* co-written with our colleague, Mary Meaney, he recounted a travel experience that is particularly salient on the topic of skillsets. Scott was fortunate enough to visit East Timor some five years after it had become a fully independent country. He was disheartened to find that the country was riddled with poverty, in part due to its poor infrastructure, especially in light of the significant reconstruction investment that it and many other nations had made on independence. He wondered why things hadn't changed.

As he was traveling through the country, he came across a field full of bulldozers, compactors, jaws, and all manner of heavy construction equipment ideal for road-making. The field was overgrown, the metal was rusting, and a few local kids were climbing on the equipment as if they were in a giant playground. "What's all this?," Scott asked his guide. "Donations from China from when we declared independence," came the response from his local guide. "What's wrong with them?," Scott asked. His guide replied, "Nothing, but no one knows how to use them."

The aspiration of many countries, including China, to help East Timor develop as a nation was clearly bold and well-intentioned. The desired change, however, fell apart because the skillset requirements to deliver the aspiration hadn't been assessed or addressed. This example may seem extreme, but to us it's emblematic of what we often see in failed change programs. Organizations make East Timor-like big investments in changing structures, systems, or processes without ensuring the skills are built to enable them to work the way they are intended. Our research backs up the premise: organizations that explicitly assess their current skill requirements against those required to fulfill their performance aspirations are 6.6 times more likely to succeed in their change efforts.[3]

Assessing the skillset requirements of your organization can be done via a three-step process. The first involves determining the skillsets that matter most to delivering on your performance aspirations (demand). The second involves understanding what skillsets you have today and where they exist outside the organization (supply). The third is then bringing the supply and demand views together to prioritize what skillsets to focus on and what needs to be done to close any gaps.

## Forecast Skill "Demand"

What skillsets does your organization need to fulfill its performance aspirations? This is a vital question to ask and answer. Consider an organization that in the short-term needs to deal with margin compression in its industry by cost-cutting, then in the medium-term is looking to grow in certain high-growth specialty markets in which it currently only has small footholds. Without having thought about the skillset requirements of the full aspiration, there's a real risk that well-intentioned leaders needing to economize and hit quarterly expectations on cost reductions will cut into the very workforce (which in the current environment feels on the fringe) with the skillsets needed to deliver the medium-term growth strategy.

Determining what skillsets are important typically involves interviewing business leaders and functional experts and asking the following: What technical and functional skills are most important to the strategy? Which skillsets require doubling down to win the war for talent? What roles create the most value and/or are most essential to risk mitigation? What does "good" versus "great" talent look like in the roles described as important? And so on.

These questions are not complex or obscure, but they often don't get asked. When they are, the answers converge very quickly. When P&G underwent its massive changes under Alan G. Lafley's initial tenure, the company quickly honed in on a shortlist of skillsets required, among them brand management, innovation, and leveraging scale. At BHP, cost-minded operational leadership was at the top of the list. For IBM, consultative sales was the key priority. At GE, it was process engineers. At Google, the priority was the ability to attract and retain talent. And so on.

The above examples may sound obvious, but be warned that sophistication is required. Consider McDonald's. That supply-chain management and marketing are strategic skillsets for the world's largest fast-food chain will come as a surprise to no one, but the company's most strategic skillset is neither of these things. As founder Ray Kroc once remarked, McDonald's isn't in the restaurant business; it's in the real-estate business. In fact, it didn't start to turn a profit until Kroc set up a realty company to purchase prime tracts of land both for his own use and for renting out to other franchisees.[4] The care that McDonald's puts into selecting exactly the right locations for the properties in its vast portfolio—more than 36,000 restaurants in more than 100 countries—enables it to maintain an edge over the competition, especially when establishing footholds in developing markets well ahead of the pack.[5]

Once you've identified the skillsets that matter, it's time to create a rough forecast of how much of each one is required. Will it be a small group of logistics engineers on whose algorithms rest huge swings in value? An army of account executives who transform the sales force into one that brings the full suite of company products and capabilities to customers? A central group of merchants savvy at managing product selection and inventory in omnichannel formats? Having a point of view on how the magnitude of priority skillsets will change over time is vital to ensuring requirements are met.

## Understand Skill "Supply" Dynamics

Having decided the skillsets that are strategically important, the next step is to undertake a structured inquiry into their current state in your organization and to understand the related external dynamics. More specifically, we advocate companies explore three areas: quality of existing skills, quantity, and comparative ability to attract the necessary quantity of the right skillsets in the talent market.

When it comes to assessing quality, this is a good time to recall the dangers of the optimism bias we discussed in the last chapter—even the best-laid change plan can be undone if an organization overestimates its skills. Objectivity is vital. For example, a global manufacturer designed a growth program that depended on sharing best practices across its plants.

It was dismayed to discover that its track record in this supposed strength was patchy at best. A mining company was convinced its health and safety-related skillsets were such that it gave the company a competitive advantage in the talent market for important frontline skills they were looking for. Unfortunately, this belief didn't stand up on closer examination and it was back to the drawing board.

How can you make a sober assessment of the skillsets in your organization? There's a vast array of tools to help you do just that—far too many, in fact, to list here. Many of them are geared to specific skills, but most fall into the categories of performance metric assessments, benchmarking, or observational assessments (grids that break an institutional capability down into its component parts and describe what "poor," "good," and "great" look like so that you can compare the description with the reality at your organization).

In order to assess the quantity of each skillset you'll need, a more numeric approach can be employed. Combining more traditional internal data sources (e.g., workforce growth data by job code, attrition rates, retirement eligibility) with external data sources (e.g., government labor statistics, studies on workforce trends) enables predictive models to powerfully forecast different supply-side scenarios and their implications. This is not to diminish the importance of talking to subject matter experts, as well; their views on where they foresee talent shortages are often very instructive.

The final aspect to consider is the comparative ability of your organization to attract the right skillsets in the talent market. This work involves using focus groups, social media analyses (sites like Glassdoor and LinkedIn can be invaluable), exit interviews, and site visits to articulate how a company's employee value proposition (EVP) stacks up against the competition in key skillset areas. EVP dimensions to consider relate to a great job (interesting, opportunities, meaning), great rewards (wages, benefits/perks, recognition), a great company (reputation, culture/values, health!), and great leaders (inspirational, supportive, empowering). A great EVP is distinctive, real (not just marketing), and targeted specifically to the skillset in question.

## Determine How to Close Gaps

At this point you have a solid handle on both the supply and demand side of the skillset equation. With this information, prioritization becomes fairly straightforward. We advocate using a simple matrix to do this, as shown in Exhibit 4.1. One axis is an assessment of the importance of the skillset (based on future demand and value at stake) and the other axis assesses the difficulty in attracting and retaining it (based on scarcity of supply and the strength of your EVP).

By way of example, consider an advanced manufacturing company who plotted over forty skill categories onto this matrix. One role in the "step

Exhibit 4.1
## Prioritizing Critical Skillsets

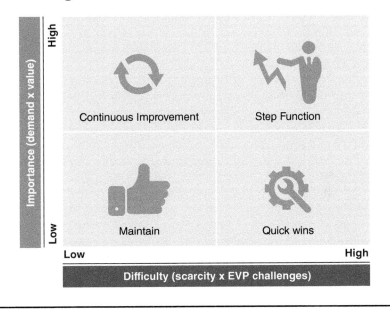

function" category was that of cyber-security expertise. It was considered important because the strategy involved pivoting to defense-industry clients who demanded a far higher level of cyber security than the existing base—to the extent that the company forecasted, it would need to grow the cyber experts by 15 percent year-on-year as a proportion of the total workforce. It was considered difficult because of the combination of its scarcity (forecasted industry talent demand shortages of over 1.8 million employees in the next five years) and the challenges the company had in attracting talent away from other opportunities in technology and government. Witness to these challenges was the fact that early career exits from the company were four times higher for cyber-security experts than the company average.

At the same time, the company had similar EVP challenges for IT talent broadly, yet the demand for IT talent and criticality to the new strategy wasn't nearly that of cyber expertise. As such, general IT skillsets fell into the "quick wins" category. In the category of "maintain" were the company's fabrication-related skillsets. The company had a broad supply base, a well-honed process for training these technicians, and the strategy was pivoted far more to services, and therefore the role was less strategically important than in the past. Further, the strong unions in these areas had ensured that the EVP in such role categories was strong. Finally, in the "continuously improve" category was systems engineering. The role was vital to success in the increasingly complex projects the company would be taking on under more and more fixed price contracts. At the same time, the nature of the work that these engineers would be doing was very attractive, supply wasn't overly constrained, and the company had a strong presence and reputation at the top universities with relevant majors.

With skillsets prioritized, the path forward to close any gaps can be explored and decided on. To what extent will you *build* the skillsets you need through reskilling, upskilling, retaining, and/or increasing deployable hours? To what extent will you *acquire* the skillsets you need through hiring individuals, tapping into new talent pools, and/or what has become known as acqui-hiring (buying out a company primarily for the skills and expertise of its staff, rather than for its products or services)? To what extent will you *borrow* the skillsets by leveraging contractors, partnerships, or outsourcing?

Take Walmart, for example. To deliver against its omnichannel strategy required a significant build-out of its digital capabilities. A vital part of its change efforts included acqui-hiring through the acquisition of more than 15 small companies, adding 3,500 employees to provide it with the search, site optimization, customer loyalty data analytics, social media analytics, and data science skills it needed. IBM, faced with a gap in the skillsets it needed at scale to perform analytics and development work, successfully partnered with Topcoder to crowdsource the UI/UX, application development, and data science skills it needed to keep pace with its growth aspirations.

Of course, there also may be overages to deal with in some areas. In these cases, the right skillset rebalancing approach may involve *redeploying* employees or *releasing* them altogether. By building a long-term, scenario-based view, you can plan these actions well in advance in order to minimize disruption and maximize fairness. For example, when tire manufacturer Michelin changed its performance aspirations such that it needed significantly fewer frontline manufacturing skillsets, it allowed factories years of notice and worked methodically through alternative paths for employees. The result was delivery of the strategy with limited headcount reductions (many workers were reskilled in new specialized lines of business) or related labor disputes.

The experience of a heavy equipment manufacturer illustrates how the steps we've described above come together in practice. The first step they took to understand skillset "demand" was to analyze the skill requirements of the enterprise strategy. This wasn't a high-level, hand-waving exercise, and instead involved forecasting full-time equivalent employee requirements over five years. In total, 33 skillsets were assessed to determine if more, less, or the same would be required going forward. A new pipeline of digital and analytic talent, a shift in emphasis from structural and production engineers to advanced manufacturing and systems engineers, and broadened procurement talent expertise would be needed, among many others.

Once the "demand" side was understood, the next step was to look at the "supply" side of skillsets. Internal and external data was combined with predictive analytics to forecast the availability of skillsets in different scenarios. Additionally, current and future talent pools were identified (both university graduates and experienced hires). Further, the company's employee value proposition was benchmarked against other companies competing for the same talent. To prioritize where to focus, the supply and demand views were integrated, and a shortlist of skillsets were chosen to focus on at the enterprise level. Specific action plans were then put in place to close the skillset gap in these areas, as well as to ensure areas of existing strength were protected.

At this point in the Assess stage, you will have a razor-sharp view of the skillset areas where you have gaps and will know how to fill those gaps. If they can't be filled, you may have to revisit the Aspire stage! Rest assured more work will be done in the Architect phase to create specific action plans to ensure you will have the right skillsets in place at the right time. Before we get there, however, there is work to do on the health side of Assess.

## Health: Mindset Shifts

Let's just call it: most leaders get squeamish when we broach the topic of employee mindsets. Some feel such is best left to organizational psychologists. Others simply have no idea what they'd actually *do* in this space. Others don't think, regardless of their importance, that mindsets can be meaningfully influenced in a reasonable time frame. As such, many leaders don't take this aspect of making change happen nearly as seriously as they should (and as a result have 30 percent success rates to show for it!).

We would go so far as to argue that this part of the Five Frames is, in fact, the most important if you want to lead successful and sustainable change at scale. We can share many concrete examples to prove our point, but the transformation metaphor of a caterpillar becoming a butterfly or a tadpole becoming a frog is most helpful. Why are these the symbols we gravitate to when talking about transformational change? What is different about them from other kinds of change, for example, changing your shirt, your tires, your password? Answer: the change is so deep and fundamental that it will never go back. The butterfly will never return to being a caterpillar. The frog will never go back to being a tadpole. In human systems, it is mindset shifts that achieve this same effect—when employees become open to new ways of looking at what's possible for them and their organization, they can never return to a state of not having that more expansive perspective.

A story from one of our colleagues perfectly illustrates this point. He was traveling in India and in one section of town, he noticed the bodies of the beggars on the street were predominantly disfigured, more so than he'd seen anywhere else. His heart went out to them. He reached into his pocket and distributed all the cash he had—he was a smart, well-intentioned person and it just felt like the right thing to do. His mindset was pure, his behavior followed.

Later, he learned that the disfigurations weren't by chance—for generations parents had purposefully disfigured their children so they could earn more from begging. On finding this out, he was horrified (as were we hearing the story), and he realized his actions had contributed to perpetuating the cruel practice. With his expanded view, he could never go back to seeing the scene the way he did, and he'd never do what he did again—the change was deep and permanent.

We realize that's a very heavy example, but we also suspect you'll never forget it, as we haven't. In the spirit of Einstein's assertion, in a 1946 telegram to a number of prominent Americans that, "Today's problems cannot be solved with the same level of thinking that created them," unless underlying mindsets change, it's exceedingly difficult to make lasting change happen at scale. Our experience is that when limiting mindsets are surfaced and reframed into more expansive, performance and health-enabling thoughts—that's where the caterpillar to butterfly effect happens.

Consider the story told by Benjamin Zander, in his book *The Art of Possibility*, about the Manchester Shoe Company. In the early 1900s, their aspiration was to grow their business by entering the African market. Two traveling salesmen were sent as a beachhead into the region. A few days later, two telegraphs came back independently. One said, "Situation horrible. They don't wear shoes!" The other said, "Glorious opportunity; they don't have any shoes yet!" The limited versus expanded mindset leads to a completely different outcome.

The data supports our assertion that mindsets matter. The companies that did no work on diagnosing mindsets also never rated their change programs as "extremely successful," whereas companies that took the time to identify deep-seated mindsets were four times more likely than those that didn't to rate their change programs as "successful."[6]

If you're a leader whose bias would have been to skip the rest of this chapter because it all just sounds too soft, we hope we've changed your mindset, and you'll continue with us. In what follows, we'll describe in depth how to uncover and reframe the critical few mindsets that will unlock health and therefore performance improvements.

## Identify Helping and Hindering Behaviors

In all that follows, we're going to work through four scenarios to bring the concepts to life and make them practical. The first will be an apocryphal story we've borrowed from Gary Hamel and C.K. Prahalad. The second, third, and fourth will be from real change programs pursued by a bank, telco, and manufacturing company respectively.

Let's start with Hamel and Prahalad's story: four monkeys are sitting in a cage with a bunch of bananas hanging from the roof, accessible by a set of steps. Whenever the monkeys try to climb the steps to get to the bananas, they are blocked by a blast of cold water. After a few days, the monkeys naturally give up—they realize there's no point in trying to get the bananas. Researchers then remove the water hose and at the same time replace one of the original monkeys with a new one. On seeing the bananas, it starts up the steps. What happens next? The other monkeys, being social creatures, pull it down before it gets blasted with water. The new monkey is startled, looks around, and starts again up the ladder. The other monkeys again keep their new companion from climbing the ladder. This happens again and again until the new monkey accepts the group code of conduct and doesn't bother to go for the bananas, either.

Over the next few weeks, the researchers remove the rest of the original monkeys one at a time and replace them with new monkeys who've never seen the jet of water. Even though there's no longer anything to stop the monkeys from reaching the bananas, each new monkey is always pulled down by the others until they submit to group norms. By the end of the experiment, there are four monkeys in the cage, none of whom have ever seen a jet of water. There are perfectly ripe bananas sitting on a platform with unobstructed steps leading to them. Yet, none of the monkeys tries to climb the steps. They've all learned the unwritten rule that, "You don't grab the bananas around here."

This story has been repeated countless times since it was published because it offers a number of lessons for change leaders, which we'll be working through in the pages that follow. At this point, however, we simply call out that the management practices of the past—the jet of water—had driven a certain set of behaviors in the monkeys. When "management" changed that practice, it's notable that the behaviors didn't change. The lesson: *mindsets ingrained by past management practices remain ingrained far beyond the existence of those practices.*

Let's make this real in the business examples we've teed up. The bank wanted to affect its customer focus management practice in support of its growth aspiration to bring "One Firm" to its clients. An inquiry into employee behaviors revealed that roughly 10 percent of the salesforce was already behaving in the desired way, with cross-sell rates that were very high. The vast majority of the salesforce sold various bundles of product with the initial sale, but very little beyond that. A small group were characterized by only selling one product to customers.

The bank then assessed what the 10 percent were doing that the others weren't. They found that two behaviors categorically differentiated the high performers from the average: the number and nature of questions they asked to profile the customer, and the extent to which they educated themselves on the bank's product set. Knowing this, the bank's leaders then created a change program aimed at giving the average salespeople support tools including scripts with good profiling questions to ask and education about the bank's broad products sets. The program was rolled out with great fanfare, effort, and cost—and sales barely improved.

We'll come back to the bank, but first let's introduce another example. As part of its health goals, a telco wanted to see a step-change improvement in its people performance review practice. Assessing today's behaviors, it saw that managers spent most of the performance review conversation explaining the complex rating process and avoiding delivering tough messages. After an extensive benchmarking process vis-à-vis best practices, the company put in place a new system—one with a dramatically simplified process and rating system, and where reviews happened every three months rather than occurring annually. Training was provided in the rollout on how to have a productive and performance-focused conversation—and the behavior change achieved was negligible. Without being able to complain about the process, leaders instead often cancelled reviews or simply spent the time on small talk and sugarcoated what otherwise should have been hard messages.

Now let's move to the third example, and then we'll talk about what all of these have in common. A manufacturer was pursuing an execution edge health recipe to support its performance aspirations, for which knowledge sharing was a vital management practice to get right. Many of today's behaviors were hindering progress: knowledge was hoarded, solutions to similar problems reinvented locally, and no one asked for, or offered, help. Having studied other companies where the opposite was true, the decision was made to invest in a knowledge-management technology platform to facilitate the documentation and sharing of knowledge. Hundreds of millions of dollars later, the system was up and running—and a complete failure in that only a select few used it.

In all of these examples, the companies did a good job of assessing the behavior change from "hindering" to "helping" needed to achieve the desired health goals. This is a very important first step in the health assessment process, but it's a mistake to stop at this level and move to solutions—as the examples illustrate. Had they taken the time to go one level deeper they wouldn't have regretted it, as we describe in the next sections.

## Uncover the Underlying Mindset Drivers

Why didn't the seemingly logical actions taken by the companies described in the previous examples work? Because they were doing the equivalent of removing the water hose in the monkey experiment while the underlying mindset of "we don't grab the bananas around here" remained. Had the underlying mindsets been addressed, the outcomes would have been profoundly different.

Before returning to the examples, it's important to establish exactly what we mean by organizational mindsets. Put simply, they are the *shared beliefs or assumptions that color employees' perceptions and predispose them to behave in a predictable manner.* To make this real, take for example one of the mindset shifts that Satya Nadella focused on when he took the helm at Microsoft. Having been inspired by Carol Dweck's research on growth mindsets, he assessed that the desire of leaders and employees to be "know-it-alls" was underlying a number of dysfunctional behaviors. By emphasizing that it would be the "learn-it-alls" who will be valued going forward, significant positive behavioral change followed related to collaboration, risk-taking, and external orientation.[7]

Having established what mindsets are, let's also talk about what they are not. They are not the equivalent of the water gun in the monkey experiment. For example, if you are inquiring about the mindsets that sit beneath a given behavior and the answer you are coming up with is "because incentive systems are out of whack," "because they haven't had good role-modeling," or "because no one set the right expectations," you are on the slow road to making change happen. These aren't mindsets; they are external factors that influence mindsets.

Making changes to these external factors will indeed have impact in the long term, but just like removing the water hose had little immediate effect on the monkeys, existing norms ingrained at a subconscious level will persist for a frustratingly long time. The fast track to making change happen involves going one step further in your assessment and answering the following question: "Because of those factors (the incentives, role modeling, expectations, and so on), what have smart, hard-working, and well-intentioned employees come to believe about themselves and their work such that they believe it's the right thing to do to act this way?" If you can name and reframe the otherwise subconscious thought patterns at play—and make reinforcing changes to the work environment, you will see rapid behavior change at scale.

The process to uncover the subconscious mindsets that drive behaviors is often visualized as an iceberg, as illustrated in Exhibit 4.2. The goal is to go beneath the observable behaviors into the depths of what sits beneath. The primary tool with which to get beneath the surface is based on an interview

Exhibit 4.2

## Uncovering Subconscious Mindsets that Drive Behaviors

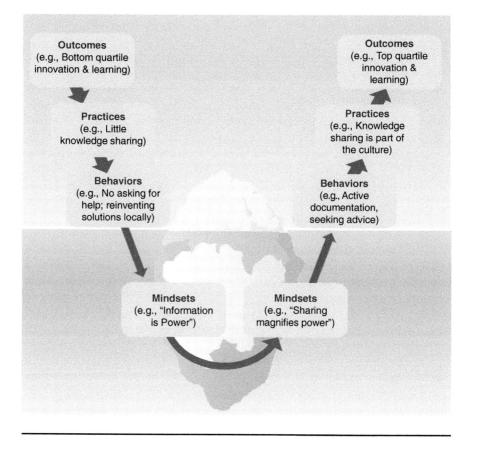

technique known as *laddering*. This approach is grounded in the theory of personal change set out by Dennis Hinkle in his 1965 doctoral thesis entitled *The Change of Personal Constructs from the Viewpoint of a Theory of Implications*. To probe ever deeper into an individual's mindsets, Hinkle developed the "laddering" method of inquiry.

The method uses multiple techniques to uncover multiple levels of *why* they hold a particular opinion. The idea is that the "ladder" of questions prompts people to reflect on their deepest motivations, and eventually leads them to state the values and assumptions through which they construct their personal world. While the technique originated in clinical psychology, it's been successfully applied in business in both marketing and the field of organizational change.

The principle behind the approach is no different than that of the "Five whys" approach that operations experts apply when the assembly line goes down. Before they try to fix a given issue, lean practitioners ask *why* as many times as it takes to understand the problem fully and get to the root cause (five questions are often enough to do the trick, hence the five whys). Take a textbook example. If a motor breaks down, a lean-minded operator won't just replace it, but will ask why? "Because it overheated," comes the reply. Then, again, why? "Because it wasn't properly ventilated." Why? "Because the machine is too close to the wall." The operator then moves the machine away from the wall before replacing the motor. Without the probing for why, the fix would have been only temporary. The new motor would have soon burned out for lack of ventilation.

Although a good analogy, digging into the "five whys" of human behavior isn't quite as straightforward as asking why five times. After all, we're looking to probe into the subconscious drivers of behavior! Using an array of interview techniques, though, allows for a skilled interviewer to get to the root causes. The *storytelling* technique elicits a colorful and detailed narrative by asking about heroes, legends, or war stories related to behaviors. *Provocations* make deliberately exaggerated statements aimed at prompting an emotional reaction in the interviewee. *Role plays* put the interviewee into a realistic work situation or someone else's shoes. *Circling* closes the loop between the current conversation and previous statements. Finally, *hypotheticals* describe imaginary scenarios and ask how they would play out.

Skilled interviewers also listen with an ear to three types of mindsets: *not allowed, can't,* and *won't.* "Not allowed" mindsets stem from perceptions of what's expected and accepted. "Can't" mindsets stem from perceptions of resource availability or capability. "Won't" mindsets typically stem from one's sense of identity, values, and perceptions of power dynamics.

Laddering interviews feel very different from traditional interviews. The former is focused on reflection—the interviewer knows he/she is on the right track when the interviewee has to pause and reflect on the question, unable to give a stock answer. The latter is typically more action-oriented, focused on gathering facts, hearing opinions, and verifying hypotheses.

By way of example, whereas a traditional interview may be along the lines of "talk to me about your sales process" followed by a set of clarifying questions, a laddering interview will say, "Imagine I'm a customer and you are going to sell me a loan that I've already shopped for online; let's role-play that interaction." The interviewer will then debrief by asking questions such as, "Where did you feel most and least comfortable in that interaction (and why)?"; "Who do you think would have handled it better (how, and why)?"; "What held you back from doing that in our interaction?"; "What do you feel was your best experience with a customer?"; "What made that different from our role-play?"; and so on.

Though powerful, the limitation of the laddering technique is that in large and diverse organizations it's hard to scale (with our large company clients we typically conduct 30 to 50 laddering interviews in the Assess phase). A complementary technique, which allows for gathering a broader and deeper fact base regarding what's going on beneath the surface, is conducting focus groups using visual cues.

The use of visual cues differs from traditional focus group techniques in a similar way that laddering interviews differ from traditional fact-finding interviews. The approach involves laying out a selection of 100 or so pictures on a table and asking participants to choose the images that best represent their feelings on whatever topic is asked about. For example, "What most energizes/frustrates you about the organization?" or, "What is your greatest hope for the organization?"

Depending on the type of change program in question, this approach can be targeted to specific business challenges. For instance, going back to our earlier examples: "Which image represents what it's like to sell to customers?"; "Which image represents how it feels to be in a performance review?"; "Which image represents how collaboration and knowledge sharing works around here?" The benefit of using pictures is that they trigger a much more honest, emotive, and visceral conversation than asking stock questions that start with, "Tell me about...."

A handy side-benefit is that the images representing the employees' ideal organization can be adopted in the communications program later, thus forging a link between employees' input and the themes in the change effort. After people have chosen images individually, the wider group can go on to create collages that summarize how they collectively feel about their work. Further, although it's common to use a skilled and objective third party to help with focus groups, we encourage the leadership team to take part in a few of them, as well. Doing so is often extremely eye-opening—the mindset equivalent to what lean manufacturing executives call *genchi genbutsu,* or "go and see," to find out what is actually going on.

The third tool for understanding mindsets more broadly in the organization comes from the social science methodology known as qualitative data analysis (QDA). This method mines rich sources of textual data (reports, websites, advertisements, internal communications, and press coverage) using linguistic techniques (known as narrative, framework, and discourse analysis) to identify recurring themes and search for causality.

One relatively basic and straightforward QDA technique that many are familiar with is the use of *word clouds.* A word cloud analyzes how often words are repeated in a particular text or texts. The more often it's used, the bigger the word is printed on a page that contains all the words analyzed. An individual word cloud can be quite insightful in that what people *talk* about no doubt informs what they *think* about, which, as we've discussed, is a major driver of what people actually *do*. It can also be insightful to compare word clouds from different sources. For example, when a public sector organization compared the word cloud related to its stated values and leadership model with that of the executive teams' various internal speeches over the previous year, it was shocked to find nary a word in common!

Taken together, laddering interviews, focus groups using visual cues, and QDA do a potent job of pointing to the underlying mindsets that drive observed behaviors. Let's go back to the stalled change programs at our bank, telco, and manufacturing company. At the bank, the assessment stage revealed that two mindsets accounted for the lack of uptake of the new sales stimulation tools and training. The first was a mindset that, "My job is to give the customer what they want," and the second was, "I should follow the 'Golden Rule' and treat my customers the way I'd like to be treated." At the telco, performance management behaviors hadn't shifted in its highly relational culture due to a deep-seated belief that, "Criticism damages relationships." At the manufacturing company, the knowledge-management system was a ghost town because of the underlying belief that, "Around here, information is power, and good leaders are powerful leaders" (as illustrated in Exhibit 4.2).

Each of these root causes has something in common with the others—that the mindset in question is pretty darn reasonable. This is a vital point: when the right tools are used, the analysis of mindsets moves beyond otherwise flippant views of, "Our salespeople are afraid to talk to customers"; or, "Our leaders are wimpy when it comes to tough messages"; or, "Our people have 'not invented here' syndrome." Too often, we run into change programs where, when we ask leaders what mindsets they are targeting, we get responses related to bureaucracy or being slow-moving. These are not mindsets. No reasonable people wake up each day saying, "My job is to be a bureaucrat" or, "Today I'm going to slow progress." As we've indicated already, an important test that you've identified a root cause mindset, which is truly an unlock to health and therefore performance, is whether a smart, hard-working, well-intentioned person could reasonably hold the belief described, and yet that very belief can also explain the performance-limiting behaviors that need to be shifted.

Once you understand the root-cause mindsets, the next step is to reframe them to expand the range of reasonable behavioral choices that employees make day in and day out. Keep in mind that in doing so, you're creating the caterpillar to butterfly effect we described earlier.

## Reframe Root-Cause Mindsets

What different beliefs would create expanded and better informed behavioral choices for our average-performing bankers? How about if they believed their job—the way they add value to others—is to "help customers fully understand their needs" versus "giving customers what they want." If they believed this, as it turns out the high performers whose behaviors were initially studied do, they wouldn't need the stock list of profiling questions because they'd ask them naturally, as a matter of course. And what if they believed, as the higher performers do, in the Platinum Rule, "Treat customers as *they* want to be treated," instead of the Golden Rule that says, "Treat others the way I want to be treated"? No doubt they'd show more behavioral flexibility in how they deal with their customers, leading to an improved experience. The health goal of increasing customer focus is, in turn, transformed.

What if our telco executives holding their performance management discussions believed, "Honesty (with respect) is essential to building strong relationships"? Surely the sugar-coating that came from thinking being honest would destroy relationships would give way to courageous conversations, which in turn would increase a baseline of trust in the organization and would allow for the people performance review practice to rocket into the top quartile.

And what if our manufacturing managers really believed "sharing information magnifies power" instead of believing "information is power" and therefore hoarding it? Were this the case, the company very likely wouldn't have needed a multimillion-dollar system to prompt them to reach out to one another and share best practices.

Savvy readers will see that beneath each of the reframes described is a deeper shift in worldview. For example, moving from a view of giving customers what they want to helping them fully understand what they really need reflects a move from a subordinate to a peer mindset. Switching from Golden Rule to Platinum Rule is changing from a me-centered to an other-centered worldview. Recognizing that honesty builds rather than destroys relationships reflects a shift from victim to mastery. And choosing to believe that power is expanded by sharing, not that information is power, focuses on abundance not scarcity. Although these represent the more fundamental shifts that create the caterpillar to butterfly transformation effect, had the changes been framed in these terms, they would just become conceptual jargon without practical meaning in the workplace.

The best naming and reframing is not only profound (using practical and relatable terms yet reflecting the deeper change in worldview), but also insightful (making the subconscious conscious in ways that expand possibility), memorable (so it can easily be raised and discussed in the context of day-to-day work), and meaningful (specific to the organization's context—evoking a "that's so us!" response.

We're the first to acknowledge that in spite of there being a practical toolkit to help leaders, working with mindsets and, in particular, the reframing step will always have a degree of art to it—probably more, in fact, than any other aspect of managing a change program. But that shouldn't deter leaders from venturing into unfamiliar territory. Remember, perfection is not the goal. Plenty of us take art classes without expecting to end up like Picasso or Rembrandt. We may not paint masterpieces worth millions, but by learning the basics of composition and technique, we can become better artists.

Further examples reinforce what good looks like when it comes to naming and reframing. A retailer found that the shift from "listening and responding" (reactive mindset) to "anticipating and shaping" (proactive mindset) that sat beneath its customer focus management practice was vital. An engineering company that wanted to improve its practices for capturing external ideas found it was consistently over-optimistic about results and underestimated competitors. Through its assessment process it realized this was driven by a "winning means being peerless" (expert) mindset, which led to increasingly insular behaviors. Changing to a mindset of "winning means learning more and faster than others" (learner), prompted employees to look for best practices in competitors and beyond. You'll notice that this is the same underlying shift (expert to learner) that Satya Nadella focused on at Microsoft, yet the articulation of how it manifested in the retailer was different, and hence the language related to the shift is specific to each company.

These business examples, while helpful, tend to be far less memorable than human health analogies. Consider the predicament of people with heart disease. Years of research have shown that most cardiac patients can live considerably longer if they change their behaviors by cutting out smoking and drinking, eating less fat, reducing their stress levels, and regularly exercising. Indeed, many make a real effort to do so. Yet, study after study has shown that 90 percent of people who have undergone surgery for heart disease revert to unhealthy behavior within two years.

That's a situation that Dean Ornish, a professor of medicine at the University of California at San Francisco and founder of the Preventative Medicine Research Institute, was determined to change.[8] He decided to try a new approach. Rather than focusing on the behaviors patients should adopt to survive, he decided to tackle their mindsets instead.

Dr. Ornish decided to reframe the underlying mindset beneath the patient narrative from, "If I behave this way, I won't die" (fear-driven mindset) to "If I behave this way, my life will be filled with joy" (hope-driven mindset). In his words, "Telling people who are lonely and depressed that they're going to live longer if they quit smoking or change their diet and lifestyle is not that motivating. Who wants to live longer when you're in chronic emotional pain?" How much better would they feel, he posited, if they could enjoy the pleasures of daily life—making love, taking a hike, playing with their children or grandchildren—without suffering any pain or discomfort?

The reframe, reinforced by the types of mechanisms we'll be discussing in the next chapter on the Architect stage, worked: 77 percent of his patients managed to make permanent changes in their lifestyles, as against a normal success rate of 10 percent.

As with the "profoundly simple" end product of the Aspire stage—a shortlist of management practices to either fix or drive to distinction—the end product of the Assess stage can typically fit on one piece of paper. An example end product is shown in Exhibit 4.3.

In Chapter 5, we'll discuss numerous ways to influence and embed mindset reframes such as these. Further, in Chapter 6, we'll share powerful techniques that prompt leaders to examine and expand their personal world-views in relation to the more fundamental underlying shifts at play (e.g., victim to mastery, me to we, scarcity to abundance, fear to hope, and so on). We note here, however, that methods to influence mindset shifts can also be "profoundly simple." At an aerospace company, while not the only thing they did by any means, one powerful intervention they made involved opting to include a laminated card on their name badge lanyards. One side of the card was red and had the performance-limiting "from" mindsets printed on it. The other side was green and had the performance-enhancing "to" mindsets. The card acted not only as a reminder of desired shifts, but also as a practical vehicle for providing feedback: in initiative meetings, employees called out when they realized old, subconscious patterns related to the "red" mindsets and related behaviors were at play by holding up their red card. This allowed everyone to pause and reset their approach. Employees reinforced "green" mindsets and related behaviors, too, thereby encouraging others that they were on the right track.

Before we leave our discussion of the Health Frame of the Assess stage, we'd be remiss not to mention that the academic underpinnings for everything we've discussed are rock solid. We haven't gone into detail on this front as our goal is to create a practitioners' guide versus an academic treatise, but those wanting more in this regard would do well to consult works such as *The Unbounded Mind* by Ian Mitroff and Harold Linstone; Peter Senge's *The Fifth Discipline*; Carol Dweck's *Mindset: The New Psychology of Success*; Edward Russo and Paul Schoemaker's *Decision Traps* and *Winning Decisions*; *Creating the Corporate Future* by Russell Ackoff; *Teaching Smart People How to Learn* by Chris Argyris; and *The Inner Game of Work* by Timothy Gallwey.

All of these books reinforce that chasing behavioral change *without* addressing mindsets is like playing Whac-a-Mole in an amusement arcade. You pound one mole (behavior) into its hole only to find many more moles

Exhibit 4.3

# Naming and Reframing Root-Cause Mindsets and Related Behaviors

| Management practice | Performance *limiting* mindsets and related behaviors | Performance *accelerating* mindsets and related behaviors |
| --- | --- | --- |
| **Bottom-up innovation** | **Protect our legacy:** *"What made us great in the past will make us great in the future"*<br>■ Move slowly and only after careful analysis<br>■ Filter new ideas to avoid risk of failure<br>■ Spend most of time on plans, updates, documents<br>■ Innovate if given permission and/or resources | **Shape our future:** *"The best way to respect our past is to proactively shape the future"*<br>■ Rapidly iterate, test & learn to improve<br>■ Raise opportunities, allow for intelligent failures<br>■ Spend most of time in ideation and prototyping<br>■ Innovate incrementally as part of standard work |
| **Openness and trust** | **Value harmony:** *"Look after each other (and self) by being 'nice' and focusing on the positive"*<br>■ Nod heads, real discussion is outside the meeting<br>■ Be positive, fit in, share good news ("smooth")<br>■ Don't push back on leaders for fear of reprisal<br>■ Take pride not asking for help/knowing it all | **Value excellence:** *"Look after each other (and self) by being transparent and asking for/giving help"*<br>■ Discuss tough issues in the meeting, then solidarity<br>■ Be honest, authentic, and direct ("straight")<br>■ Constructively disagree regardless of hierarchy<br>■ Seek interdependence/support to deliver 1+1=3 |
| **Personal ownership** | **Work hard, complete tasks:** *"Understand expected actions & targets, give 110% in pursuit"*<br>■ Leaders dictate what to do & how to do it<br>■ Show success by activity/busyness, report-outs<br>■ Rituals and reports continued w/out asking why<br>■ Blame others re: ultimate company results | **Work smart, deliver outcomes:** *"Understand expected outcomes and rationale, then deliver"*<br>■ Leaders set objectives & reasons, then coach<br>■ Demonstrate success through delivery of outcomes<br>■ Constant prioritization based on activity value-add<br>■ Passion that no one wins if the company doesn't |

popping up all around you. As Gallwey himself explains, "There is always an inner game being played in the mind no matter what outer game is being played. How aware you are of this game can make the difference between success and failure."[9]

We close this section with one of the most iconic mindset-related vignettes of all time to drive home the point one final time. Until the mid-1950s, the four-minute mile was regarded as beyond human achievement. Even medical journals judged it unattainable. Yet, in May 1954, a medical student named Roger Bannister smashed through the barrier with a time of 3 minutes, 59.4 seconds. In his memoir, Bannister explained he did what was once thought impossible by spending as much time conditioning his mind as his body. He wrote, "The mental approach is all-important … energy can be harnessed by the correct attitude of mind."[10]

What is perhaps more amazing is that two months later, the four-minute barrier was broken again, by Australian John Landy. Within three years, 16 runners had followed suit. So, what happened here? Was it a sudden spurt in human evolution? A new super-race of genetically engineered runners? Of course not. It was the same physical equipment, but with a different mindset: one that said, "This can be done." No doubt there are some "four-minute mile"-like mindsets sitting beneath the behaviors you see in your organization that, if broken through, will unlock a whole new level of performance in a similar manner to Bannister's effect on the running community.

With that, we hope by this point you're well and truly convinced that assessing mindsets isn't something that should be written off as too soft or considered optional for change success. Missing this step will doom any change program to stalling or unacceptably slow and frictional progress until it's finally revisited, either explicitly or implicitly. As we've shown, there are many well-established methods and tools that have been tested and proven in other fields, even if they are not yet widely applied in the business world. In fact, that they aren't mainstream makes them all the more advantageous to you in making change happen better and faster than your competition (how's that for a reframe?!).

## Master Stroke: Balance Your Inquiry

We now turn our focus to the most important lesson from the field of predictable irrationality that should be considered during the Assess stage of making change happen. This change leader master stroke is best illustrated by a study carried out at the University of Wisconsin during which two bowling teams were filmed in action. Each team was then given its own video to study. One team got a video that showed only its mistakes; the other got a video that showed only its successes. After studying the videos, the teams competed again as the researchers looked on. What did they find? Both teams bowled better games than they had previously—studying game tapes is a good thing to do! What is a surprise to many, however, is that the team that studied its successes improved twice as much as the team who studied its mistakes.[11]

Researchers such as David Cooperrider, Suresh Srivastava, Diana Whitney, and others draw out an important point related to this research: if you want to motivate changes in behavior, it's powerful to call out what's working and ask, "How do we get more of it?" (a *constructionist* approach) versus to only point out all of the flaws and ask, "How do we fix this?" (a *deficit-based* approach). The latter works well for technical systems, but in human systems, a relentless focus on what's wrong invokes blame and creates fatigue. The former, though, invites people to leverage their experience and build upon their successes.

Make no mistake, however; we aren't suggesting change leaders only focus on strengths or calling out what's working. In fact, we feel strongly that the way many leaders interpret "strength-based" thinking misses the mark. Strengths overplayed become weaknesses and there are such things as Achilles' heels that simply need to be fixed or you won't be successful. There is also a significant amount of behavioral research that suggests humans are far more risk-averse in pursuing upsides (going for the light on the hill, building on my strengths) than avoiding downsides (getting off the burning bridge, addressing my weaknesses). And don't get us started on how the optimism bias plays into all this (even in calling out problem areas, if there isn't a clear "from" in which an employee can see their role, they will likely see the "to" as something they already embody. More to come on this dynamic in Chapter 6).

Our recommendation is that leaders in the Assess stage put roughly equal emphasis on assessing what's broken and therefore needs fixing and what's working well that they want to see more of. Our assertion is backed by facts: large-scale change programs that emphasize an organization's strengths as well as its weaknesses are three times more likely to be successful than those that focus on one or the other, and a positive correlation holds regardless of whether it is a "good to great" or a "turnaround change program."[12] We suspect that had the researchers at the University of Wisconsin included in their study a team who studied both their strengths *and* weaknesses, that team would have improved even more than the others.

The true change leader master stroke lies one step beyond just calling out both sides of the deficit and constructionist equation. Instead, it lies in the idea that T.H. White, former president of GTE phone operations, describes in saying, "If we dissect what we do right and apply the lessons to what we do wrong, we can solve our problems and energize the organization at the same time … we cannot ignore problems, but we just need to approach them from the other side."[13]

Sounds good in theory, but how does this work in practice? Consider a financial services organization that aspired to a "One Company" vision that would leverage the company's breadth of products to serve customers and capture more scale efficiencies. Leveraging the OHI methodology, three management practices were prioritized as its health aspiration: openness and trust, customer focus, and strategic clarity.

In the first instance, the underlying mindset that drove the siloed behavior that diminished trust was a strong accountability muscle. Employees believed their job was to "run my area like I own it" (mine). Reframing the mindset to, "Run my area like I own the company" (ours) asked leaders to maintain the accountability strength and redirect it to the collective, and far more collaboration ensued. To increase customer focus, the discipline that accompanied the current "know your numbers" mindset (internal focus) was redirected to a mindset of "know your customer" (external), which dramatically changed how and where people spent their time. The short-termism that got in the way of strategic clarity was due to a mindset of, "Execution matters most—it *is* our strategy" (act first). The benefit of this mindset, however, was a strong ethic of getting things done. When that strength was redirected by emphasizing a mindset of, "Execution *of* our strategy matters most" (think first), smarter decisions on behalf of the enterprise were implemented quickly.

By way of another example, let's go back to our heavy equipment manufacturer that we mentioned in the skillset section. The company's vision involved becoming a top quartile industrial company, not just the best in their industry. Their health aspirations involved creating a step change in strategic clarity, role clarity, and performance management.

When it came to a lack of strategic clarity, it was the relentless focus on getting every detail right—a mindset of "no stone left unturned" (diligence) that had employees too focused on day-to-day execution to see the bigger picture. A shift to "focus on the big rocks" (discernment) asked leaders to put the same level of focus on longer-term efforts. Role clarity was being inhibited by a highly relational culture where things got done by "working the system" (informal). If those relationships were instead leveraged in service of "making the system work" (formal), role clarity would become self-generating. Performance management was inhibited by the problem-solving culture that focused on "fix the problem" (reactive) leading to deficit-based conversations and punitive actions being the norm. Taking the strong desire to solve problems and asking leaders to think of it slightly differently, to "prevent the problem" (proactive), unlocked profoundly different behaviors in performance management and beyond.

■ ■ ■

At the end of the Assess stage of transformation, you'll have answered the question, "How ready are we to go there?" in relation to your performance and health aspirations. You'll have identified the vital skill requirements required to fulfill your performance aspirations. You'll have taken a long, hard look at the state of these skills in your organization and in the marketplace today and going forward. You'll have determined how you'll fill any gaps or deal with any overages.

You'll also have uncovered the underlying mindsets that drive the limiting behaviors you observe in relation to your health goals. These will have then been reframed so as to unlock more constructive behaviors going forward. And you'll have done all of the above through a balanced approach to inquiry—enabling you to leverage your organization's strengths to address its weaknesses.

The journey through the Assess stage can be the most challenging in the whole change program—both because the work of long-term strategic workforce planning and exploring unspoken assumptions is typically not something an organization has a lot of experience doing, and because of the desire to "get on with it" in terms of taking action toward the aspirations that have been set. If you choose to skip this stage, however, we can assure you that you'll be revisiting it once your change efforts stall, and at that point the work will be harder as high hopes will have begun to harden into cynicism and disengagement.

Done well, however, the view at the end of the Assess phase is universally positive. In the words of one executive giving feedback on the company's skillset focus areas and mindset reframes, "Finally, we are discussing the undiscussables. These are the fundamental issues and dealing with them will drive lasting change."[14] It's now time to discuss the central question of the Architect stage of the change journey: "What do we need to do to get there?" (Exhibit 4.4)

Exhibit 4.4

# A Proven Approach to Leading Large-Scale Change: The Story So Far

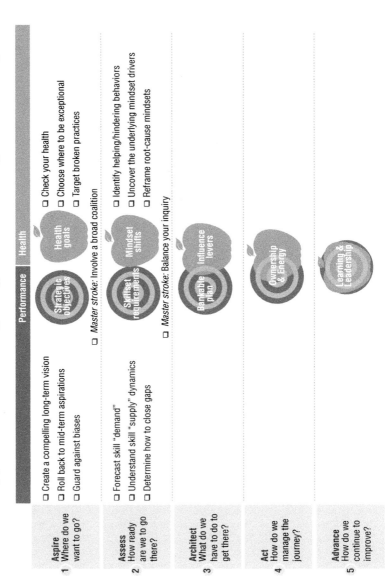

| | Performance | Health |
|---|---|---|
| **Aspire** 1 Where do we want to go? | Strategic objectives | Health goals |
| | □ Create a compelling long-term vision □ Roll back to mid-term aspirations □ Guard against biases | □ Check your health □ Choose where to be exceptional □ Target broken practices |
| | *Master stroke:* Involve a broad coalition | |
| **Assess** 2 How ready are we to go there? | Skillset requirements | Mindset shifts |
| | □ Forecast skill "demand" □ Understand skill "supply" dynamics □ Determine how to close gaps | □ Identify helping/hindering behaviors □ Uncover the underlying mindset drivers □ Reframe root-cause mindsets |
| | *Master stroke:* Balance your inquiry | |
| **Architect** 3 What do we have to do to get there? | Bankable plan | Influence levers |
| **Act** 4 How do we manage the journey? | Ownership & Energy | |
| **Advance** 5 How do we continue to improve? | Learning & Leadership | |

# Chapter 5

# Architect

## *What Do We Need to Do to Get There?*

When ownership of the global auto manufacturer, Volvo Cars, was transferred from Ford to Geely, the new Executive Management Team faced many challenges. The company's market share was declining, sales volume was low, quality was decreasing, and the brand was considered by many to be stuck somewhere in the middle between the premium and mass markets. Internally, the organization lacked direction and confidence. Any path forward had to include large-scale change.

In the Aspire stage of Volvo's journey, the Executive Management Team looked to the intersection of opportunity, capability, and passion and honed in on an overarching change vision of becoming the most progressive luxury car brand in the world. The future was rolled back to include medium-term aspirations such as having a top-tier premium auto brand perception, increasing volumes from less than 400,000 vehicles to more than 800,000 vehicles globally, and reaching top quartile car industry profitability.

On the health side, the OHI and related analytics revealed the company was overall in the third quartile of organizational health. Despite its challenges, the Executive Management Team chose to see the opportunities. As the CEO put it, "We're not healthy—but at least we are not dead!" Drawing on predictive analytics, senior leaders chose to pursue the "market shaper" recipe. Priority management practices included dramatically increasing customer focus, role clarity, talent development, and strategic clarity, among others.

In the Assess stage, skillset requirements were understood and plans were made to fill gaps. These included bringing in a significant amount of talent from outside the industry. As CHRO Björn Sällström remarked, "Technically, cars today are very different from 10 years ago. Once you needed mechanical engineers. Today there's a greater need for software engineers because cars are computers more than anything."[1] On the health side, a deep dive into the underlying mindsets beneath the priority management practices revealed a shortlist of priority "from–to" shifts. These included shifts from "put procedure first" to "use good judgement" and "rely on your expertise/what you know" to "continuously learn/engage customers," among others.

As the organization moved into the Architect stage of the journey, the first order of business was to determine specifically what would Volvo actually *do* differently to get from where it was to where it wanted to be. The first-level answer to "What will we do?" was that step-change improvement would be driven in four thematic areas: "improving profitability and efficiency," "revitalizing the Volvo brand," "reinforcing our product strengths," and "driving global growth and sourcing." Against each of these thematic areas, a concrete set of initiatives was identified to pursue. For example, to reinforce product strengths, three initiatives were defined: electric vehicle strategy, quality improvement, and car architecture renewal. Initiatives to improve profitability and efficiency included revenue management, R&D efficiency, and materials cost. And so on. Once identified, the full set of initiatives was programmatically sequenced to consider interdependencies, build momentum through quick wins, and create coherent change journeys for employee segments. The initiatives were then staffed by top talent and detailed implementation plans were developed.

Health-related interventions took the form of role-modeling actions, storytelling, reinforcing mechanisms (changes to structure, process, systems, and incentives), and skill-building. These actions were carefully hardwired into the detailed implementation plans of the portfolio of performance initiatives. For example, all initiatives were designed to include multiple iterations of customer feedback given their health goal of increasing customer focus. Even back office initiative teams would have to attend dealer showroom trainee days, car shows, and complete required reading of automotive magazines. Further, relevant growth initiatives were staffed where possible to create "matched pairs" of expat and local leaders to maximize the talent development benefits. And so on.

In addition to the health-infused portfolio of performance initiatives, a set of broad-based, integrated performance and health interventions were also designed during the Architect stage. These included: providing change leadership coaching for the top 150 leaders, cascading the change story in a way that every member of the global leadership team would be prompted to write their own personal change story in the context of the larger story, linking compensation and consequences to health outcomes, creating rotational programs between departments, and creating a robust change communications program (Internet, posters, town halls, management chats, screen savers, coffee talks, and so on), among others.

At this point, Volvo had a well-architected change program—one where performance and health were woven together such that employees would experience the work as a single, unified effort. It was now ready to move to the Act stage.

■ ■ ■

As the Volvo example shows, it's in the Architect stage in the journey that an organization's efforts to improve performance and health come together. They begin to interlock and reinforce one another as the performance initiative slate becomes a vehicle for shifting mindsets and behaviors, via the levers of what we call the "influence model." Furthermore, health-related actions are designed to reinforce the performance agenda, and both the performance and health elements are contextualized into a single, integrated narrative that encompasses all aspects of the change program.

## Performance: Bankable Plan

At this stage, you know where you want to go (strategic objectives are clear) and you know how ready you are to go there (skillset requirements are known). From a performance standpoint, it's time to create what we call a "bankable plan" that lays out clearly the "what by who by when" of going from where you are today to achieving your first mid-term aspiration. Creating such a plan involves defining the portfolio of initiatives, programmatically sequencing activity, and reallocating resources to deliver.

### Define the Portfolio of Initiatives

In the Aspire stage of the change journey, you identified your *long-term* change vision. Recall the visions from Chapter 3: GNP wanted to become "1 on 3 in 5"; Tata aspired to be a "globally diversified automotive giant"; Microsoft looked to "build best-in-class platforms and productivity services for a mobile-first, cloud-first world"; and so on. The future of these long-term visions was then rolled back to break the path down into a series of *medium-term* aspirations. For example, the first phase of Tata's journey was to "stem the bleeding," the second to "consolidate our position in India," and the third to "expand operations internationally."

Now it's time to look at the *near term*—what is the specific work that needs to be done in the next 12–18 months to move the organization toward its aspirations (that you decided in the Aspire stage) and build the required skillsets (that you identified in the Assess stage)? There are three important considerations in doing so. First, choose a balanced portfolio of initiatives to pursue. Next, structure the program into a coherent set of themes that essentially shows how each brick (initiative) fits together to build the cathedral (the mid-term aspiration). Finally, use a bottom-up process to develop implementation plans for each initiative.

To determine what is the optimal portfolio of initiatives, we suggest leaders consider value, risk, and time frames of impact. This can be done efficiently by plotting potential initiatives on two axes, time and familiarity, and doing so by visually representing the relative impact potential of each, as shown in Exhibit 5.1. The grid they produce will reveal at a glance whether the initiatives are balanced, like the large grid in the exhibit, or unbalanced, like the six smaller grids on the right.

The *time* axis helps ensure that the portfolio is balanced between efforts that meet current earnings expectations, efforts that yield medium-term impact, and efforts that create long-term value. The initiatives are about what we do in the near term, but we can't neglect that there may be things we need to be doing today if we are to achieve long

## Exhibit 5.1

## **The Portfolio of Initiatives**

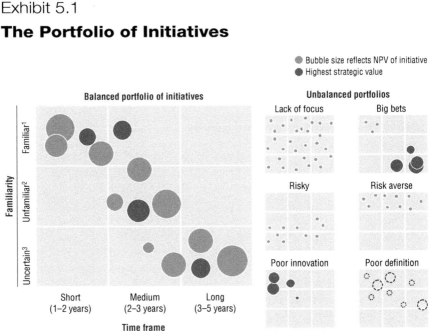

1 **Familiar:** Distinctive knowledge (superior to competition); initiative already possessed or easily acquired; some execution risk
2 **Unfamiliar:** Knowledge surpassed by competitors; attempt small to moderate investments to gain familiarity
3 **Uncertain:** Difficult to estimate probability of success; combat uncertainty by diversifying and learning from experience; attempt small initial investments to gain familiarity

lead-time impact further out. The *familiarity* axis ensures that the portfolio isn't biased toward big bets on the future on the one hand, or incremental improvements that stay too close to the current state on the other. The *value*-creation potential of each initiative is denoted by the size of the circles plotted on the grid, and this ensures that the activity will ultimately lead to the needed impact.

Once the optimal portfolio of performance initiatives is determined, it's vital to create a coherent overall change-program structure to house the initiatives. Without this, you'll run the risk of the "100 lost projects" syndrome: many initiatives embarked on but few completed thanks to a lack of role clarity, coordination, and motivation. Here's an experiment that illustrates the point. Take a look at the picture on the left in Exhibit 5.2. What does it show? Some abstract shapes? A pattern of light and dark? What if we asked you to talk about the picture for a few minutes? Could you find much to say, or summon much enthusiasm?

Now look at the picture on the right of Exhibit 5.2. If we gave you that additional information, would it make any difference to your conception of the left-hand side? Of course it would. You'd be able to describe the reflection of the house in the water and the trees in the foreground. Seeing the big picture—literally—helps us see how each piece fits in, gives each more meaning, and generates more energy in those working on it. It's no wonder that programs are 6.1 times more likely to be successful if they are well structured.[2]

## Exhibit 5.2
## Seeing the Big Picture

A simple but powerful approach to provide structure to a change program is provided in Exhibit 5.3. The mid-term aspiration is clearly stated at the top and is then broken down into a set of performance themes. These themes provide sensible groupings for specific initiatives and measures of success.

This example comes from a commercial insurance brokerage with a long-term vision of becoming a digital and data-driven risk solutions provider. It had a medium-term aspiration of increasing earnings by operating as one firm, not as a federation of acquired businesses. The initiatives were structured around three thematic focus areas: cross-sell, working together, and technology optimization.

The "cross-sell" theme had metrics related to both number of products per client and customer retention. Initiatives included customer segmentation, product bundling, key account management, and so on. The "working together" theme had metrics related to expense ratio and compliance. Initiatives to support this included putting in place a new regional office model under a single brand (retiring all pre-acquisition heritage branding),

## Exhibit 5.3
# Performance Initiative "Placemat"

| Mid-term aspiration: | Deliver double-digit operating income growth by operating as one Firm | | |
|---|---|---|---|
| Performance Themes | Cross-sell | Working together | Technology optimization |
| Initiatives | Customer segmentation strategy | Incentive alignment | Systems integration |
| | "Best in front" strategy | Regional office partnership model (single brand) | Technology road map |
| | Key account management program | Process standardization | Cyber-security upgrade |
| | Sales and product knowledge skill building | Functional CoEs | Data and analytics strategy |
| | Product bundling | Centralize transactional activities | Employee enablement retooling |
| Measures | • Cross-sell rates<br>• Customer loyalty | • Expense ratio<br>• Compliance | • Systems duplication<br>• Risk incidents |

process standardization, setting up centers of excellence, and standardizing transactional activities, among others. The "technology optimization" theme had metrics such as the number of duplicate systems and risk incidents (e.g., outages, breaches). Some of the initiatives to impact these were a new data and analytics strategy, improved cybersecurity, and putting in place a technology roadmap.

We refer to this format as the "Performance Placemat." The name comes from the idea that if you cannot explain the structure of a change program on a single page—the size of a typical placemat used at a dining table—it's too complicated. As P&G's Alan G. Lafley describes it, the placemat provides "a Sesame-Street-level of simplicity" to the change agenda.

Once you have your performance placemat, the next step is to plan each of the initiatives in detail. This is best done by those who will ultimately be responsible for executing against the plan. Doing so builds ownership in the spirit of the "write your own lottery ticket" effect we described at the end of Chapter 3. It also ensures the right knowledge is brought to bear so the plans are as robust as possible. Allowing staff to contribute to planning the initiatives they will be involved in is 3.4 times more likely to be considered successful.[3]

A detailed initiative plan typically includes a crisp description of what success looks like and how it will be achieved. Activities to deliver the desired results are itemized and timelines for their completion determined. Impact milestones along the way are noted so progress against more than just activity can be measured. Accountabilities are also assigned, including what targets and measurement mechanisms will be used to evaluate success during the journey. Furthermore, resource (money and people) requirements are specified, stakeholder involvement is clarified, and interdependencies with other work are noted. Change programs that plan their initiatives at this level of rigor are 3.5 times more likely to be successful.[4]

## Programmatically Sequence Activity

Once there is a first draft of the detailed initiative plans, it's vital to take a top-down look at whether all of the initiatives sync up such that they create a coherent program of work. Change programs that put a focused effort on effective prioritization and planning of implementation from the top down are 1.7 times more likely to be successful.[5]

There are numerous rules of thumb for sequencing initiatives that should be employed at this point. For example, ensure you have a set of "quick wins" (improvements that have visible, immediate benefit that are achieved early in the program of work) to build momentum. Also, take on some "sacred cows" (something unreasonable but that people believe is beyond criticism) early in the program to signal that this is serious and demands people's time and attention. Furthermore, take on high-value projects first, all other things being equal. And so on.

Most change leaders would think to sequence activities in these ways. Too few, however, recognize that these sequencing principles seek to optimize from the change architect, or "sender," point of view. It's also vitally important to apply sequencing principles that take the "receiver" point of view. This means asking how will various internal and external stakeholders experience the program of work if implemented as planned?

Consider you are an employee who is doing your best to manage the day-to-day running of the business. You are also aware you need to support work related to changing how the business is run. The organization restructure initiative team has planned that your area will be taking part in a de-layering workshop next week. The technology infrastructure initiative has also informed you that you'll need to attend a day of training on the new CRM tool being rolled out. The product development initiative team requires that you notify customers personally about a new product that is being launched that week, as well. The salesforce effectiveness team has scheduled you for your negotiation skills workshop at the same time. And it just so happens that it's the week of the annual industry conference that is vital to attend to see and be seen with your key clients. Suffice to say, were this the case, you'd be more than a little frustrated with the lack of coordination of the change program being pursued—and those leading initiatives will also no doubt be frustrated that the frontline isn't getting on board with their efforts, unaware of the impossible position the overall program was putting you in.

Poor sequencing often doesn't just lead to internal frustration, but to customer frustrations as well. A large medical device company, for example, found when they rolled out the initiative-by-initiative plans that they would require the frontline to spend more than 70 percent of its time on internal activities in certain periods. Changes were then made to plans so that the amount of time taken away from customer-facing activities would never be more than 30 percent in any given period. Similarly, an insurance company found that the launch of a new product was planned by one initiative to take place just before a CRM system changeover planned by another, a move that would have introduced significant risk to customer experience—prompting the order in which these efforts were implemented to be flipped.

Conducting an analysis of impact from the receiver perspective is easier than one may think. There are now a number of web-based tools and structured methodologies to draw on. McKinsey & Company's *Change Navigator* is an example of one of these tools that provides a one-stop shop for applying common rules of thumb from the sender perspective in addition to quantifying the change impact and workload implications for key stakeholders—so that ultimately the work of change can be sensibly balanced from all viewpoints.

## Reallocate Resources to Deliver

Once the initiative plans are finalized and sequenced appropriately, the next step is to ensure the work is properly resourced. Too often, change programs are cited as "the most important thing we can be doing," and meanwhile, they end up staffed by lower performers so that business as usual can be run by the superstars. Furthermore, despite many organizations seeking to reduce an excess of employees, ironically their change programs are often starved when it comes to allocating resources.

Consider one company we know that prioritized expanding in China. It set an ambitious sales growth target for the country and planned to meet it by supplementing organic growth with a series of acquisitions. Yet, it identified just three people to spearhead this strategic imperative—a small fraction of the number required. This may sound irrational, but it's often exceedingly difficult to reallocate talent. Even if a reduction in resources benefits the company as a whole, ambitious leaders are unlikely to agree to letting their top talent go without a fight. The fight is worth fighting, however, as change programs that allocate sufficient personnel to support initiatives are 3.6 times more likely to be successful,[6] and those that report their best talent was deployed to carry out the plan report success rates 5.5 times higher than those that don't.[7]

This same dynamic is true not just for human resources, but also capital and operating expenditures. For example, a review of the performance of more than 1,600 U.S. companies over a 15-year period shows that for one-third of businesses, the amount of capital received in a given year was almost exactly that received the year before—the mean correlation was 0.99. For the economy as a whole, the mean correlation across all industries was 0.92. In other words, there were only modest shifts in resource allocation made. Meanwhile, no doubt, enormous amount of change was being aspired to. This finding is consistent across industries as diverse as mining and consumer packaged goods.[8]

To break through this tendency, we advocate that change leaders make explicit choices as to which areas, amongst those that did not rise to the level of the performance placemat, they'll *prune* (take resources away from), so that they can *nurture* the priority change areas.

For example, Alan G. Lafley, former CEO of Procter & Gamble, credits increasing profits by 70 percent and revenues by almost 30 percent in the first five years of his tenure as much to what he stopped as to what he started. On his performance placemat were four core businesses (fabric care, baby care, feminine care, and hair care) and 10 out of more than 100 countries. These were the businesses and geographies that would have differential investment and leadership attention. The feelings of those who didn't make the list weren't pandered to as they were simply told, "Just keep doing a good job where you are." He sums up his philosophy as follows: "Be clear on what you won't do—what needs to stop ... Most human beings and most companies don't like to make choices, and they particularly don't like to make a few choices they really have to live with ... If we caught people doing stuff we said we were not going to do, we would pull the budget and the people and we'd get them refocused on what we said we were going to do."[9]

This philosophy is strikingly similar to that of former Apple CEO, Steve Jobs, who said, "I'm as proud of what we don't do as I am of what we do ... saying no to 1,000 things to make sure we don't get on the wrong track or try to do too much ... it's only by saying no that you can concentrate on the things that are really important."[10] Along the same lines, management thinker Jim Collins notes that great companies create a "stop doing" list to complement their "to do" list.[11] Take, for example, an insurance company who put acquisitions on the "stop doing" list until they could prove the ability to grow organically, and discontinued any investment in language and/ or artifacts related to previously acquired companies. Or the technology company who put any innovation projects not sponsored jointly by an external business partner on their "stop doing" list. Or the industrial company who stopped subscale acquisitions and putting product investment above services investments. All of these decisions free up time and resources to focus on the "to dos" of delivering the performance placemat.

The facts back up the philosophy. Successful change leaders are 1.8 times more likely than others to have explicitly communicated what their expectations were about what to stop, as well as what to start.[12]

## Health: Influence Levers

At this point, on the health side of things you've decided on the vital few management practices that will unlock high health and, in turn, improve delivery against your performance aspirations. You've also named and reframed the underlying root-cause mindsets that will enable you to make rapid and lasting progress. In the Architect stage, you will build a plan to influence the target mindset shifts and their related behaviors.

Based on our research and experience, there are three things to consider in building this plan. The first is to understand the full set of levers available to you to reshape the work environment. The second is to use these levers to hardwire health improvements into how performance initiatives will be implemented. Third is to create and interactively cascade a robust and compelling change story that brings everything together into a single, integrated program. At this point, performance and health efforts become one. Change leaders who take these actions are twice as likely to report that their change programs were successful.[13]

## Determine How to Reshape the Work Environment

Employees' mindsets and behaviors are shaped significantly by their work environment, just like Chapter 4's monkeys in the cage were shaped by theirs. By way of analogy, imagine that you go to the opera on Saturday and a sporting event on Sunday. At the climax of the opera—the very best part of the event—you sit silent and rapt in concentration. You and the audience then offer a genteel clap. At the climax of the sporting event—the very best part—you leap to your feet, yelling and waving and jumping up and down. You haven't changed; you are the same person with the same feelings, values, and needs. But your context has, and so has your mindset about the behavior that's appropriate for expressing your appreciation and enjoyment, and therefore the behaviors you choose to exhibit and practices you choose to participate in.

To continue with the analogy, the biggest tripwire for organizations looking to improve their health is that they end up leaving employees caught somewhere between an opera house and a sports stadium—not a comfortable place to be if you're trying to make decisions as to how to think about your situation and what to do in it. Communicating to employees that you want them to adopt sports-stadium practices and related mindsets and behaviors is no use if your evaluation systems and the leadership actions they see are that of the opera house. If you want your people to think like sports fans, you need to create a stadium environment that encourages and enables them to think and act differently.

Through years of research and practical application, we have developed what we call the "influence model." It identifies the four levers that can directly influence employee mindsets and behaviors (Exhibit 5.4). Taken together, these levers shape the employee work environment and, as such, all are important.

*I will change my mindsets and behaviors if I have...*

- **Understanding and conviction.** Can employees say, "I know what is expected of me, I agree with it, and I want to do it"? The main vehicles for fostering understanding and conviction are a compelling, meaning-laden narrative, an interactive way of communicating (to create the "lottery ticket" effect) and embedding its message through ongoing language, rituals, and communication of what success looks like.

- **Reinforcement from formal mechanisms.** Do the organization's formal mechanisms reinforce the shifts in mindsets and behaviors that employees are being asked to make? Formal mechanisms include financial and non-financial rewards, recognition, and consequences, processes, structures, and systems.

- **Confidence and skills.** Do employees have the skills they need and safe places to practice thinking and behaving in the new way? Confidence and skills can be developed by adopting a "field and forum" approach to skill-building; tending to each of the technical, relational, and adaptive aspects of applying new skills; and refreshing the talent pool as needed.

- **Role modeling.** Do employees see their leaders, opinion-leading colleagues, and staff that they respect and take their cues from thinking and behaving in the new way? Effective approaches to role modeling include having the senior team undergo a visible transformation, taking symbolic actions, and selecting and nurturing influence leaders.

## Exhibit 5.4
## The Four Levers of the Influence Model

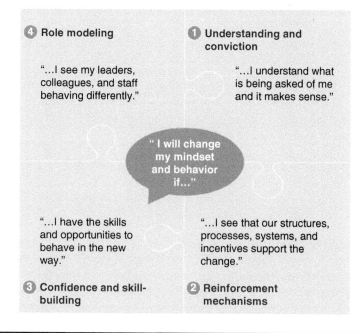

To see how the four elements fit together, let's assume you are one of the vast majority of people who believe "skydiving isn't worth the risk." Let's say we want to shift your mindset to believe that it is absolutely worth the risk, so you jump out of a perfectly good airplane.

What if, in order to build *understanding and conviction*, we show you reliable data from a source you trust that shows the chances of being injured in skydiving are far less than the chances you'll die in a car accident in your lifetime (which is indeed true, by the way!). We then make the jump more meaningful by telling you that your jump will be part of a skydive for charity event, during which we'll donate US$1 million to the charity of your choice for every jump you do.

As a *reinforcing formal mechanism*, you'll also personally receive a million dollars into your bank account for each jump should you be willing to receive it. On the downside, if you don't jump you'll owe us 50,000 dollars (sorry!). You will also have world-class safety equipment, including an automatic military grade backup chute.

Your *confidence and skills* will be developed through training with a world-champion skydiver who will give you in-depth lessons before you jump (including numerous simulations) and ease any underlying fears you may have. In fact, you'll be jumping in tandem, securely attached the whole time to this elite professional who has successfully conducted more than 2,000 jumps.

Finally, you will have the *role modeling* of your boss, two of your colleagues, your immediate family, and your closest friends jumping with you. What's more, they've already done a few jumps and absolutely loved it—and are encouraging you to do so!

At this point, would you be willing to jump out of a perfectly good airplane? The past 100 years of behavioral and cognitive psychology would say that you would be very likely to do so.

Many leaders wonder which lever of the four is most important. Evidence shows that they all matter with minor statistical variations as to what degree, and there is no particular order in which they need to be experienced—the key is to ensure they all are present. Further, change efforts not thoughtfully engineered on all four levers can cause more harm than good. Recall the previous analogy of employees being stuck somewhere between the opera house and the sports stadium.

To make this real, imagine pursuing a cost-cutting program while executives fly around in corporate jets to cushy offsite meetings to discuss who and what will be cut. Or pushing for cross-business collaboration when incentives squarely reinforce putting silos first. Or asking the frontline to take on risk-management responsibilities without giving them the training needed to enable them to do so. In these situations, the only thing meaningfully achieved is increased employee frustration, cynicism, and resistance to future change.

Having established each of the four elements of the influence model and the importance that they all work together, let's dive into each of the four levers of the influence model in some detail.

## Understanding and Conviction

The work of Stanford social psychologist Leon Festinger demonstrates the need people have to align their actions with their beliefs. Half a century ago, Festinger proposed the theory of "cognitive dissonance": that individuals seek consistency among their thoughts, opinions, and beliefs (or cognitions) and their behaviors, and try to eliminate any inconsistencies or dissonance between them. Festinger noted, "It's difficult to behave in a different way if the behavior is inconsistent with your view of the world."[14]

The implication of this finding for a change leader is that if employees don't believe in the overall purpose of the change, they will suffer cognitive dissonance when asked to support it. If they do believe in it, on the other hand, they will be inclined to change their behavior to serve that purpose. Therefore, it's imperative for anyone leading a major change program to take the time to think through the "change story"—what makes it worth undertaking—and what is the role of the individual's actions in its unfolding that makes it worthwhile to play a part.

The advantage of a story—as opposed to a report or an analysis—is that it can convey emotions as well as facts. We therefore respond to it in a different way; we don't just process the information intellectually, we relate it to our personal experiences and beliefs. According to our survey, programs that communicate and embed an emotionally compelling narrative about the desired change are 3.8 times more likely to succeed than those that don't.[15] Further, when change leaders are asked what they would have done differently in retrospect, the number one vote-getter is "spending more time developing and communicating the change story," cited by 44 percent of change leaders.[16]

In this section, we'll focus our discussion on the content needed for a great change story, but that won't be the whole story. We'll expand on this when we talk later in this chapter about interactively cascading the story (and why a traditional cascade never works). We'll then talk about how to maximize the meaning quotient of the story when we get to this chapter's "Master Stroke." Then, in Chapter 5, we'll talk further about how to keep the narrative alive through on-going two-way communications. It's simply that important!

It's important to keep in mind that if the leader doesn't provide a story, employees will create their own. For instance, an innocent comment from a leader about the need to be more cost-conscious can spark near-hysteria as it spreads through an organization. Before long, it can turn into a story like, "All the work in our division is going to be outsourced and we're all about to lose our jobs." Sounds far-fetched? It's not—we've seen it happen. Had the comment been placed in the context of a robust change story, this kind of misunderstanding would never have arisen.

So let's get to the content needed. Good change stories use concrete, evocative, and immediate language to answer employees' fundamental questions: Where are we today? Why do we have to change? What are we changing to? By when? How will we measure success? How do we get there? What does it mean for me and my team? How will we be supported? What won't change? Why does this matter? Exhibit 5.5 further illustrates the core architecture of a great change story.

As you can see, in answering these questions you are drawing on all of the work you've done to date in the Five Frames and putting it into a single, unified change narrative. The work done in the Aspire stage answers many of the where, why, what, and when questions. A large retailer, for example, could tell the story about how much their company had to be proud of in expanding its physical footprint, but the industry was changing in ways where a physical presence wasn't enough, and their position at the top was not secure. As such, the goal was to become the most admired omnichannel retailer in five years' time. On the health front, the goal was to be top quartile on three management practices: competitive insights, operational discipline, and challenging leadership. Progress toward the performance and health aspirations would be measured against shareholder return, access differentiation (as measured by customer research), and OHI targets.

Answers to the rest of the questions come from the work done in the Assess and Architect stages. The retailer in question could articulate clearly that getting there involved delivering against a portfolio of initiatives that included growing in three specific categories (food, general merchandise, and apparel), becoming a serial acquirer of relevant start-ups, doubling down on winning in two major geographies, shifting the value proposition to value-oriented customers, and building skillsets in market optimization, analytics, and supply chain. They could also name and reframe a set of underlying mindsets needed to enable and accelerate progress ("smooth talk" to "straight talk," "listen/respond" to "anticipate/shape," and "retail is detail" to "retail requires results"). Not only that, but they could specify how the work environment would be reshaped to support the shifts (actions related to reinforcing mechanisms, building confidence and skills, role modeling, and fostering understanding and conviction). Finally, they could articulate a deeper sense of why making the change happen would matter—using techniques we'll discuss further in the "Master Stroke" section at the end of this chapter.

We emphasize that what we are talking about here is not a PowerPoint presentation. Often, it's a text narrative with an accompanying video that tells the story in an emotive, authentic (not "salesy") format. The company story is typically followed by the leader putting their own personal overlay

Exhibit 5.5

# Elements of a Great Change Story

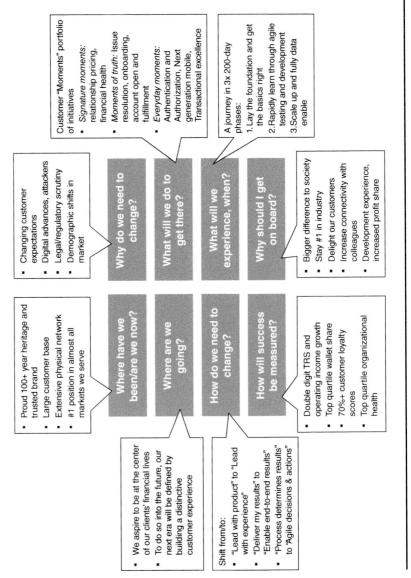

on it, saying "what it means to me is …" As Corrado Passera, the former CEO of Italian bank Banca Intesa, notes, a good story is "not like an analyst's presentation, with figures and graphs," but is rather "a book written in human language telling people where we are, where we want to go, and how we are going to get there."[17]

## Reinforcement Mechanisms

When it comes to reinforcement mechanisms to influence desired mindsets and behavior shifts, change leaders should consider how to alter rewards and consequences, formal structures, business and management processes, and enabling systems and tools.

It's hardly news that *rewards* and *consequences* have a big effect on our thoughts and behaviors. B.F. Skinner and other behavioral scientists have argued that human behavior is a reaction to stimuli such as praise, rewards, punishments, and so on. When these stimuli change, so does the behavior. According to Skinner, our environment sends us signals that make us more likely to behave in certain ways.[18] Combine this with the assertion from academics Richard Pascale, Jerry Sternin, and Monica Sternin that, "It's easier to act your way into a new way of thinking, than think your way into a new way of acting,"[19] and the power of rewards and consequences on shaping mindsets is clear. Paul Allaire, former CEO of Xerox, sums it up: "If you talk about change but don't change the recognition and reward system, nothing changes."[20]

Our advice for leaders is to link rewards and consequences both to the "what" and the "how" of the desired change. The former relates to contributions to achieving performance objectives and the latter to health objectives. A simple but effective matrix can be used to show employees where they stand and what the related consequences are, as shown in Exhibit 5.6. Change programs that hardwire change-related targets into individual employees' incentives are 4.2 times more likely to be successful.[21]

The hardest employee profile to deal with on this matrix is s/he who is delivering performance but detrimental to health. Successful leaders don't shy away from this challenge. Cisco's former CEO and chairman John Chambers, for example, was known for withholding managers' bonuses if their behaviors weren't in line with expectations, even if they delivered results. Former CEO of EMC, Joseph M. Tucci, simply says, "You have to get rid of them."[22] Dismissing employees is never easy, but as GE's former CEO Jack Welch reflects, "Anyone who enjoys doing it shouldn't be in the job, but nor should someone who can't do it."[23] Successful change leaders don't wait for formal reviews to reward desired mindsets and behaviors, however. For example, when Continental Airlines made it to the top five for punctuality, CEO Gordon M. Bethune sent a US$65 check to every employee in the company. Nor do they rely exclusively on financial rewards.

Exhibit 5.6

# Linking Behavior to Rewards and Consequences

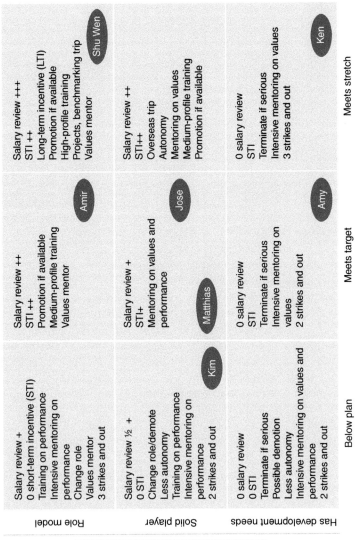

At ANZ Bank, John McFarlane gave every employee involved in the change program a bottle of champagne for Christmas with a card thanking them for their work on changing the company. Indra Nooyi, former CEO of PepsiCo, went as far as sending the spouses of her top team handwritten thank-you letters. After seeing the impact of her success on her mother during a visit to India, she began sending letters to the parents of her top team, as well. We'll speak more about how to maximize the impact of non-financial rewards during a change program in Chapter 6's "Master Stroke."

Beyond incentives, an organization's *structure, processes,* and *systems* can have a profound influence on employees' mindsets and behaviors. Let's start with structure. If customer focus is an important management practice, changing the primary axis of organization from being a product structure organizing around customer segments may have a significant impact on related mindsets and behaviors. Adjusting the annual strategic planning process to include as much information required on customer experience impact as well as financial impacts would also influence employees. Changing talent development processes to include rotations into customer-facing positions as part of management development programs also sends a signal. Further, implementing a customer relationship management (CRM) system to help them have better information with which to engage with customers will also have real impact. It's easy to see how these changes, in particular if taken together, can make a big difference.

Even seemingly innocuous processes and systems can have a surprisingly powerful effect on mindsets and behaviors. When PricewaterhouseCoopers was making the transition to a more entrepreneurial culture, one partner complained that although he liked what was happening, he felt he was not treated like a partner but like a salaried employee. If he wanted to give his assistant flowers for working until midnight, he needed three signatures for the expenses system. If he wanted to meet a client in another city, that was another three signatures. He felt he wasn't trusted. As a result, he didn't feel empowered to proactively take initiatives to build the firm. It had never occurred to anyone that the expenses system was transmitting powerful mindset and behavior cues that were incompatible with an entrepreneurial culture.

It's worth bearing in mind that formal processes can affect mindsets and behaviors by their absence as well as their presence. Netflix, an online movie and TV streaming service, has no formal policy on vacations, for instance. Former chief talent officer Patty McCord wryly observed, "There is also no clothing policy at Netflix, but no one has come to work naked lately."

## Confidence and Skill-Building

The third lever that leaders can use to shape mindsets and behaviors relates to increasing employees' confidence in their ability to think and behave in the desired ways. Change efforts that invest in doing so are 2.4 times more likely to succeed.[24]

As individuals, we like to do things we feel competent at, especially when others are watching. Scott, for example, is a guitarist outside of work and is quick to take any stage he can find to play for an audience. At the same time, he has no natural ability to dance. Therefore, anytime there's an event where dancing is involved he conveniently has other commitments to tend to!

To illustrate how skills and confidence are intertwined, consider the adult learning cycle: we start unconsciously incompetent ("I didn't know this was important"), then become consciously incompetent ("I realize this is important and that I'm not very good at it"), then move to being consciously competent ("I can do it if I concentrate on it"), and finally we get to a point where we are unconsciously competent ("It comes naturally to me"). Think about driving, for example. At some point as teenagers it dawns on us that having to rely on our parents to act as taxi drivers is holding back our social life. Our first time behind the wheel, however, we realize what looks effortless is actually quite hard—we are not confident, and we are not competent. After some practice we can do it, though it takes our full attention: checking the mirrors, remembering to signal before turning, working out who has priority at a junction. As we gain more experience, we get to the point where we can multitask while driving, arriving at point B from point A without having given the journey significant thought and having been fully confident in our ability to get there.

So how do we move employees through this process in relation to the mindsets and behaviors we desire to see? Studies have confirmed that only roughly 10 percent of what is shared in speech-based training sessions such as lectures, presentations, demonstrations, and discussions, is retained after three months. When learning by doing—through role plays, simulations, or case studies—65 percent is retained. And when classroom learning is immediately put into practice for a few weeks at work, almost everything is retained.[25] This finding resonates with the human experience, as the Chinese proverb that says: "Tell me and I'll forget; show me and I may remember; involve me and I'll understand."

In practice, the "learning by doing" method is referred to as *field and forum*, which brings classroom learning, coaching, on-the-job training, and special projects together into a coherent program. A large-scale change program is an ideal situation in which to deploy such an approach. Every initiative on the performance placemat represents a rotational assignment for those involved. Each initiative has a clear beginning, middle, and end, and thus lends itself to periodic in-person classroom style learning in "forums." Each requires accelerated delivery of impact, which creates an ideal crucible for the application of learnings in the day-to-day ("fieldwork"). The transparency of results enables multiple cycles of action and reflection that maximize learning. Successful change programs are 3.2 times more likely to report that they explicitly used performance initiatives as a vehicle to build change-related skills and confidence than unsuccessful ones.[26]

In applying a field and forum approach to building skills and confidence, three types of competencies should be incorporated: *technical, relational,* and *adaptive.* The vast majority of leaders tell us that it's the latter two of these that are most lacking in change programs and are the hardest to build.[27] As such, we'll talk in depth about relational and adaptive skills both in Chapter 6 (when we talk about making the change personal for leaders) and Chapter 9 (when we talk about your role as a change leader). For now, however, let's bring the combination to life in the context of a large-scale change in an industrial company.

The company needed to build skills and confidence to support its lean manufacturing initiative. Examples of the mindset shifts desired included from "success is about what we do" to "success is about both what we do and how we do it"; "problems mean failure" to "problems mean opportunities"; "cost, quality, and service are inversely related" to "quality, cost, and service are directly related"; and "time with managers equals trouble" to "time with managers helps me/us get things done."

To influence these shifts, skills and confidence were built in each plan that the initiative rolled out to over the course of three forums with fieldwork in-between. The first forum educated those involved in the *technical* skills of leading change (performance and health approach) and lean (e.g., 5S, Kanban, eight kinds of waste), *relational* skills (e.g., self-awareness and awareness of others, empathy, creating trust), and *adaptive* skills (e.g., telescope and microscope perspectives, productive tension, resilience). The fieldwork that followed involved applying the tools learned during the forum to the work of meeting targets for cost, quality, and service. Between forums, activities such as getting peer feedback and completing a series of e-learning modules were also incorporated to help them reflect on their experience and further build on forum learnings. Anyone who completed the coursework and hit their performance targets was awarded a "green belt" in lean.

The next forum sought to develop deeper skills in designing technical systems and leading projects and teams. The fieldwork included redesigning areas of the plant floor and overseeing teams dedicated to specific improvements. Quantitative targets were set in terms of financial results and people and project leadership. Those who achieved these targets became "brown belts" in lean. The final forum built advanced skills such as shaping plant-wide improvement programs to address strategic issues, applying improvement concepts to complex operations, and coaching and mentoring. As before, fieldwork was used to put these lessons into practice. Those who met the quantitative improvement goals emerged from the program as "black belts." These black belts then served as faculty for future skills and confidence-building programs during the roll out.

The academic underpinnings for the field and forum method of building confidence and skills are strong. Those interested should consult the work of David Kolb and Chris Argyris related to experiential and action learning. Also, Victor Vroom's "expectancy theory" is very relevant, as he puts building skills on an equal footing with other influence levers when it comes to motivating behavior.[28] For more on relational skills, look into Daniel Goleman's work on the learnability of emotional intelligence that builds on the multiple intelligences research of Howard Gardner. For adaptive leadership, see the directly related work of Ron Heifitz, situational leadership work from Hersey and Blanchard, shared leadership approach of Henry Mintzberg, and more distributed leadership of James Spillane.

## Role Modeling

The final lever that leaders can use to influence mindsets and behaviors is role modeling. Employees need to see the people they admire and take their cues from behaving in new ways. Niall FitzGerald, former CEO of Unilever, underscores the importance of role modeling: "One of the things that leaders don't fully recognize is that when they speak or act, they are speaking into an extraordinary amplification system. The slightest thing you say, the slightest gesture you make, is picked up on by everybody in that system and, by and large, acted upon."[29]

Academics in the field of social psychology agree. Stanford professor emeritus Albert Bandura argues that social behavior is primarily learned by observing and modeling the behavior of relevant others.[30] Similarly, Konrad Lorenz, a professor of psychology and Nobel Prize winner, concludes from his work on imprinting that people take their cues from those they consider as "significant" and model their behavior accordingly.[31] Our research into transformation programs also bears out the importance of role modeling. Programs in which leaders model the desired changes are 5.3 times more likely to be successful.[32] Two particular groups have disproportionate impact on others' thoughts, behaviors, and practices in change programs: senior leaders and influence leaders.

There are many examples that bring to life the power of *senior leader* role modeling. Take, for example, when McDonald's founder Ray Kroc noticed litter in the parking lot at one of his restaurants: he called the manager and his driver over, and the three of them picked it up together. As word of the incident spread, so did the realization that cleanliness and order really mattered. In a similar vein, the founder of IT company Hewlett-Packard, Bill Hewlett, once took a bolt-cutter to a lock on a supply-room door to signify that management and frontline staff could trust one another. When N.R. Narayana Murthy, former chairman of Infosys, takes his wife on business trips, he pays the difference between a single and a double hotel room out of his own pocket, so setting a symbolic example of integrity—a value highly prized in his company's leadership model. As he puts it, "Credibility comes from eating one's own food before recommending it to others."[33]

We'll be spending more time discussing the role of the most senior leader in successful change programs in Chapter 8—yes, it's so important that we dedicate an entire chapter to it! Why? When asked to rank the groups and people based on how important they are to the success of change programs, 70 percent of respondents put the most senior leader as number one.[34] Further, those programs where the most senior leader is strongly involved in role modeling are 2.6 times more likely to succeed.[35]

Individual senior leaders aren't the only role modeling leverage point, however. The way senior teams work together has a powerful role modeling effect, as well. In the survey mentioned, senior teams rank number two on the list of groups and people who are important to change program success.[36] It's worth noting that when change leaders are asked what they would have done differently in retrospect, 41 percent report that they would have spent more time aligning the senior team.[37] As such, rest assured we will also spend more time talking about creating high performing senior leadership teams in Chapter 8.

Also vitally important are the influence leaders deep in the organization; any change leader should find out who they are and work with them explicitly. We define influence leaders as those who, regardless of their official title or status, have a wide circle of personal contacts who respect and emulate them. When they are engaged in helping motivate employees to change, efforts are 3.8 times more likely to be successful.[38] These leaders play a vital role in generating ownership and energy during the Act stage, and because of this we'll be talking extensively about how to identify and mobilize influence leaders in Chapter 6.

Finally, it's important to consider that everyone in an organization has the power to role model, and when large groups of people do so together it can have a profound effect on the organization more broadly. Robert Cialdini, a well-respected professor of psychology and marketing, examined the power of "social proof"—a mental shortcut people use to judge what is correct by determining what others think is correct.[39] No wonder TV shows have been using canned laughter for decades; believing that other people find a show funny makes us more likely to find it funny, too. We'll also discuss how to leverage this phenomenon further in Chapter 6, when we cover how to make the change personal for a critical mass of leaders.

Finally, we'd be remiss not to mention how the increasingly connected digital world of today provides more opportunities than ever to share information about how others think and behave. Have you ever found yourself swayed by the number of positive reviews on Yelp? Or perceiving a Twitter user with a million followers as more reputable than one with only a dozen? The impact is real, and can and should be taken advantage of in leading change. Use of these methods is in its relative infancy, and we encourage leaders to experiment. No doubt that in the third edition of *Beyond Performance*, we'll be filling many pages with your examples!

## Hardwire Health into Performance Initiatives

Some leaders learn of the influence model and are quick to design a host of interventions on each of the four levers to drive desired changes in mindsets and behaviors. After all, the goal is to clearly indicate whether employees are in an opera house or a sports stadium, not to leave them somewhere in the middle. This inclination, however, is typically not constructive in practice. It leads to a laundry list of health-related initiatives that are separate from, and additional to, the initiatives on the performance placemat. Not only does this create an initiative overload, but also means that employees experience two separate programs of work, one for performance and one for health, which is not the path to successful change—health is meant to be a means to performance.

We advocate as a rule of thumb that 80 percent of the work on improving an organization's health should be done by the performance initiatives—not because of *what* those initiatives do, but because of *how* they are executed. In fact, *every* performance initiative that touches employees—be it a customer-service enhancement, a salesforce effectiveness drive, an IT upgrade, or a cost-cutting effort—creates an opportunity to influence mindsets and behaviors. By carefully hardwiring health interventions into performance initiatives like these, the work of health becomes less about doing new things and more about doing things that need to be done differently, in healthier ways that lead to more significant and sustainable performance impact. In the Architect stage, then, efforts on performance and health become integrated into a singular change effort.

The process of hardwiring health into performance initiatives is surprisingly straightforward, though too seldom done in practice. It involves applying a simple analytic tool to the performance initiative plans that we discussed earlier in this chapter, as shown in Exhibit 5.7. Target health shifts are the columns, and the four levers of the influence model are the rows. The cells of the resulting matrix are then completed so that the work done in implementing the performance initiative is done in a way that improves as many of the health priorities using as many influence levers as possible

Exhibit 5.7

# Hardwiring Health into a Performance Initiative: Service Operations Example

What the performance initiative will do to explicitly improve our health in each of our priority areas:

Practices *(Reframed mindsets)*:

| Influence levers: | Knowledge sharing<br>("I win only when we win") | Personal ownership<br>("If it is to be, it's up to me") | Talent development<br>("Coaching makes the best better") |
|---|---|---|---|
| **Role modeling** | ▪ Executives sponsor best practice visits | ▪ Someone takes a question-led approach (vs. telling) | ▪ Someone shares their own "learning edge" |
| **Understanding and conviction** | ▪ Knowledge sharing examples proactively disseminated<br>▪ No success rewarded unless radiated | ▪ "How I make our customer promise come alive" discussion sessions<br>▪ "Passionate people serving people passionately" top-line adopted | ▪ "In the spirit of coaching champions" language top-line adopted<br>▪ Success stories highlight how coaching helped |
| **Confidence and skills** | ▪ Directory of "who does and knows what" created and shared | ▪ Relational skill-building program | ▪ Stars and strugglers both given coaches<br>▪ "Coaching 15" expectation (formal 15-minute feedback conversation) |
| **Reinforcing mechanisms** | ▪ Cross-functional brainstorming sessions added to approach | ▪ Agile approaches leveraged let teams decide the "how" of delivering targets<br>▪ SOP books symbolically destroyed in favor of "operating principles" | ▪ Quality of coaching built into evaluation criteria of project leader<br>▪ Milestones trigger 360 review to further improve effectiveness |

and practical. Typically, when an initiative leader and team consider their initial performance plan against the matrix, there is a lot of white space. Sometimes there are even contemplated actions that, if taken, would have otherwise run counter to health aspirations (sending sports stadium signals into the opera house!). The work isn't done until each cell of the matrix contains at least one powerful idea to ensure the initiative will have positive impacts on both performance and health.

Let's make this concept real by way of an example. Consider the U.S. financial services provider who had a performance initiative (one among many initiatives) to apply lean manufacturing techniques to their processing functions. The company also had a set of health goals, including improving openness and trust. In order to apply lean principles to operations improvement, a standard practice was to hold regular *kaizen* events. These were short-duration, frontline-driven improvement efforts to address specific operational issues. Using the matrix above to brainstorm how to hardwire health into the lean initiative, they decided to focus every other kaizen event on improving trust in the team and with management.

One such session resulted in increasing frontline involvement in determining how targets were set, a process that previously felt ad hoc and "from on high." Another resulted in changing the performance review process to start with a self-assessment, which turned the review into more of a conversation. Yet another resulted in the adoption of a monthly "ask me anything" session with management to increase the communications flow. Still another prompted kaizen boards (used for the visual management of the area's KPIs) to be updated to include the team's view on six trust measures: communication, support, respect, fairness, predictability, and competence. Not only did the health-infused performance initiative ultimately deliver a 20 percent reduction in costs and raise service and quality standards, but it also increased OHI scores on the open and trusting management practice by over 50 percent—ultimately delivering a top-quartile result.

Now consider an automotive company who had one of its performance initiatives focused on safety, and one of its health objectives was to increase its external orientation. By brainstorming ideas against the matrix for hardwiring external orientation into the safety initiative, the company decided to staff the working team not just with their own employees, but also with a safety expert from a mining company who was focused on improving safety practices. The idea was a win for the performance and health of the automotive company and a win for the mining company, which gained a development opportunity for its employees and benefited from the flow of new and different safety ideas back to their organization.

Ensuring there is at least one good idea in each block of the matrix (i.e., the intersection of each influence model lever and each health priority) for every initiative on the performance placemat (typically anywhere from 10 to 25 initiatives), has an extraordinary cumulative power. Consider the math: if your change program is comprised of 20 performance initiatives and you have 3 health objectives, there will be 240 high-impact health interventions (3 health objectives × 4 levers of the influence model × 20 initiatives) that employees will experience in a manner that is *fully integrated* with the implementation of performance initiatives.

This same approach can be used to hardwire health into business as usual processes such as recruiting, onboarding, training, performance management, and strategic planning. It takes the idea of "doing what we'd do anyway, but differently" further—and one can imagine even with just this list of processes, another 60 health interventions would be experienced by employees (3 health priorities × 4 levers of the influence model × 5 processes). It's easy to see how this can play a significant role in reshaping the work environment.

This doesn't mean there aren't any health actions taken outside of those hardwired into performance initiatives and other business processes. As we'll see more in the next section and chapter, we advocate that there is a set of broad-based, predominantly health-related actions to take (to do the other 20 percent of the work!). These typically involve interactively cascading the change story, maintaining a high impact two-way communications program, and making health objectives personal to a critical mass of leaders.

## Interactively Cascade the Change Story

The transition between the Architect and Act stages of a change program is typically marked by the broad-based sharing of the change narrative deep into the organization. We talked about the content of a great story earlier in this chapter when we discussed the influence model lever of fostering understanding and conviction. A great story is only great, however, to the extent others are aware of, understand, and believe in it!

Getting the change story out and embedded into the minds and hearts of employees at this point in the change process enables everything that happens in the Act stage to be contextualized by "what it all means." A key characteristic of a good process for sharing the story is that it encourages employees to feel a sense of authorship, like the lottery-ticket writers in Chapter 3. That's the thinking behind the "interactive cascade" approach that we recommend, as illustrated in Exhibit 5.8. This process turns writing and telling a relevant change story into something in which everyone in the organization participates.

Before we dive into the specifics of the approach, let's first establish why it works. While every organization's OHI is different, one finding is true across virtually every organization of the thousands who have employed

## Exhibit 5.8

# The Interactive Cascade Process

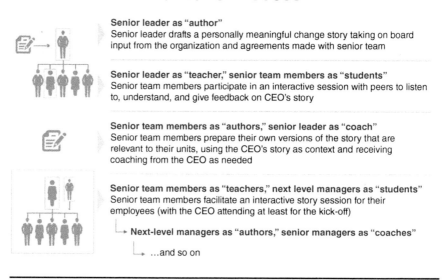

**Senior leader as "author"**
Senior leader drafts a personally meaningful change story taking on board input from the organization and agreements made with senior team

**Senior leader as "teacher," senior team members as "students"**
Senior team members participate in an interactive session with peers to listen to, understand, and give feedback on CEO's story

**Senior team members as "authors," senior leader as "coach"**
Senior team members prepare their own versions of the story that are relevant to their units, using the CEO's story as context and receiving coaching from the CEO as needed

**Senior team members as "teachers," next level managers as "students"**
Senior team members facilitate an interactive story session for their employees (with the CEO attending at least for the kick-off)

└→ **Next-level managers as "authors," senior managers as "coaches"**

└→ ...and so on

the tool: strategic and role clarity diminish the further down you go. Why? The company story stops resonating at some point, largely because it feels high-level and not relevant to the day-to-day work that needs to get done. An interactive cascade, however, ensures the narrative is tailored to each area and includes group and individual reflection as to "what does it mean for us/me." Programs are 5.5 times more likely to be successful when everyone in the organization understands how their work relates to the overall change aspiration.[40]

In their seminal work, Canadian organizational psychologists Natalie Allen and John Meyer propose that there are three types of commitment simultaneously at play in the workforce: continuance (just enough commitment to ensure they keep their jobs); normative (coming from a feeling of obligation to the organization rooted in the norms of reciprocity), and affective (based on emotional ties one develops with organizations primarily via positive work experiences).[41] Viewed through this lens, the interactive story cascade's power comes from addressing multiple types of commitment simultaneously, far more so than more traditional cascade approaches.

So how exactly does it work in practice? The company change story (that includes all of the integrated performance and health elements described earlier in this chapter) acts as a common and consistent foundation for everything that happens. It is often written in prose and shared as a pre-read for the first meeting of the interactive cascade. The process then begins with the senior leader personalizing the company narrative in their words. What does the company's change story mean to her/him? Why is the change necessary? Why is s/he committed to it? What does s/he need to change in their own thinking and behavior to make it happen? What changes is s/he expecting of their team? The senior leader's direct reports are free to ask questions, and then discuss what the change program means for the team. Then time is given for them to think through what the change means for their specific area of responsibility. At the end of the session, having fully understood the story and its implications, each participant shares their individual commitments to the change.

After the session, each of the participants prepares to host a similar session with their teams. They begin by telling the story in their words, both overall and specifically as they see it relating to their area of responsibility. They then answer questions, and the team members who have just heard the story discuss what it means for the team and for them as individuals. The session then closes with their individual commitments. Level by level, the process cascades throughout the whole organization. Being involved in writing the narrative builds conviction among the "authors," as well as ensures that the story is applicable to every part of the organization and every person in it.

By way of example, consider how Symantec (the manufacturer of Norton antivirus software and a global leader in IT security, storage, and systems management) used this approach. After a broad coalition of senior managers had spent several months defining a change story drawing on input from the organization, they held a series of four-day events to communicate it to the company's 14 divisions. During the first two days of each event, managers were exposed to the new performance and health aspiration, the core initiatives, and the mindset and behavior shifts needed to make it happen. The managers also grappled with the question, "What does it mean for us in our division?"

In the last two days of each event, everyone in the division right down to the frontline came together to translate the company's direction into job-level objectives for all employees. The entire process was completed in 13 weeks, and then the content from the cascades was built into the company's orientation program for new hires.[42] The impact was felt almost immediately. Symantec went on to gain the number one spot in the worldwide security market and increase its market share by 6 percent within a year.[43]

Cascading the story in such an interactive way undoubtedly takes longer than pushing it directly through the organization. However, savvy leaders realize that even if it takes twice as long, it's likely to have far more impact in building people's commitment to the outcome. Indeed, recall that the lottery ticket experiment from Chapter 3 indicates the impact is likely five times higher—which makes the interactive cascade approach a solid return on investment by any standard.

It's notable, however, that it's not just the lottery ticket effect that accounts for the interactive cascade's power. In the words of organizational psychologist Noel Tichy, whose theory of leadership recommends having a teachable point of view, a story for your organization, and a well-defined teaching methodology (all of which are wrapped into the interactive story cascade approach), "The very act of creating a Teachable Point of View makes people better leaders ... Leaders come to understand their underlying assumptions about themselves, their organization, and business in general."[44] Indeed, the mental work of figuring out one's point of view, and then the creative work of putting it into a format that is accessible and of interest to others makes better leaders in the process.

## Master Stroke: Appeal to Multiple Sources of Meaning

A disproportionate amount of this chapter has been dedicated to the change narrative—to its content and how it can be interactively cascaded through the organization. This is because these are the things that will provide coherence and give meaning to everything that employees will experience in the Act stage of the change program. Without these, change efforts are likely to end up in Joel Barker's "action without vision that merely passes the time" mode. Done with mastery, "vision with action that changes the world" is in reach.

But is there more to achieving mastery than we've discussed? Indeed, there is, and it comes from appreciating yet another learning from the field of predictable irrationality. Consider that most company change stories tend to fall into one of two classic narratives. One of these narratives is "good to great," which goes something like this: "Our historic advantage is being eroded by intense competition and changing customer needs. If we change, we can regain our leadership position, dominate the industry for the foreseeable future, and leave our competitors in the dust."

The other narrative is "the turnaround," which goes something like this: "We're performing below the industry standard, so we need to transform ourselves to survive. Incremental change won't be enough; investors won't keep pouring money into an underperforming company. Given our assets, market position, size, skills, and staff, we can do much more. We can become a top-quartile performer in our industry by exploiting our current assets and earning the right to grow."

Most executives read these stories and feel that they are compelling. The truth is that they are not. In fact, these stories fall flat with the vast majority of the workforce. Research by a number of leading social scientists such as Danah Zohar, Chris Cowen, Don Beck, and Richard Barrett helps us understand why.[45] These classic narratives revolve around the *company*—beating the competition, leading the industry, attracting investors. This is but one source of meaning that motivates people to change, and there are at least four others. People also want to hear about the impact changes will make on *society* (improving people's lives, building a community, stewarding resources), the *customer* (providing superior service, better products, closer relationships), their *working team* (creating a sense of belonging, a caring environment, harmonious working conditions), and *me personally* (better development opportunities, increased pay and bonuses, more empowerment to act).

In surveys of hundreds of thousands of employees to discover which of these five sources of meaning motivates them most, the surprising result is a roughly consistent 20 percent split between dimensions. Regardless of level (senior management to frontline), industry (health care to manufacturing), and geography (developed or developing economies), the split stays broadly the same.[46]

The implication for leaders is profound. It suggests that the company-focused story, which is the one most have been trained to tell—will tap into only about 20 percent of what motivates their workforce. To get people truly on board, change leaders need to be able to add that missing 80 percent and draw on *all* of the sources of meaning that their employees care about. In other words, they need to be able to *tell five stories at once*. If they can pull that off, they'll unleash tremendous amounts of change energy in the organization. If they can't, it will remain latent.

When a large U.S. mortgage company embarked on a program to increase its efficiency by reducing overheads and reengineering processes, it devised a story that ticked all the boxes according to conventional wisdom on change management. Costs were up and revenues were down, so the burning platform seemed obvious, and so did the message: if we don't get leaner, we won't survive. Three months into the effort, though, the story didn't seem to be working and the change program was stalled. Employee resistance was strong—hardly anyone was submitting improvement ideas and people were still keeping performance information to themselves.

Desperate to break through the barrier, and with the benefit of having been exposed to the five stories at once approach, the team recast the narrative. Instead of focusing on the company's need to stem the unsustainable growth in expenses, they broadened the story out to include elements on the missing four sources of meaning. The new story touched on the benefits change would bring for individuals, emphasizing this was a once-in-a-career opportunity to turn around a company and create bigger, more attractive jobs. It touched on a better life for working teams, with less duplication of effort, greater delegation of responsibility, and a stronger sense of accountability. It touched on the improvements that customers would experience in the form of greater simplicity, fewer errors, and more competitive prices. And it touched on the benefit for society: enabling more people to achieve their dreams of home ownership.

This relatively simple and easy-to-achieve shift in approach had a dramatic impact. Within a month, employee motivation levels had soared from 35 percent to 57 percent. What's more, the program went on to achieve efficiency improvements of 10 percent in the first year—far surpassing the company's initial expectations.

We should make it clear that "telling five stories at once" is not about spin or somehow being disingenuous. The message that a leader communicates must be true to the actions being taken (nowhere in the mortgage company's narrative did it shy away from the change program being about reducing costs, but it gave five reasons why doing so would lead to a more exciting future). It must be sincere—the leader needs to fully believe in what they are saying. John Mackey, CEO of Whole Foods Market, notes that any "lack of honest, authentic communication and transparency usually boomerangs … and undermines trust and creates cynicism."[47]

■ ■ ■

At the end of this, the Architect stage of your change program, you can answer the question, "What do we need to do to get there?" On the performance side, you have constructed, structured, sequenced, and resourced a balanced portfolio of performance improvement initiatives. On the health side, you have used the four influence levers available to you to hardwire health improvements into how the portfolio of performance initiatives will be implemented, you have written a compelling change story laden with five sources of meaning, and you are in the process of cascading the story interactively throughout the organization.

At this point, the distinction between what is performance and what is health has faded into the background as a single, integrated change program that addresses both equally in an integrated manner has been developed. From here, in the words of P&G's Alan G. Lafley, "It's about executing with excellence"[48] in the Act stage. As such, we now move on to the central question of: "How do we manage the journey?" (Exhibit 5.9).

Exhibit 5.9

# A Proven Approach to Leading Large-Scale Change: The Story So Far

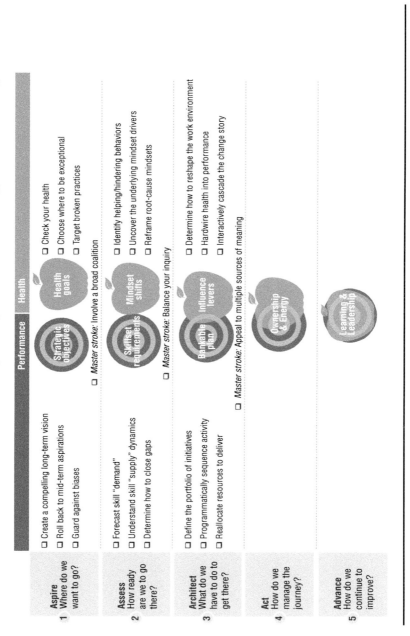

| | Performance | Health |
|---|---|---|
| **Aspire** 1 Where do we want to go? | Strategic objectives | Health goals |
| | □ Create a compelling long-term vision □ Roll back to mid-term aspirations □ Guard against biases | □ Check your health □ Choose where to be exceptional □ Target broken practices |

□ *Master stroke: Involve a broad coalition*

| | Performance | Health |
|---|---|---|
| **Assess** 2 How ready are we to go there? | Skillset requirements | Mindset shifts |
| | □ Forecast skill "demand" □ Understand skill "supply" dynamics □ Determine how to close gaps | □ Identify helping/hindering behaviors □ Uncover the underlying mindset drivers □ Reframe root-cause mindsets |

□ *Master stroke: Balance your inquiry*

| | Performance | Health |
|---|---|---|
| **Architect** 3 What do we have to do to get there? | Bankable plan | Influence levers |
| | □ Define the portfolio of initiatives □ Programmatically sequence activity □ Reallocate resources to deliver | □ Determine how to reshape the work environment □ Hardwire health into performance □ Interactively cascade the change story |

□ *Master stroke: Appeal to multiple sources of meaning*

| | | |
|---|---|---|
| **Act** 4 How do we manage the journey? | Ownership & Energy | |

| | | |
|---|---|---|
| **Advance** 5 How do we continue to improve? | Learning & Leadership | |

149

# Chapter 6

# Act

## *How Do We Manage the Journey?*

Majid Al Futtaim (MAF) is a multicountry conglomerate based in Dubai that owns and operates shopping malls, retail, and leisure establishments in the Middle East, North Africa, and Central Asia. When CEO, Alain Bejjani, took over, he realized virtually every sector in which MAF was operating was going through tremendous disruption. His goal was to "future-proof" the business, and as such he set out on a large-scale change effort that started with creating a "North Star" aspiration for the company.

In the Aspire stage of the journey, a broad leadership coalition started by looking 25 years out, and then translated an overall high-level vision of "creating great moments for everyone, every day" into a series of more tangible mid-term aspirations. For the first five years of the journey, three themes reigned supreme: improving customer experience, unleashing the power of digital and analytics, and world-class leadership and talent development (a reflection of their desire to create the "Leadership factory" health recipe).

During the Assess stage, a shortlist of skillsets that needed to be built was identified to enable the strategy: customer service, predictive analytics, and human capital management. Mindsets related to moving from an employee to an owner's viewpoint, from a maximizing the sum of the parts to a $1 + 1 = 3$ mentality, and a transactional to relational way of operating were uncovered as vital to health improvements.

In the Architect stage, a balanced portfolio of initiatives was developed that included changing the role of the holding company, rolling out a new leadership model and leadership development approach, embedding analytics into decision-making, delivering a signature customer experience, and so on. Each initiative was planned in a way that influenced both performance and health; meanwhile, the performance management system was also redesigned to ensure feedback and incentives would be in place related to both elements. Furthermore, a powerful change narrative was developed and communicated via cascading interactive town halls down through all of its 45,000 employees.

MAF then moved into the Act stage of their change journey. This was guided by a central team of 50 people who not only tracked progress on both performance and health but also problem-solved together on real issues affecting the change program as initiatives were piloted and scaled. For example, an initiative related to creating a data lake for people analytics was quickly seen to be ineffective, and alternate approaches asking employees to simply volunteer new information were adopted, eventually providing much more recent and robust data. The team represented all functions, businesses, and countries, and was coordinated by a small program management office.

All of this work happened in the context of an intensive two-way communications program that used fresh and punchy approaches to maintain and refresh messages such as humorous videos, Facebook, and comic strips. More traditional approaches were also employed such as town halls, leadership lunches, and "Ask anything" forums. Further, a group of influence leaders from across and deep in the businesses, functions, and geographies, were trained to be change champions to drive understanding and generate energy as initiatives rolled out. All of these leaders, plus thousands of others, also took part in Personal Insight Workshops (PIWs) at the newly created MAF Leadership Institute. The PIW field and forum program made the desired mindset and behavior shifts personal by first equipping leaders with world class relational and adaptive change leadership skills, and then prompting personal insight and commitment into what each individual leader could uniquely do that would have the biggest impact on change success.

Toward the end of the Act stage of the transformation, MAF began to turn its sights to the Advance stage, which—as planned—would bridge it into the Aspire stage of its next S-curve on the path to realizing its 25-year "North Star."

■ ■ ■

As MAF's experience shows, the bulk of the Act phase is all about—you guessed it—acting on the plans that have been developed in the Architect stage. To ensure the execution of those plans stays on track and that efforts are adjusted as needed, there are two areas change leaders should focus on: creating ongoing ownership and generating energy to drive the change forward.

## Performance: Ownership Model

As Richard Evans, former chairman of United Utilities, a water services provider, remarks, "If people don't take ownership, they don't deliver to their full potential."[1] As we've pointed out previously, many "write your own lottery ticket" features of the Aspire, Assess, and Architect stages will have already instilled a significant degree of ownership. Even when a change program has done this, however, it can't take for granted that ownership will continue throughout the Act stage. In order to assure it does, change leaders should establish strong governance, thoughtfully choose scale-up methods, and monitor and adjust the program accordingly.

## Establish Strong Governance

A strong governance structure will enable change efforts to remain coherent, coordinated, and actively managed during the Act stage. Change programs with a governance structure that provides clarity regarding roles and responsibilities are 6.4 times more likely to be successful.[2] While the governance should be tailored to context, the vast majority of successful programs include the following four elements: an executive steering committee, change management office, executive sponsors, and initiative owners and their teams.

1. **An executive steering committee (ESC)** is typically made up of the most senior leader and a senior executive team (or their equivalents if a change effort is taking place lower in the organization).[3] The ESC owns the overall direction for the change program and makes critical ongoing decisions such as approving changes in execution plans, reallocating resources, resolving issues across initiatives, and reshaping the portfolio of initiatives over time. This body is also the ultimate authority for holding those involved in the change program accountable for results. It should also frequently and openly communicate progress and success during the Act stage. Programs where the ESC plays this role are a whopping eight times more likely to be successful than those where it doesn't.[4]

2. **The change management office (CMO)** is charged with coordinating the overall program, tracking its progress, and ensuring that issues are followed up on and resolved. Its role also involves facilitating transparent and effective interactions between the ESC and all relevant initiatives. The CMO sometimes assists with implementation by brokering the sharing of best practices across the portfolio and acting as a consultant and thought partner to initiative teams. It seldom leads initiatives itself except in rare cases where there is no natural owner for them elsewhere. The CMO typically has a full-time senior leader in charge of it who is responsible for the overall change program. Reporting to the role are one or more communications and change leads and an

implementation monitoring role (tracking activities, metrics, budgets, and impact) at minimum.

3. **Executive sponsors (ES)** provide guidance, judgment, and leadership to initiative teams by reviewing progress, suggesting and validating changes to execution plans as more is learned, and keeping a tight focus on business impact. They may be members of the ESC or senior leaders a level down who have direct-line ownership of a particular initiative (or bundle of thematically related initiatives). Whereas the ESC looks to optimize the full portfolio of initiatives, the ES role looks to maximize the impact of a particular initiative.

4. **Initiative owners (IO) and their teams** are responsible for executing the initiative plans and delivering the desired impact. Team members are typically from the line, but may also include representation from staff functions. IOs will typically have been involved in formulating their initiative charter; identifying resources, operating expenses, and capital requirements; determining the scale-up approach; and developing timelines and milestones (as described in the previous sections). They operate as "task and finish" teams and should be constituted to be able to do both the problem-solving and people-solving required for impact.

Within this structure, accountability for impact should rest as far as possible with line management and be built into the relevant budgets. We use the cheesy-sounding formula BBB—"benefits baked into budgets"—as a reminder that no aspect of a change program is complete until its benefits have been fully reflected in the relevant budgets. This also helps ensure that the CMO provides support and oversight, but the line retains full ownership for impact.

Getting governance right pays big dividends. Programs that are characterized by clear roles and responsibilities are six times more likely to be successful than those that aren't and programs that have effective CMOs are twice as likely to be successful as those that don't.[5]

To see how the governance model comes together, consider the case of a retailer that was restructuring its global operations. It had embarked on the change program in the wake of three consecutive quarterly losses, and after an OHI survey had identified numerous health issues, the CEO set up an ESC comprised of senior leaders from both the retailer and its parent company.

The retailer then created a CMO and asked the widely respected senior manager of the most profitable business line to head it up. He promptly enlisted a top performer from his own department as well as two highly regarded middle managers from other departments to be part of the CMO's staff. He also hired an external change expert and a retail turnaround specialist to work on the project so that best-in-class advice would be readily at hand. Otherwise the staffing of the CMO was kept light to ensure that it didn't become a permanent structure within the organization or prevent project ownership from lying where it should, with the initiative teams and with line management.

Each initiative in the program had a clear IO and an ES who supported both the IO and CMO in ensuring that the relevant initiative team was fully committed to delivering against targets and had the resources it needed to do the job. The initiative team also included on the team a "project amplifier" whose role was to propagate the initiative at grassroots level and relay the concerns of the wider organization back to the initiative team.

Adopting such a clearly structured ownership model helped the retailer to reorganize its 75,000-strong workforce and cut costs by 12 percent within six months. The company also saw significant improvements in its health across the board. The light yet robust program structure proved easy to dismantle, and the responsibility for continuing to deliver and track the ongoing initiatives and generate continuous improvement was then placed firmly in the hands of the business.

## Choose Scale-Up Methods

For the vast majority of initiatives, the Act phase will involve a "test, learn, and scale-up" approach to implementation. This approach makes eminent business sense: when you try out a prototype in a pilot location, you can learn from it and refine your approach before you start rolling it out more widely. If things go well, successes can be replicated elsewhere; if things go awry, you can confine mistakes to a small area and limit any damage. Early results also help to build people's appetite for change, smoothing the way for full-scale implementation. Too often, though, organizations are impatient to get a pilot under their belt, so they press on with the rest of the implementation. Be warned that driving it too fast or without sufficient care and attention can quickly lead to unintended consequences.

Consider the experience of Achmea, a large Netherlands-based insurance group. Spurred on by radical reforms in the healthcare market introduced by the Dutch government, it launched a change program in the health division. One of the most important initiatives was a call center transformation aimed at achieving a 25 percent gain in efficiency while improving customer experience at the same time. The initial pilot was a huge success and was celebrated as showing tough targets could be met. Before long, though, they ran into a roadblock: the approach taken by the manager who led the effort was hard to replicate elsewhere because he had achieved the changes through his personal influence, rather than by introducing systems to support the desired shifts. As Jeroen van Breda Vriesman, the former leader of the health division, wryly admitted: "We couldn't duplicate the improvement achieved by the manager who did it on his own."[6]

Achmea's experience provides an important lesson: a successful pilot doesn't necessarily make for a successful rollout. To be robust, the pilot phase should consist of not one but two tests—a double pilot. The first pilot is a *proof of concept* designed to establish whether the idea you are testing truly creates value. The second pilot is a *proof of feasibility* designed to test the robustness of the rollout approach, ensuring that the bulk of the desired impact can be captured in a way that is fully replicable. The end products from this pilot are not only the desired impact, but a fully codified, industrial strength, easy-to-deploy approach to roll out. Often this second pilot is also used to "train forward" those people who will lead the rollout in subsequent waves of implementation. In Achmea's case, this lesson was well learned, ultimately leading to a multi-year programmatic rollout so successful it hosts visits from other company executives looking to learn from, and replicate, their methodologies.

As Aristotle described, "Well begun is half done," and the double pilot approach ensures you're on the right path. To get to "done," however, there is still the actual scale-up. After carrying out detailed reviews of dozens of successful implementation programs and observing hundreds at a distance, we've identified three broad "flavors" for scaling up change program initiatives (Exhibit 6.1). The three models are linear, geometric, and "big bang":

1. In **linear** scale-ups, the second pilot (proof of feasibility) is replicated in one area after another across the organization. In this approach, the next area isn't started until the previous area is done. This approach is the best choice if: an initiative is to be rolled out in only a few areas; capable team members are in short supply; the company is not facing a crisis; the stakes (risk or rewards) are high; deep, expert-led dives are needed; there is strong resistance to change; and the toolkit and solutions being used need extensive customization.

2. In **geometric** scale-ups, implementation takes place in waves, with each successive wave much bigger than the last (say, two sites in the first wave, four in the second, 16 in the third, and so on). This approach makes sense if: multiple areas share a few common features; many areas need to be transformed and a linear approach would take too long; capable implementers are readily available; and the organization has the capacity to absorb the changes.

3. In **"big bang"** scale-ups, implementation takes place across all relevant areas at once. It takes many resources, but only for a relatively short time. This approach makes sense if: multiple areas share many common features; the need for transformation is urgent; little resistance is

Exhibit 6.1

# Three Models for Program Scaling

| Model | Description | Resource requirement | Number of units impacted |
|---|---|---|---|
|  | **Linear**<br>Sequential interventions with stable resource requirement | | 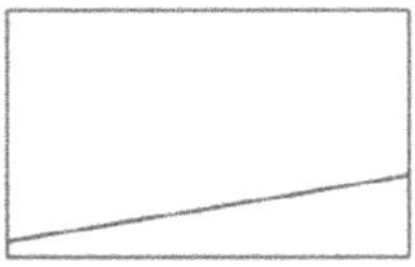 |
| 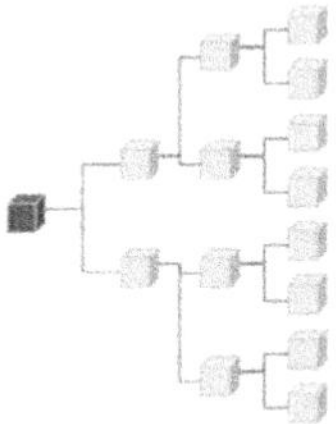 | **Geometric**<br>Successive waves of interventions with increasing resource requirement | 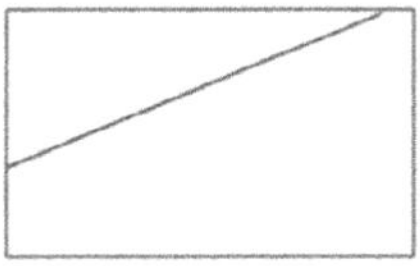 | 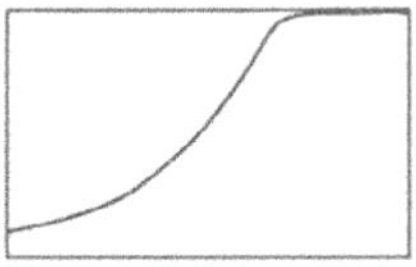 |
| 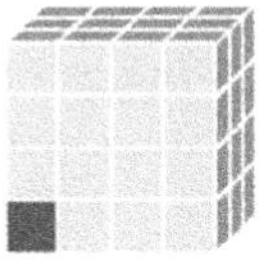 | **"Big bang"**<br>Concurrent interventions with intensive short-term resource requirement | 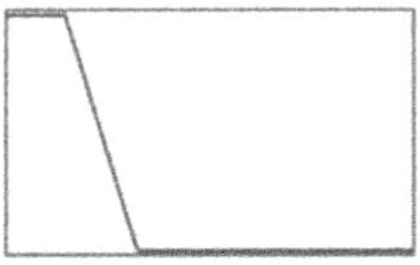 | 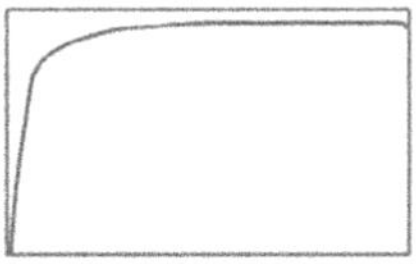 |

expected (or an appetite for change already exists); a standard toolkit and approach can be employed.

A multinational energy company, for example, used the linear approach to roll out a unified people-management software system that was replacing an array of freestanding national systems. Senior management were aware that if they switched to the new software in all their global operations in one go, or even if they proceeded on a regional basis, they might create serious technical repercussions and overload the project team with demands for troubleshooting. Since changing to the new software would be a major shift, the company also wanted to ensure that all its country-level organizations would buy into the effort, and that any concerns that might emerge at one location could be fully addressed before the rollout moved on to the next. In addition, implementation called for considerable support from an external provider that had limited resources to devote to the effort.

The same company chose a geometric approach when implementing its new global procurement strategy. By conducting an analysis of vendor relationships, it had uncovered similarities between markets in terms of buying patterns, levels of procurement sophistication, and vendor choice. Grouping markets that shared these similarities into clusters would enable it to increase its leverage with vendors. Once it had identified these clusters, it used the geometric approach to roll out the project within individual regions and countries. This enabled the procurement teams to get up to speed quickly, allowed approaches to be refined as the effort progressed, and ensured that cost savings could be captured from an early stage.

Yet another of the energy company's initiatives related to a revamping of its public relations processes. It had recently come out of a crisis situation that it hadn't been equipped to handle due to the decentralized approach to managing its public image. As a result, one of the change program initiatives was to centralize all of its public relations and stakeholder management efforts, roll out a new set of policies and guidelines, and conduct a company-wide (all geographies, all business units) push to ensure the general public and key stakeholders were aware of the changes being made at the company to improve transparency and accountability. A big bang approach was taken to implementation, enabling it to be fully executed during a two-month period.

Since our first edition, a buzzword related to how to test and learn has become prominent in the management lexicon: *agile*. For those not familiar with them, agile teams have their genesis in the world of software development where largely self-organizing and cross-functional teams integrate requirements and solutions in collaboration with end users. Agile teams are highly empowered, are ultimately held accountable for outcomes, and the means to achieve those outcomes aren't dictated to them. Scaling via the deployment of agile teams is well-suited for working on complex problems in dynamic environments where close collaboration with end-users is feasible. They are less suited for initiatives related to more routine operations (e.g., purchasing, accounting, de-layering).

There is some speculation that agile working methods will spell the end of traditional hierarchies and become the predominant management philosophy by which organizations are run. We're not convinced. Even those enterprises most known for employing agile methodologies—for example, Google, Amazon, Spotify, Netflix, Bosch, Tesla, SAP, Salesforce, Saab, and so on—still choose to operate with a mix of agile teams and traditional structures.[7] In the words of Columbia Business School professor Rita Gunther McGrath, "On the one hand, [growth companies are] good at experimentation [and] can move on dime. On the other hand, they're extremely stable."[8] Regardless, if an organization is thinking about embarking on a change program to shift its overall management approach from one of a traditional hierarchy to self-governing agile teams, we'd point out that it's got the highest probability of successfully making such a change if it employs the Five Frames of Performance and Health approach to do so!

## Monitor Progress and Dynamically Adjust

To enable the governance model to work effectively and to monitor test, learn, and scale-up impact, the CMO needs to play an integrative measurement and planning role. A foundational part of this role is the rigorous tracking of progress and impact through clear metrics and milestones. Change programs characterized by this are 7.3 times more likely to succeed.[9] This role is akin to the role your car's onboard computer plays while driving, which reports back to you how the vehicle is functioning—speed, fuel, engine temperature, oil pressure, tire pressure, and so on.

There is more to the CMO's role than just monitoring, however. As Julio Linares, former managing director and COO of Telefónica de España, warns: "The market is going to change constantly, and because of that you need to make a constant effort to adapt to the market. Of course, some parts of the program will end, but new ones will come up."[10] Let's extend the driving analogy. Even with the best-laid plans and a well-functioning vehicle, a long journey seldom goes as you expect. The weather changes without warning, heavy traffic holds you up, roadworks prompt a detour, and after all that, you need a break. Even with a sound on-board computer in your vehicle, imagine such a drive in the pre-mobile phone era—this volatility could set your arrival back by days. Today, your satellite navigation plans ahead to let you know which detours to make, and your mobile phone allows you to call ahead and rebook whatever is needed all while driving. By this analogy, the CMO needs to play the role of both the vehicle's on-board computer and the mobile phone with satellite navigation. When this is done well, change programs are 4.6 times more likely to succeed.[11]

What does this look like in practice? To start with, in the wry words of N. R. Narayana Murthy, former chairman of Infosys, "In God we trust; everybody else brings data to the table."[12] Managing the program dynamically depends on good data. You have to be clear from day to day how much progress you've made against your plans. That means regularly measuring the impact of your change program on at least four key dimensions (Exhibit 6.2):

- **Initiative progress.** Track progress not just in terms of time (milestones) and budget (money spent versus planned), but also against key operational performance indicators (e.g., cycle time, waste, wait times, quality).

- **Health impact.** Are management practices and their underlying mindsets and behaviors shifting to support the improvements in performance that you want to see? Targeted analytics, surveys, focus groups, and observation can give you a good read. Note that in Chapter 10, we provide more detail on how to measure health improvements over time, given it's an area in which many leaders have less experience.

- **Performance impact.** Measure key business outcomes such as revenue, cost, and risk to confirm that improvements are happening where you expect and not causing unforeseen consequences elsewhere in the organization.

- **Value creation.** Keep a constant eye on the ultimate outcome that matters. In large-scale company-wide change programs, this measure is shareholder value creation. In not-for-profit and governmental organizations, it is likely related to other stakeholders. Whatever the ultimate measure for your change program, it's vital to have a clear-eyed view of the ultimate outcome that matters most amidst all of the other data.

The specific metrics that should be monitored within each of these dimensions will be unique to your change program. That said, we warn that less is more. Too often, change-program metrics cascade into an unwieldy number of complex permutations. An analysis of all of the data in McKinsey

---

## Exhibit 6.2

# Measuring Impact in Four Dimensions

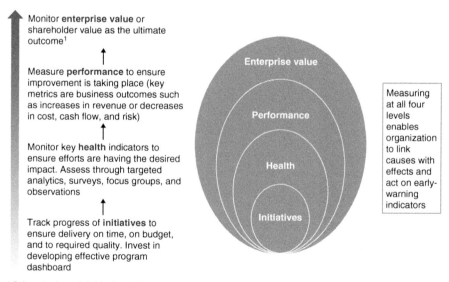

Monitor **enterprise value** or shareholder value as the ultimate outcome[1]

Measure **performance** to ensure improvement is taking place (key metrics are business outcomes such as increases in revenue or decreases in cost, cash flow, and risk)

Monitor key **health** indicators to ensure efforts are having the desired impact. Assess through targeted analytics, surveys, focus groups, and observations

Track progress of **initiatives** to ensure delivery on time, on budget, and to required quality. Invest in developing effective program dashboard

Enterprise value

Performance

Health

Initiatives

Measuring at all four levels enables organization to link causes with effects and act on early-warning indicators

1 Or impact on key stakeholders for not-for-profit and public sector organizations

& Company's WAVE tool, an automated change-program-management solution used by thousands of companies globally, shows that only 29 percent of the metrics organizations claim to follow are actually used in the management of the effort. The rest become statistical noise, increased bureaucracy, and even a source of confusion and waste in the process.

Once you have the right metrics in place, the next question to answer is how often to measure and review them? The answer is also context-specific. That said, as a rough guide in large-scale change programs, initiative measures should be reviewed weekly by initiative teams, health and performance monthly or quarterly by sponsors and steering committees, and enterprise value once or twice a year by everyone involved in the change program. Reviews should serve two purposes. One is to enable you to enforce accountability, identify issues, and determine remedies. The other is to identify best practices to share, spotlight successes to celebrate, and instill a culture of continuous learning and improvement.

Even though every major initiative planned in the Architect stage will have a solid business case, robust set of execution milestones, and monthly schedule for expected value captured on the bottom line, you should anticipate that a number of initiatives will run into trouble somewhere during the Act stage of the journey. Based on the data in McKinsey & Company's WAVE tool, 28 percent of well-planned initiatives don't deliver the results forecasted. This means that during the journey, you can count on the fact that new ideas will need to be generated and initiatives be stood up along the way. It's the CMO's role to ensure the required adjustments to the program are made in a timely manner to assure the overall aspiration will be achieved. This will mean shutting down some planned initiatives, launching new ones (ensuring health is hardwired into them), and reallocating resources accordingly.

We've talked about how the expected impact from initiatives plays out in the Act stage, but what about the timing? Our data shows that, on average, 31 percent of initiatives will have their execution end date changed once during the lifecycle of the initiative, 28 percent will see it happen twice, and 19 percent three times. The CMO's role is to ensure these changes happen for the right reasons, are decided on early (no last-minute delays or surprises), and rigorous problem-solving is applied to get things back on track. This is one of the reasons we advocate that initiative metrics be monitored weekly—regardless of whether there is a major milestone, asking for brief updates on progress and offering support often enables potential issues to be identified early, which is when they can be solved with minimal effort. With even five minutes of discussion, we've seen well-facilitated discussions enable initiatives to go from "red" (meaning they are at high risk of falling behind) to "green" (indicating a forecast of smooth sailing ahead).[13]

## Health: Energy Generation

Change programs require employees to keep everyday business on track while at the same time they change how everyday business is done. This additional work, by definition, requires more energy. As such, an important role of the change leader during the Act stage is to ensure that the change program generates more energy than it consumes. It's all too common that after the launch of the program employees lose sight of the bigger picture and begin to feel they are being asked for "pain with no gain," fostering cynicism and fatigue. We characterize this period as the "Valley of Desolation" (Exhibit 6.3).[14]

To minimize the depth of and time spent in the Valley of Desolation, we advocate change leaders create energy by mobilizing influence leaders, making the change program personal for a critical mass of leaders, and rigorously reinforcing it through ongoing two-way communications.

Exhibit 6.3

## The "Valley of Desolation"

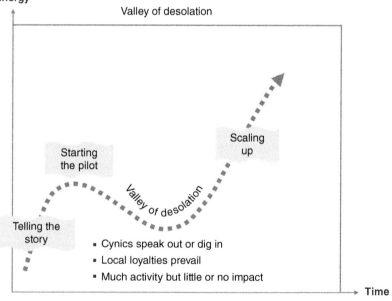

Energy

Valley of desolation

Starting the pilot

Scaling up

Telling the story

Valley of desolation

- Cynics speak out or dig in
- Local loyalties prevail
- Much activity but little or no impact

Time

## Mobilize Influence Leaders

As we mentioned in our discussion of role modeling in Chapter 5, senior leaders aren't the only ones that employees take cues from. There are influence leaders deep in the organization that, if they are excited about and on board with the change program, can have a disproportionate effect on the energy levels of everyone else.

Influence leaders are people who, regardless of their official title or status, have a wide circle of personal contacts who respect and emulate them. Journalist, author, and public speaker Malcolm Gladwell's best-selling book, *The Tipping Point*, describes three types of influencers: the "Mavens" are discerning individuals who accumulate knowledge and share advice; the "Connectors" are those who know lots of people; the "Salespeople" are those who have a natural ability to influence and persuade others. All of these types can be powerful energy and impact generators in your change program. As we mentioned in Chapter 5, our research indicates change efforts that engage influence leaders to help motivate employees are 3.8 times more likely to be successful.[15]

To illustrate how influence leaders can have disproportionate impact, consider the example of doctors and NGOs working on a change program related to maternal healthcare in sub-Saharan Africa. None of the interventions they had been pursuing via traditional campaigns, such as doctors and pamphlets, were working. Taking the influence leader lens, they realized that hairdressers were extremely influential amongst the target group of young women. As it turned out, one of the few places women felt they could talk to other women openly about such matters was at the hair salon. Knowing this, the doctors and NGOs focused their education campaign on hairdressers—and the message finally got through as hairdressers spread the story.

Another example comes from our work in the sawmills in Northern Canada. During the Act stage, as part of a lean operations implementation, we were helping frontline supervisors run their daily huddles differently (using data and visual boards). Although doing so led to improvements, there was little excitement for the new approach and it was clear that sustainability was in jeopardy. We made sure the chain of command, everyone from the mill manager to the department heads, was sending the right messages and role modeling accordingly. Employees had been educated on the new methods, as well, so they knew what to do. Management suggested we discuss the approach with the union leaders, which we did, but still met with limited cooperation.

What we hadn't appreciated was that a big part of the local workforce came from the nearby First Nation community who were indigenous to the area. For them, the social hierarchy was more important than the company's formal hierarchy, and it turned out one of the forklift operators in the yard was the local Chief. He hadn't yet been involved in the process given the nature of the geometric scale-up method chosen at the mill, and as such hadn't given his approval to the new working methods. On knowing this we met with him, explained the methodology and rationale, got his guidance on the process, and within days the new practices were broadly adopted.

Our Canadian experience shows that influencers are sometimes hidden. So how do you find such influence leaders? An analytical technique known as social network analysis (SNA) can be used to help identify who they are and who they influence. A fairly simple application of a SNA is referred to as "snowball sampling." The snowball approach is based on a simple survey technique used originally by social scientists to study street gangs, drug users, and sex workers—hidden populations traditionally reluctant to participate in formal research. In that context, the method employs brief surveys (two to three minutes) that ask recipients to identify acquaintances who should also be asked to participate in the research. Thus, one name or group of names quickly snowballs into more, and trust is maintained, since referrals are made anonymously by acquaintances or peers rather than formal identification.[16]

In business settings, the methodology is easily adapted to better understand the patterns and networks of influence that otherwise operate below the radar. Organizations can construct simple, anonymous e-mail surveys to ask, for example: "Who do you go to for information when you have trouble at work?" or, "Whose advice do you trust and respect?" By asking employees to nominate three to five people (or more in very large organizations) who are also surveyed, executives can quickly identify a revealing set of influencers across a company. When the names of nominees start to be repeated—often, after only three to four rounds—the survey can end.

McKinsey's proprietary *Influencer* tool uses the snowball methodology to identify influence leaders. Having used it in hundreds of client situations, we can say with certainty that leaders often find the results surprising, along the lines of our experience in the sawmills. For example, influencer patterns almost never follow the organizational chart. Yet most leaders we encounter feel they already have a good idea of who the influence leaders are in their organizations. Fortunately, there is empirical evidence from the Influencer tool to illuminate the truth—leaders are typically unaware of 40 percent of the key influencers in their organizations.

To illustrate further, a simplified network map is shown in Exhibit 6.4. It would have been impossible to identify Smith as an influence leader from the formal organization structure on the left. However, the network map shows the web of connections that make Smith the most influential person within the group, and thus the highest point of leverage for positive role modeling (or the highest point of vulnerability in the case of negative role modeling).

# Exhibit 6.4

## Identifying Influence Leaders Using Social Network Analysis

Hypothetical example

**Formal organization structure**

**Business-unit leader**
Nielsen

| | **Operations** Curtis | **Sales** Fisher |
| **R&D** Lewis | | |

**R&D** Lewis

**Americas** Riley
Spears
Stevens
Gordon
Rodriguez
Smith
Blair
Daniel

**Europe** Boutin
Robert

**Operations** Curtis
Choi
Marley
Krauss

**Sales** Fisher

**Americas** McConnell
Schmitz

**Europe** Levy

**Informal structure showing social networks**

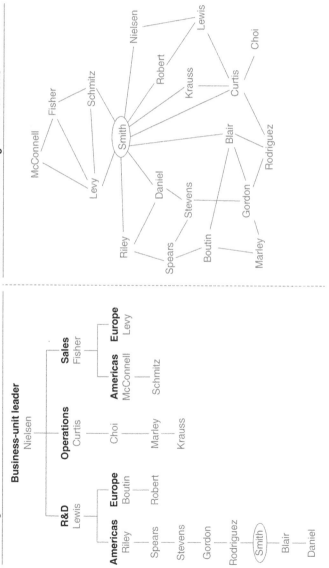

Source: Adapted from Rob Cross and Andrew Parker, *The Hidden Power of Social Networks* (Boston: Harvard Business School Press, 2004).

Once you've identified the influence leaders, there are many ways to get them mobilized. If you can get some of these people to participate in pilots or be early adopters of new tools and approaches, it can be very powerful. At the very least, you can create a two-way pipeline that provides early access to information and enables you to gather important feedback on the program as it is implemented. How does the frontline really feel? What do employees want more or less of? Where will be the most productive places to pilot? And so on. It is also ideal to bounce any new ideas to enhance implementation efforts off this group to ensure they will be as powerful as possible, as well as broadly accepted.

At the Australia and New Zealand Banking Group, commonly known as ANZ Bank, 180 influence leaders were identified. This group was charged on top of their day jobs to work with the CMO and with business leaders to ensure the company's large-scale change program was executed successfully. One of the early experiences for these change leaders was to take part in a pilot of a workshop program to make the change program personal for leaders, something we describe in detail in the next section that can be an extremely powerful vehicle to mobilize change leaders.

## Make It Personal for a Critical Mass

Victor Frankl, an Auschwitz survivor who went on to write *Man's Search for Meaning*, wrote: "Between stimulus and response there is a space. In that space is our power to choose our response. In our response lies our growth and our freedom." We find it helpful to use a shorthand version of Frankl's quote to reflect this: S (stimulus) + T (how one chooses to think about the stimulus) = R (response). When it comes to making change happen at scale, this equation poses an  interesting challenge.

Let's think about what we've done so far in the Five Frames process. On one hand, we've named and reframed the underlying mindset shifts (the "T") and related behaviors (the "R") we want to see during the Assess stage. For a very select few employees, simply surfacing these shifts will be enough for them to choose to change. Most, however, will require more encouragement and proof points before they are willing to make different choices. What's the reason why? Who else is on board? Do my incentives reinforce the shifts? Am I confident I'll be successful? And so on. Therefore, in the Architect stage, we used the influence model to plan a host of changes to the work environment (the "S") to reinforce the desired shifts.

There are three aspects of human behavior, however, that we still need to consider if we're to maximize the chances of rapid, significant change. The first relates to the story of the monkeys and bananas from Chapter 4 that illustrated how mindsets created by one set of stimuli (the water jet) last far longer than the presence of the stimulus itself. The lesson here is that if we leave it to changes in the "S" to shift the "T," we'll very likely be waiting a long time. The second aspect is that changes to the "S" won't impact everyone the same way. If one goes back to the opera house versus sports stadium metaphor, not everyone in a sports stadium chooses to act the same way, even though they are surrounded by the same environment.

The third aspect is perhaps the most vexing. It's that the influence model itself relies in part on role modeling (in addition to fostering understanding and conviction, building confidence and skills, and putting in place reinforcing formal mechanisms), yet at the outset of the change program, the "S" to influence the first role models likely doesn't yet exist. It's their "T" and the related "R" that will become someone else's "S," but how can the process be kickstarted? Make no mistake; it's a lot harder than simply asking leaders to think and behave differently. In fact, the single biggest barrier to rapid personal change is overcoming most leaders' propensity to say, "Yes, that's the problem. If only *others* would change their behaviors, we'd solve it."

For example, at one company we asked leaders to estimate how much time they spent tiptoeing around other people's egos: making others feel that "my idea is yours," for instance, or taking care not to tread on someone else's turf. Most said 20 to 30 percent. Then we asked them how much time people spend tiptoeing around their egos. Most were silent. This same phenomenon accounts for why in low-trust teams everyone can agree that's the case, but each team member reports that they as individuals are trustworthy. Or why in self-professed bureaucratic organizations you'll be hard-pressed to find anyone who identifies themselves as a bureaucrat or creating the bureaucracy that plagues progress.

What's going on here? Psychology explains this dynamic as a very predictable, and very human "self-serving bias." This is a similar phenomenon to the optimism bias we discussed in Chapter 3 that expects the best possible (versus most probable) outcome will emerge. In this case, however, it's more personal in that it involves viewing one's own actions favorably or interpreting events in a way that is beneficial to themselves. It explains why 88 percent of drivers rate themselves in the top 50 percent of safe drivers on the road.[17] It's why 25 percent of students rate themselves in the top 1 percent of the ability to get along with others.[18] It's also why when couples are asked to estimate their contribution to household work, the combined total routinely exceeds 100 percent.[19] These are all statistical impossibilities, of course, and show that in many behavior-related areas, we as human beings consistently overestimate how much we are part of the solution, not the problem. The facts show role modeling change is one of these areas: on average a full 86 percent of leaders report that, "Leaders role model desired behavior changes," whereas the same question asked of those that report to the leaders in question only receives a 53 percent average positive response.[20]

If your efforts take direct action on leaders' and employees' "T" in addition to the "S," change becomes faster, more reliable, and more significant. But are there any methods out there that can overcome the self-serving bias such that leaders and employees become aware of and fully commit to what they can and should change *personally* to role model and bring to life the desired mindset and behavior shifts, even while changes in their "S" are not yet in place? We've searched long and hard for ways to accomplish this efficiently and effectively.

Our journey has led us to have deep conviction regarding the application of what we call Personal Insight Workshops (PIWs). We've now conducted thousands of these workshops worldwide and have never been disappointed with the impact they have. Let's explain what they are and why they work. PIWs most often take place offsite in small groups of 20 to 30 employees over 2–3 days. They are led by facilitators experienced in the principles of adult learning, knowledgeable in techniques developed in the field of human potential, and well-versed in applying the "U-process"—a social technology developed during a 10-year partnership between Generon Consulting, Otto Scharmer and Peter Senge from MIT, and the Society for Organizational Learning. This "U-process" involves three phases.

The first phase is called *sensing* (typically 30 percent of the workshop time is spent here). This typically involves a senior leader, who has already been through the workshop, telling both the company's change story and his/her own. This opens the space for inspiration and learning. Next, the "hard facts" and specifics regarding the organizational context are shared to reinforce the tangibility of the story. Participants then have time to clarify their outstanding questions. Note that the nature and duration of the sensing phase differs greatly if an interactive story cascade (as described in the previous chapter) has already happened and the PIW is the next step of the journey. In some programs, however, the two are combined.

At this point, the session turns inward for the second phase, known as *presencing* (typically 40 percent of the workshop time is spent here). Here, participants explore their personal "iceberg" of behavior—what uniquely drives them as individuals (in terms of thoughts, feelings, beliefs, and needs). Questions are addressed through a series of interactive modules: When do I feel in "flow" and when do I move into fight, flight, or freeze responses? What triggers me into one state versus the other? Is there a way to remain at a point of choice instead of reactively responding? What new behaviors and outcomes would be possible if that was so? How would those new behaviors and outcomes create a more powerful personal legacy in the workplace, and how do they link to the bigger organizational change we've discussed?

These modules are structured to make participants aware of their personal orientation toward the fundamental underlying mindset shifts at play in the change program (e.g., victim to mastery, me to we, scarcity to abundance, fear to hope, and so on), and in doing so, generate personal insights unique to each leader in relation to how they can be the best role models and have the most impact possible (moving participants from being "unconsciously incompetent" to "consciously incompetent" in adult-learning terms).

With these questions answered, the PIW transitions into its third and final phase, known as *realizing* (typically 30 percent of the workshop time is spent here). Here, the participants make explicit choices about how their personal leadership mindsets and behaviors will shift and identify "sustaining practices" that will facilitate them acting on the insights they've had. They then reflect on their personal networks in the context of ensuring they will have the challenge and support they'll need to stay the course coming out of the workshop. This support network also includes sub-groups from the workshop known as "mini-boards" (named in the spirit of them acting as a sort of personal board of directors) that are formed to provide peer coaching beyond the workshop—supporting the individual to move from being "consciously incompetent" to become "consciously competent." Further, any collective action the group will take on behalf of the organization is discussed and decided upon. The session then closes with each individual sharing the insights they've had and the commitments they are making and, in doing so, are positively acknowledged by their colleagues.

PIWs have been applied successfully in contexts as wide-ranging as helping end Colombia's civil war to helping frontline operations leaders fully embrace their role in leading a customer-experience change program. We acknowledge the approach sounds about as "soft" as any we've described in this book, but also know that these workshops have universally been met with rave reviews from organizations filled with the likes of Dutch engineers, American investment bankers, Middle Eastern government officials, and South Korean conglomerates. Example feedback includes: "The most valuable program I have ever been part of—this will take us to an entirely different level"; "Life-changing for me and transforming for the company"; "An eye-opening, intense and wonderful journey"; "We went deep and got real. I loved that we work on real issues and not general leadership theory"; and, "I know what they mean when they say corporate transformation requires personal transformation."

Should every leader go through a PIW? While many organizations ultimately choose to put all their employees through them because of the profound impact they see from doing so, the vast majority of impact potential can be realized by putting a critical mass of leaders through the program. The exact number for a specific organization will differ somewhat based on how distributed their leadership model is, but a general rule of thumb from the social science of epidemiology (how ideas and patterns of behavior spread in a social network) is that once roughly 25 to 30 percent of leaders have been through the program, the shedding of the "if only *they* would change" mentality spreads to all leaders and is replaced by a profound sense of "if it is to be, it's up to me."[21] One can see why this is the case if one recalls our previous point that any shift in an individual's "T" influences the "S" of all those around them (i.e., it amps up the impact of the role modeling influence lever).

For leaders involved directly in planning and executing performance initiatives, the PIW experience is often integrated into a broader field and forum journey to build skills and confidence—like those we described in Chapter 5. For influence leaders, the experience is often part of a series of upskilling and engagement events that they participate in over time. As mentioned, this group is often the ideal pilot group for the PIW approach—if it's not going to work for your organization, this group will let you know (or let you know what needs to change for it to have impact). And if they think it's profoundly impactful, they'll spread the word and get others excited, such that you'll likely be hard-pressed to keep up with demand! In truth we've never had a pilot group go through the experience and report back a "Don't roll this out" recommendation.

Not every successful change program we have seen uses PIW techniques, but at the same time in our experience every change program that has used this approach has been successful. In particular, when organizations are grappling with how to thaw what's often referred to as "the frozen middle" (a change-resistant middle management layer), we've seen PIWs cut through like a hot knife through butter.

So powerful is this approach that McKinsey & Company has created a new business unit of its own that does nothing but deliver PIWs and related coaching. The business unit, named *Aberkyn* (a name with Celtic and Norse origins meaning where communities connect to their source), is a global group of over 100 expert workshop designers, facilitators, and coaches. Working with our McKinsey Academy group, Aberkyn is also in the process of enhancing the PIW process with data and analytics-driven approaches. For example, significant work is being done to incorporate the neuroscience of behavioral "nudges" (subtle interventions that guide choices without restricting them) to allow for more mass customization and embedding of PIW techniques across the entire workforce. No doubt those methods will be written about extensively in the third edition of *Beyond Performance*!

Even if not via the PIW methodology, if you're leading a large-scale change program, we urge you by whatever means possible to catalyze a critical mass of leaders to make the change personal. If you don't, you'll very likely have a lot of leaders, no matter how well-intentioned, nodding in agreement with the changes you are saying are important but inside thinking those changes are everyone else's to make but theirs. When 30 percent or more of your leaders know, are committed to, and *act* on the one thing that each one of them can do uniquely as individuals that will make the biggest impact toward achieving your performance and health aspirations, you'll find yourself already a long way down the path to success!

We hope our explanation of the why, what, and how of PIWs has been compelling. That said, we often liken the PIW experience to that of tasting an apple. You can explain that it's sweet, sharp, fresh, juicy, and so on, but if the person you're talking to has never eaten an apple, they won't fully "get" what it tastes like until they take their first bite. We therefore encourage change leaders to actually "taste the apple" and attend a PIW in order to decide if it should be part of their change leadership menu. We host a number of multi-client PIWs through the year expressly to enable leaders to do so.

We close by acknowledging that the "Make it Personal" approach may feel even softer to hard-nosed leaders than our treatment of mindsets in Chapter 4. Rest assured, however, that performance and health outcomes are ultimately unlocked. In the words of Frans van Houten, CEO of the multinational technology company Philips, when talking about the company's application of the PIW process that was known internally as the Accelerate Leadership Program (ALP), "The beautiful thing is that when you take people through this and people have discovered where they have blind spots, they come up with a breakthrough action plan for themselves *and* for their teams, and productivity goes up in a wonderful way. I can correlate business performance with teams who have done this and teams that have not—it makes a real difference."[22]

## Maintain High Impact, Two-Way Communications

The final element that change leaders should tend to with rigor and discipline in the Act stage is engaging the workforce in high impact, two-way communications. Change programs that make the organization feel engaged and energized through communications and involvement are four times more likely to succeed than programs that don't do these things.[23] But, you may ask, haven't we already won most of this battle by all of the "writing their own lottery ticket" work done in the first three stages of the change journey? Interestingly, all that work can create a problem in this stage—one that is up to you as the change leader to ensure doesn't come to fruition.

Consider an experiment that involved a group of people divided into two sets, "tappers" and "listeners."[24] Tappers were asked to drum out with their fingers the rhythm of a well-known tune such as "Happy Birthday to You." Listeners had to guess what tune was being tapped. Once they knew what songs they would be tapping, the tappers were asked to predict what proportion of the songs their listeners would guess correctly. They predicted half. Over the course of the experiment, the actual result was just 2.5 percent. Only 1 person in 40 correctly identified the tune. What's more, as the tappers tapped, they visibly became frustrated with their listeners. "How can they not get it? It's so clear what this is," they would think to themselves. Meanwhile the listeners remained bewildered as they continued to hear an unintelligible Morse-type code.

Why the huge gap between expectation and reality, and why was it such an emotive experience for the participants? It's because once we know something, we find it incredibly hard to imagine not knowing it. It's easy for us to hear the tune as we tap (and, conversely, it's impossible for us to not hear the tune as we tap), but the listener hears only a sequence of apparently random beats. This phenomenon is known as "the curse of knowledge."

We see the curse of knowledge playing out in change programs all the time. Leaders who know the story inside out and are passionate and excited to get on with making it reality assume incorrectly that other people will take it in quickly and see all the implications that they see. As with our tappers and listeners, that's unfortunately not how it works. When people hear a story for the first time, they are so busy processing what they hear and trying to work out what it means that they can't possibly appreciate all the nuances. More often than not, what leaders consider to be carefully crafted messages that make so much sense to them aren't heard by employees as anything other than a string of seemingly disconnected ideas.

Having established that the curse exists, is there a way to break it? We suggest a combination of four approaches to do so: relentless repetition with the right mindset; repeating simple and memorable language; balancing "telling" with "asking"; and using multiple, well-orchestrated channels. It's not rocket science, but that doesn't mean it's easy.

Firstly, leaders who have to tell and retell a story over and over again should remind themselves to approach it with a "beginners' mind"—and not lose sight of what it's like to tell and hear the story for the first time. As Alan G. Lafley, former CEO of P&G, notes, "Excruciating repetition and clarity are important—employees have so many things going on in the operation of their daily business that they don't always take the time to stop, think, and internalize."[25] Paolo Scaroni, who has led three Italian public companies through major change as CEO of Techint, Enel, and Eni, agrees as he indicates the key to successful communications is "repeat, repeat, and repeat … throughout the organization."[26]

The second way to ensure the message sticks is to coin and relentlessly repeat language that is simple and memorable. Consider Walmart's "10-foot rule," which reminds frontline employees of the company's customer service aspiration: whenever you are within 10 feet of a customer, look them in the eye, smile, and ask how you can help. At Microsoft, at the end of every meeting the question is called as to, "Was that a growth mindset or a fixed mindset meeting?" This acts not just as a reminder of the desired shift, but also prompts the act of continuous learning that a growth mindset is meant to manifest. As Willie Walsh, former CEO of British Airways, explains, "The simpler the message, the easier it is to deliver. The simpler the message, the more likely it is to be consistent. The simpler the message, the easier it is to control and manage the communication."[27]

The language *not* used can be just as powerful as that which is. When Australian telecommunications and media company Telstra wanted to improve internal collaboration, it banned people from using the word "they" in conversations about other teams and units to remind employees to work as one organization. Posters proclaiming, "No 'they,'" like the one below appeared everywhere, and people started to call attention to references to "they" and "them" even in casual conversations.

A third way to overcome the curse of knowledge is to move from "telling" to "asking." This has the benefit of also leveraging the "lottery ticket" effect to build ownership. With this technique, even chance conversations can be put to good use. At Emerson Electric, CEO David Farr makes a point of asking virtually everyone he encounters the same four questions: "How do you make a difference?" (to find out whether people are aligned on the company's direction); "What improvement ideas are you working on?" (to emphasize execution edge health recipe); "When did you last get coaching from your boss?" (to probe on the people development management practice); and "Who is the enemy?" (emphasizing collaboration—the right answer is to name a competitor and not some other department!). This sends a clear message that these issues matter. If employees don't have good answers for you right at that moment, you can bet they will when they are asked next time.

The fourth way to overcome the curse of knowledge is to ensure the story doesn't just come from leaders and instead is reinforced through as many channels as possible: speech, print, online, actions, symbols, rituals, and so on. Using multiple channels reinforces the consistent message. Back to the tappers and listeners analogy, it ensures the song being tapped is heard multiple times using different instruments. We'd be remiss not to mention that the most progressive two-way communications programs take what's known as a "transmedia" approach—not just telling the same story through multiple channels but telling different aspects of the story through different channels that all add up to the integrated picture in ways that otherwise wouldn't be possible to build.

We encourage companies to get creative in the channels they use, in particular given the many options that social media provides. We've seen very successful two-way communications strategies involving blogs, tweets, videos, podcasts, "jams" (online, topical, time-bound problem-solving sessions often involving thousands of employees—like IBM's ValuesJam example we shared in Chapter 3), online change-focused Wiki-like resource centers tailored to employee segments, and so on. These are made even more powerful when interwoven with in-person formats such as large group offsites, unannounced "walking the floor" visits, brownbag lunches, and the like.

Equally important to the more top-down oriented channels is the creation of bottom-up-led channels. What does this look like in practice? At Neustar, former CEO Lisa Hook sponsored a video competition to help communicate the company's story and strategy (employees submit a video recording, employees are able to vote online, a winner from the top five is selected by the ExCo, and the CEO gives an award at the annual All Hands Meeting). At Australia's largest telecommunications company, Telstra, a "rogue" comic strip was created by employees to express and correct cynical views of the change program. At McKinsey & Company, "citizen journalism" is encouraged, where employees share their own stories and others that interest them—including being able to submit requests for "investigative reports" by the firm's communications team. Admittedly, bottom-up efforts are still kicked off by the corporate center, but after that they must be left to spread through the organization under their own steam. To get them started, some infrastructure and funding may be needed. Companies often give an influence leader in each area a small budget and what is often referred to as "freedom within a framework," which means they can decide how to create energy for change in accordance within a few broad guidelines about which aspects of the story to emphasize.

One often underestimated channel is that of embedding new rituals into the organization. For example, a mining company we worked with, for whom safety was an important theme of their change program, made it a point to open all meetings with an announcement about emergency exits and safety hazards. Viewed as a one-off activity, this might seem a waste of time given that serious accidents don't often happen in meeting rooms.

Regarded as a ritual, however, it went a long way to embed the mindset that safety matters.

Another often underutilized channel is the outside world. As Banca Intesa's former CEO, Corrado Passera, reflects, "Internal results undoubtedly matter, but even they won't count for much if everyone keeps reading in the newspapers that the business is still a poor performer, is not contributing to society, or is letting down the country as a whole."[28] Beyond the press, change leaders should look for ways to leverage customers, users, patients, voters, and other stakeholders to generate energy for change.

The power of a multi-channel or transmedia strategy is maximized when it's designed by taking a "receiver" view—like what we advocated when we discussed sequencing the change program in Chapter 5. The "receiver" view starts with an employee segment and maps the coherence of the communications journey they will be taken on to ensure it moves them from understanding to commitment to action. For example, employees may learn of the change program in an offsite interactive story cascade session. Then they read about it on the company home page as they log in. At lunch, they see posters on the walls. At home, they read about the plans in the press. Next, they take part in a skill-building "field and forum" journey that starts with a PIW that helps them be a better change leader themselves. As time goes on, they notice how the environment is changing. People work in open-plan offices, not behind closed doors. The corporate jet goes up for sale. All of these things are set in the context of the overall change story. If, from the receiver view, all of the communications and experiences combine to help employees clearly understand the meaning of the change story, convince them that it is real, and motivate them to play a role, then the communications plan can be seen as robust.

As we bring our discussion on high impact, two-way communications to a close, savvy business readers will no doubt be scratching their heads as to why we haven't made a fuss about the importance of celebrating successes. Yes, celebrating successes is important—it puts a spotlight on what you want to see more of, shows that doing what's desired matters, shares best practices, and increases motivation. Further, when coupled with "how do we get more of this?" messaging it taps into the "studying our strikes" bowling-team effect that we described at the end of Chapter 4. That said, we've seen too many change communications programs take the mantra of celebrating success and become nothing more than a cheerleading program, which employees quickly tune out as not credible.

In the words of one of our communications colleagues, "Everyone loves ice cream, but if fed it for every meal, they get sick of it. It's important, and healthy, that they have broccoli, too." Sober, substantive messages linked directly back to the change story, repeated with a "learner's mindset," done with simple and memorable language, balancing telling and asking, using multiple channels orchestrated to take the receiver on a sense-making journey—and the curse of knowledge is lifted!

## Master Stroke: Motivate Through Social Contracts

Upton Sinclair once wrote, "It is difficult to get a man to understand something if his salary depends upon him not understanding it."[29] As we pointed out in the Architect chapter, when talking about the formal reinforcement mechanisms of the influence model, if a change program's objectives are not linked somehow to employee compensation, this sends a strong message that the change program is not a priority, and motivation for change is adversely affected. Unfortunately, however, there is generally limited upside in linking change objectives to financial compensation. The reason for this is both practical and psychological.

In practice, there are always limitations to just how much compensation upside can be offered, and, within those limitations, compensation and rewards typically need to be linked to a wide array of metrics (e.g., overall company performance, individual area P&L, customer, quality, cost, risk, safety, social responsibility, diversity, talent). Practically, this means that the link to compensation of any one metric is typically not of significant relevance in the overall scheme of the plan. Of course, there is an option to change the approach that most companies use, but that's often far easier said than done as it typically requires board approval and is not without risk and potential unintended consequences. Furthermore, from a psychological point of view, it's been shown that the benefit of wealth on our feelings and happiness greatly decreases beyond levels of US$75,000, making every additional dollar of reward linked to change outcomes less valuable and motivating than the last.[30]

The good news is there are easier, relatively inexpensive ways to motivate employees that draw on lessons from the field of predictable irrationality, which brings us to our change leader master stroke for the Act stage of the journey. The key is to establish what employees perceive as a social—as opposed to market—exchange with the organization when it comes to delivering the change outcomes that you seek.

To see the difference, imagine you are invited to your mother-in-law's house for a special dinner. She has spent weeks planning the meal, and all day cooking. After dinner you say thank you and ask how much you owe her. How would she and the family react? Chances are she'd be mortified, as would everyone else. The offer of money changes the experience from a social interaction built around the notion of a reciprocal long-term relationship to a market transaction that is financially based, shallow, and short-lived. Yet, what if you had brought your mother-in-law an expensive bottle of wine as a contribution to the feast? She'd probably have accepted it graciously. The offer of a gift rather than payment indicates that social and not market norms are in play.[31]

Consider another example. A day-care center decided to impose a US$3 fine when parents were late picking up their children. Instead of encouraging them to be punctual, it had the opposite effect. Late pickups went through the roof. Why so? Before the fine was imposed, a social contract existed between daycare staff and parents, who tried hard to be prompt and felt guilty if they weren't. By imposing a fine, the center had inadvertently replaced social norms with market norms. Freed from feelings of guilt, parents frequently chose to be late and pay the fine—which was certainly not what the center had intended.[32]

As these examples show, when it comes to change, using social rather than market norms to shape behavior is both cheaper and often more effective. Some may look at the day care example and think to themselves, "They should have made the fee bigger than three dollars!" Indeed, they may have inadvertently offered cheap babysitting, but the social versus market contract effect holds in example after example. Consider how the American Association of Retired Persons (AARP) once asked some lawyers if they would offer their services to needy retirees at a cut-rate price of around US$30 an hour. The lawyers declined. Then the AARP asked if they would offer their services for free. Most of the lawyers agreed. So, what was going on here? When compensation was mentioned, the lawyers applied market norms and found the offer lacking. When no compensation was mentioned, they used social norms and were willing to volunteer their time.

What this means in practice is that small, unexpected non-financial rewards and recognition by peers and superiors have a surprisingly powerful motivating effect. In Chapter 5, we mentioned how ANZ bank's John McFarlane gave every employee a bottle of champagne for Christmas and PepsiCo's Indra Nooyi sent the spouses of her top team handwritten thank-you letters. At an Australian mining company, management sponsored a relatively impromptu "pit top bar-b-que" for employees and their families (named such as it took place near the top of the open pit mine) to celebrate the achievement of a particularly important change-program milestone. Employees recounted that time together for years afterward, whereas the bonus payments related to change-program milestones in general were long forgotten.

Other examples can be as simple as taking someone to lunch, taking extra time to get to know more about them and their aspirations, giving unexpected recognition in public settings, providing an experience to share with family or friends (e.g., sporting events, theater tickets, a restaurant gift certificate), allowing additional schedule flexibility, and so on. Ultimately, social-contracting methods needn't be complicated. As Sam Walton, founder of Walmart, put it, "Nothing else can quite substitute for a few well-chosen, well-timed, sincere words of praise. They're absolutely free—and worth a fortune."[33]

■ ■ ■

Whereas the first three stages of the change journey typically take months, the Act stage usually lasts for years. There's no denying it can feel like a long haul, especially after the initial excitement wears off and yet the mid-term aspiration is a hard road away. At this point, there's comfort to be had in Benjamin Franklin's adage, "Energy and persistence conquer all things." By combining ownership creating and energy generating approaches in the Act phase, your change program will remain on a path to glory.

When we're talking to companies about the Act stage, we often liken it to what happens when a champion sports team takes the field. Aspirations have been shared, skill and will requirements are clear, and there's a game plan in place. But once the whistle blows, it's not often that the points scored come from well-rehearsed set plays. Whether it's a key rebound in basketball, a pass interception returned for a touchdown in American football, or a goal coming out of a fullback's solo run in soccer, it's the improvising within the game plan that usually makes the difference between winning and losing. The same holds true for organizations. Your job at game time is to make the necessary adjustments as the game proceeds and to keep the players motivated to give 110 percent in the pursuit of success.

At the end of the Act phase, you'll be well on your way to achieving or exceeding your change aspirations. It's time to start planning on what will happen when you get there. How do you make sure you keep winning and stay on top? That's what we turn to next as we discuss the Advance stage and answer the question, "How do we continue to improve?" (Exhibit 6.5).

## Exhibit 6.5

# A Proven Approach to Leading Large-Scale Change: The Story So Far

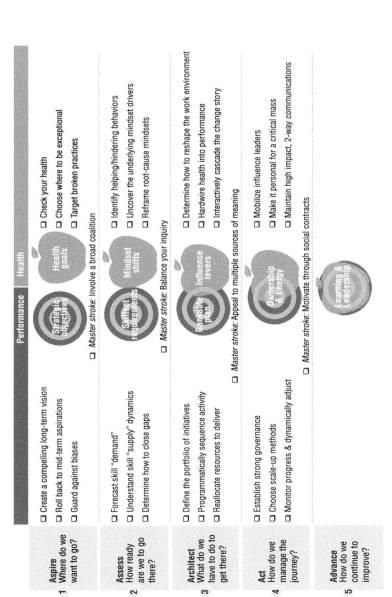

| | Performance | Health |
|---|---|---|
| **Aspire**<br>1 — Where do we want to go? | **Strategic objectives**<br>□ Create a compelling long-term vision<br>□ Roll back to mid-term aspirations<br>□ Guard against biases | **Health goals**<br>□ Check your health<br>□ Choose where to be exceptional<br>□ Target broken practices |
| | *Master stroke:* Involve a broad coalition | |
| **Assess**<br>2 — How ready are we to go there? | **Skillset requirements**<br>□ Forecast skill "demand"<br>□ Understand skill "supply" dynamics<br>□ Determine how to close gaps | **Mindset shifts**<br>□ Identify helping/hindering behaviors<br>□ Uncover the underlying mindset drivers<br>□ Reframe root-cause mindsets |
| | *Master stroke:* Balance your inquiry | |
| **Architect**<br>3 — What do we have to do to get there? | **Bankable plan**<br>□ Define the portfolio of initiatives<br>□ Programmatically sequence activity<br>□ Reallocate resources to deliver | **Influence levers**<br>□ Determine how to reshape the work environment<br>□ Hardwire health into performance<br>□ Interactively cascade the change story |
| | *Master stroke:* Appeal to multiple sources of meaning | |
| **Act**<br>4 — How do we manage the journey? | **Ownership & Energy**<br>□ Establish strong governance<br>□ Choose scale-up methods<br>□ Monitor progress & dynamically adjust | **Ownership & Energy**<br>□ Mobilize influence leaders<br>□ Make it personal for a critical mass<br>□ Maintain high impact, 2-way communications |
| | *Master stroke:* Motivate through social contracts | |
| **Advance**<br>5 — How do we continue to improve? | **Learning & Leadership** | |

# Chapter 7

# Advance

## *How Do We Continue to Improve?*

When John McFarlane took over the ANZ bank, it was the worst performer of Australia's big four banks, regarded as the highest-risk bank investment by the market, and in strategic disarray. It was grappling with almost A$2 billion of bad debt and a cost-to-income ratio of roughly 63 percent.[1]

The bank set its sights on a five-year aspiration to double its profitability and market capitalization and reduce its cost-to-income ratio to below 50 percent. To achieve this performance aspiration, health improvements were needed in relation to people development, openness and trust, risk management, and customer focus. In the Assess stage, it became clear that a raft of skills needed to be built in risk, technology, sales, marketing, HR, and so on. Mindset shifts would be required, too. For example, from "risk is the risk function's job" to "risk is everyone's job"; "it's respectful not to disagree in public" to "we have an obligation to dissent in meetings"; and "process is a necessary burden on customer service" to "process is a tool to help us responsibly serve our customers," and so on.

The core architecture of the change program was a portfolio of initiatives organized around three themes: perform, grow, and breakout. In the "perform" theme, topics were tackled such as overhead cost reduction, collections management, and lean service operations. Examples in the "grow" theme were, among others, initiatives directed at customer service, sales force effectiveness, and international portfolio restructuring. The "breakout" theme included a number of initiatives related to employees such as creating an internal job market, developing a new leadership model and 360-degree review process, and creating and implementing a new diversity strategy. Each of the initiatives was hardwired to influence the desired mindset and behavior shifts, sequenced, and resourced with rigor.

The plans were then implemented in the Act stage, during which a change management office (CMO) played an integration role across all of the various efforts, including providing a monthly "Perform, Grow, and Breakout" scorecard and adjusting the program over time based on the results being delivered. A robust, two-way communications program was also put in place. A unique feature of the program was the implementation of the "stupid rule button" that enabled employees to quickly eliminate standards, processes, and protocols that didn't make sense. Influence leaders were identified and mobilized, and in total over 6,000 leaders went through Personal Insight Workshops (PIWs). In the words of the leader of the program, "We realized the program had to be an 'inside/out' journey. In other words, it's the individual who transforms, and in turn, the organization."[2]

Just under four years after ANZ's large-scale change program had begun, the turnaround was declared complete. More than a year ahead of schedule, its goals had been met. But the story doesn't end there. In the Advance stage, ANZ ushered in an era of continuous improvement. For instance, while the central change management office infrastructure wound down, a group of 180 breakout champions continued in roles designed to foster continuous improvement on top of doing their normal "day jobs." To facilitate best practice identification and sharing, performance results from 21 specialist business units were shared broadly on an ongoing basis via an online "executive desktop." Investments were also made in a customer management system that enabled cross-functional teams to regularly convene, reflect on, and improve the end-to-end customer experience. The internal job market was enhanced to ensure the most value-creating roles were known and the best talent was placed in those roles.

During the six years of McFarlane's CEO tenure *after* the change program that turned around the company was complete, ANZ steadily continued its upward trajectory. Profit after tax grew at a cumulative average growth rate of 15 percent, market capitalization doubled again, and customer satisfaction soared from 65 percent to 78 percent. Further, the bank was receiving over 10,000 applications annually for its 250 graduate leadership program positions, indicative of how its continued health and high performance made it a talent magnet. At the end of McFarlane's 10-year tenure as CEO, the bank that had been called the "lame duck" by the Australian press a decade earlier was now referred to as "a highly polished money-making machine."[3]

■ ■ ■

Not all companies fare as well as ANZ in their post large-scale change program era. We recall talking to the executives of a North American engineering business when they were in celebration mode. They had taken their company from being characterized by stalled momentum and restive shareholders to one that had increased EBITDA by more than $100 million, and its cash flow by $150 million—all in 18 months! A few years later, however, the company was filing for bankruptcy. Once the intensity of the change program was over, slowly but surely the company slipped back to old ways, siloed thinking again prevailed, and a hierarchical and political culture flourished and slowed the gears of good decision-making to a halt.

Unfortunately, this engineering company isn't alone in their experience. As we described in Chapter 1, where we introduced the "big idea" of performance and health, there are plenty of companies who hit the financial targets of their change programs only to find that a year or two later, results have slipped and they are in need of yet another major change. Back to our caterpillar to butterfly analogy, real transformation eluded them.

It's not hard to see how this could happen at the end of a program. The CMO role winds down such that the previous cadence of weekly scrutinizing initiative progress gives way to the old monthly budget reporting and quarterly review process. Resources become more hardened into roles with an annual talent assessment being the only clearinghouse for rotations. Performance transparency diminishes into PowerPoint presentation-led dog and pony shows. New ideas don't have anywhere to go to get funding and people behind them. And so on. When asked what they wish they had done differently, a full 39 percent of change leaders reflect that they should have spent more time thinking about how to make the transition to continuous improvement a success.[4]

The good news is that if you've followed the Five Frames process up to this point, you've already done the vast majority of the work required to avoid this fate. Not only will you have achieved your performance aspirations, but new skillsets will have been built, limiting mindsets will have been irrevocably shifted, leadership capacity will be increased, and overall health will have improved greatly—the organization is now run in a way that makes it easier than ever to align itself, execute without friction in the system, and renew itself as needed to shape and adapt to its environment.

To ensure that the performance and health trajectory continues to improve after the formal change effort is wound down, however, change leaders are well advised to put a few final pieces of the puzzle in place by establishing a continuous learning infrastructure and ensuring the right leaders are placed in the roles that are most critical to value creation going forward.

## Performance: Learning Infrastructure

Making the transition from the intensive work and constant upheaval of a transformation to a period of continuous improvement requires transitioning from a programmatic approach to change to one that, as ANZ's John

McFarlane puts it, "unleash[es] the potential of some very talented people by giving them a lot of freedom to take their businesses where they've got to go."[5] This doesn't mean simply stepping back and letting leaders do as they please, however. Just as freedom in a society requires a legal infrastructure, so the kind of freedom in organizations McFarlane describes requires a learning infrastructure. Change leaders are wise not to leave this to chance, even if pushed by line leaders to leave everything to them. To borrow a phrase from the father of modern continuous improvement processes, W. Edwards Deming, "A bad system will beat a good person every time." So what does a good system look like? One that embeds knowledge sharing, institutionalizes improvement processes, and facilitates continuous learning.

## Embed Knowledge Sharing

Systems for sharing knowledge and best practices ensure that relevant improvements in one area are quickly adopted across the organization. Microsoft employees are familiar with the phrase that sums up the power of getting such systems: "Knowledge shared is knowledge squared."[6]

In Germany, Volkswagen has created its own Lean Center, a model factory designed to spread best practices in manufacturing efficiency, ergonomics, and quality, and educate employees about lean, clean process flows that can be applied to all nine brands in the carmaker's group. P&G operates a web-based knowledge repository, stages regular reviews to share best practices between brand managers, and constantly updates its international training programs to reflect best practices. In industries characterized by partnerships with customers and suppliers, approaches like these are often extended beyond the company to allow knowledge to be shared and leveraged from one end of a process or relationship to the other.

Although the approaches used for knowledge sharing vary widely, the research is clear that the systematic sharing of knowledge and best practices matters: change programs that put them in place are 4.2 times more likely to be considered a sustainable success.[7]

## Institutionalize Improvement Processes

Processes and expertise to enable continuous improvement allow employees at any level to change things for the better. Toyota's manufacturing environment is a great place to see this at work. If employees spot a problem on the production floor, they are expected to sort it out there and then: stop the line, get into a huddle to identify the cause, take corrective action, and track progress until the problem is resolved. Such processes can be adopted in any business setting.

Paradoxically, the companies that excel in making continuous improvement everyone's job tend to charge certain people and groups—often former members of the CMO—with helping it to happen. Estimates suggest that two-thirds of Fortune 500 organizations have dedicated expertise whose mandate it is to foster, enable, and drive continuous improvement, typically a core team of skilled individuals who direct and coordinate improvement activities.[8] Motorola, for example, has three such teams: kaizen teams that address relatively simple challenges; lean teams that focus on cross-functional projects; and Six Sigma teams that perform deep process analytics to resolve complex challenges.

## Facilitate Continuous Learning

Methods that facilitate continuous learning give an organization a chance to pause, step back, and take stock of what's working, what isn't, what it means, and what to do about it. The U.S. Army's After Action Reviews (AARs) serve precisely this purpose, and involve interested observers as well as soldiers from all ranks. They turn training activities into a learning process that asks what was planned, what actually happened, why, and what could be done better next time. The aim is not to judge success or failure, but to focus on learning from the experience so that the organization is better equipped to meet similar challenges in the future. Such sessions don't necessarily have to take place after the event: "pre-mortems" can also be held to challenge assumptions (managers ask members of their team to play devil's advocate and compete to articulate plausible ways that a project might go wrong).

Continuous learning should also happen looking outside the walls of an organization. One international airline studied how pit stops were orchestrated in the Indianapolis 500-Mile Race to help it develop a more efficient luggage-handling system. In much the same way, a construction company took route-planning lessons from a pizza-delivery chain and was able to raise its rate of on-time cement deliveries from 68 percent to 95 percent.[9]

All three elements of a learning infrastructure we've described will be highly tailored to your organization's context; some will need to stress particular elements more than others. The key to success is to ensure that all are thoughtfully designed and mutually reinforcing. Take Google's approach to continuous improvement. When a significant mistake is made within the engineering group, such as a visible service disruption or a slow customer resolution, a postmortem is undertaken to identify what happened, why, its impact, how the issue was resolved, and what will be done to prevent the problem from recurring (continuous learning). However, the postmortem doesn't stop there. The postmortem is stored in a Google Doc that allows for open commenting and annotations, e-mail notifications, and real-time collaboration. The report is further shared to the organization through a monthly newsletter and through postmortem reading clubs (knowledge sharing). Finally, select postmortems are treated to a "Wheel of Misfortune" exercise where a previous postmortem is reenacted quarterly with newer site engineers who try to determine the root cause of the problem and generate even more novel and effective solutions (improvement processes).

Consider also how a heavy equipment manufacturing company moved through the Advance stage of their large-scale change program by creating what was referred to as the continuous product improvement (CPI) process. The process enabled dealers and service representatives to communicate issues raised by customers to the wider organization. When a problem arises, a CPI team from the company contacts the customer to understand its scale and impact, launches an investigation, and in due course, reports back to the aggrieved customer with its findings and solutions (improvement process). It also shares the information with dealers worldwide to assist other customers facing similar issues (knowledge sharing), and with new product development so that relevant findings can be used to improve future design and manufacturing (continuous learning).

Putting in place a learning infrastructure requires as much energy and focus as any other stage in a change program. It's well worth the effort, however. Companies that build the capacity for continuous learning into their organization are 2.6 times more likely to report their success is sustained long after the change program ends.[10]

## Health: Leadership Placement

As you near the end of the change program, you'll face the question of where and how to place initiative-dedicated talent back into more permanent roles. The question is a vexing one on many dimensions.

Consider an initiative leader, Svetlana, who has been driving the supply chain rearchitecture and digitization effort for the company full-time for the last 18 months, and is wrapping up her efforts. Thanks to her leadership, delivery time frames will no longer be jeopardized by single-source suppliers, and margins will be improved due to the vertical integration strategy of which she has led the implementation. Everyone feels great about the impact achieved, but what's next for Svetlana? The head of the Supply Chain function is a good 10 years from retirement, and thanks to the great job done, there are far fewer senior positions available in the function and those left have been recently filled as part of the initiative work. And what of the 20–30 Svetlana-equivalents who have been working on other initiatives, and whose technical, relational, and adaptive leadership skills you've invested in heavily throughout the course of the change program?

Getting the leadership placement aspect of the Advance stage right typically involves an approach that echoes the one used in the Architect stage, where talent was reallocated to deliver the portfolio of change initiatives. The concept is fairly simple: ensure the right talent is in the right roles when viewed through a value-creation lens. And don't just do it once: institutionalize the process so that you can dynamically adjust how you're deploying talent to optimize performance as you continuously improve going forward.

Be warned, however, that doing this is far easier said than done. Consider the CEO of a healthcare company who we asked to list the top 20 most talented leaders in the company. We then asked him to list the top 20 most important roles in the company—the roles that created the most value. When asked how many people on the first list were filling the roles on the second, the CEO went pale. He didn't have to do the math to know the answer wasn't one the board or shareholders would be happy to hear. Further, once the CEO had gone through the steps we'll describe in the following section—prioritizing roles by value, matching talent to priority roles, and operationalizing the process—he realized both of his lists regarding roles and talent were wrong to begin with!

## Prioritize Roles by Value

The process for prioritizing value-creating (and enabling) roles starts with defining the value agenda for the organization—understanding how and where value will be created going forward. This process looks at the variables that drive value (in a publicly held enterprise, these include revenue, operating margin, capital efficiency, and so on), and the drivers of those variables. Once the value drivers are well defined, roles can be scored for the extent to which they impact those drivers (and any significant drivers that don't have roles lined up against them can be flagged for new roles to be considered).

Leaders who undertake this process for the first time should prepare themselves for a host of insights that will very likely make them rethink the business. One profound insight relates to the extent value creation follows hierarchy. Based on our experience working with clients to prioritize roles by value, of the top 50 value-creating roles you can expect to find 10 percent in the ranks directly reporting to the CEO (CEO-1), 60 percent at the CEO-2 level, and 20 percent at the CEO-3 level. What about the last 10 percent, you ask? Companies who put a sharp lens on understanding value creation by role often identify roles that don't exist yet, but should. These are typically roles that capture value that comes from working across existing organizational boundaries or are aimed at capturing new sources of value driven by industry trends (e.g., data and analytics) or that couldn't have been targeted before the change program put in place the right foundations.

Another profound insight relates to the value creation role of functions versus business units. The American football film *The Blind Side* offers a vivid illustration of the dynamic at play. In the opening scene the viewer is asked who they think is the highest paid player on the team. Those familiar with the game typically think to themselves, "the quarterback," because that's the most central person in executing the majority of the plays. The narrator of the film reveals that's absolutely right, and then asks, "Who is the second highest paid?" Most viewers' minds go to running backs or wide receivers, as they work most directly with the quarterback to move the ball forward toward scoring the points needed to win. This, the viewer finds out, is wrong. It's actually the left tackle (if the quarterback is right-handed), a player who doesn't touch the ball at all. Why? Because they protect the quarterback from what he can't see (his "blind side"), which are the things that are most likely to get him injured.

In the business context, the quarterbacks, wide receivers, and running back equivalents are most often thought of as revenue-generating businesses. The "left tackles" aren't often obvious, and most senior leaders are hard-pressed to think who they might be. In the Navy, it may be the ship-bound IT outage engineer, who prevents unintended catastrophe for the captain, crew, and humanity at large. In financial services, it may be the head of the government relations function whose sensing and shaping with politicians and regulators can dramatically alter the fortunes of the company and the industry. These are roles that create value by protecting or enabling it, the quantification of which during the prioritization process enables them to be seen on an equal playing field, so to speak!

With the concepts clear, let's talk about how all this works in practice. We once asked the CEO of an insurance brokerage to identify the most important roles in his company—those where A-players should most certainly be deployed. The CEO neglected to mention the account manager for a key customer, in part because the position was not prominent in any organizational chart. By just about any other criterion, though, this was one of the most critical to current performance and future growth. The role demanded a high degree of responsibility, a complex set of interpersonal and technical skills, and an ability to respond deftly to the client's rapidly changing needs. As it turns out, the CEO was unaware of the incumbent account manager's growing dissatisfaction, and there was no succession plan in place. When she suddenly took a job at another company, the move stunned the senior team. As performance suffered, they scrambled to cover temporarily, and then to fill, this mission-critical role.

In light of her departure, the CEO and top team decided to get serious about taking a value-creation lens to prioritizing roles. They realized that given their strategy centered on building their small business platform and achieving disproportionate growth in China, the value at stake in roles related to those areas looking forward was far greater than roles it currently considered to be its core businesses and geographies. It also discovered that what was previously considered more of a "second-class" function, Service Operations, would require first-class innovation to enable needed efficiencies to be achieved to provide investment in the company's growth platforms. Further, they realized that a global sales and marketing role was needed to drive the sharing of best practices across regions and business lines, a role that didn't exist in the organization today.

## Match Talent to Priority Roles

Once you've got a handle on what roles the most value will hinge on into the future, it's time to ensure you have the right talent in those roles. Doing so happens in two steps. The first is to be clear on the jobs to be done (JTBD) to deliver the value. For example, let's say the head of a product line role is a priority role and is expected to deliver value on the order of $150 million, which translates to year on year 10 percent growth for the next 3 years. The JTBD may include making operations more agile, which will reduce costs by 5 percent, delivering one-third ($50 million) of the needed value. Another JTBD may be driving improved sales and marketing that will increase revenue by 5 percent to deliver another $60 million in value. If momentum growth of the business was, say, $20 million in value, then that leaves a $20 million value creation expectation to come from breakthrough innovation.

Once you know the JTBD of the 50 highest value-creating roles, you can then determine what Knowledge, Skills, Attributes, and Experiences (KSAEs) are best suited to getting the JTBD done. For example, in the product leader role mentioned above, the knowledge and skills needed may relate to business development, agile working methods, and target scanning and due diligence (assuming growth will require M&A). The attributes may be someone with global mindset, intellectual curiosity, and great team-building skills. The experience may be having run a $100 million or more P&L, led an integration, and built and executed a high-impact sales model.

We suggest this level JTBD and KSAEs be drilled down to for the top 50 most value-creating (or enabling) roles. This number works because it is big enough to take an organization far beyond the "usual suspect" positions, and it means that the collection of roles will typically account for a large portion of overall value delivery for the company. It's a small enough number, however, such that the most senior leader can play a hands-on role in relation to hiring, retention, performance management, and succession planning related to the roles in question.

Once the KSAEs of each of the top 50 value-creating roles are known, the talent match process involves looking to see which leaders in the organization are the best match—regardless of where they currently sit. Conversations become very specific and fact-based. Comments such as, "Javier's been a successful CFO in a smaller business unit; I think he's ready to move to the bigger role" can be met with data that Javier's current role drives value through acquisitions, and yet the vacant role requires driving value through aggressive cost-reduction—is he still the best choice?

Fair warning, however, that for companies who have never gone through a process like this, it can get quite uncomfortable. The data-driven process makes it hard to ignore that some incumbents might not be up to the future demands of the job and that leaving them in place would put a significant amount of value at risk. Typically, 20 to 30 percent of those in critical roles today are not well matched.

Further revelations from the process will come in the form of being able to identify systemic gaps in knowledge, skills, and attributes across the entire leadership bench. This is highly instructive for retooling the leadership development agenda to add maximum value to the organization going forward. Also, the talent match process enables significant enhancements to succession planning. Career paths can be created to develop needed KSAEs for various roles, and previously hidden candidates can be flagged through analytics as viable options to fill vacancies.

## Operationalize the Process

Operationalizing the talent match process ensures that the talent matching isn't a one-off or simply relegated to a once-a-year talent-review-related event. Instead, it ensures that talent is managed as rigorously as the finance team deploys capital on an ongoing basis.

Operationalizing the process shouldn't harken in a new era of giant printed binders and Excel spreadsheets. Everything we have just described lends itself to digital enablement: simple, highly interactive user interfaces, backed by a powerful data and analytics engine. There are many such solutions available to organizations, one of which is McKinsey's *Talent Match*, which has been developed precisely for these purposes. By populating it with the KSAEs for your priority roles and your people, and by combining it with additional information about their performance and preferences, a dynamic model of your leadership bench is created. With a swipe of a touch screen, you can see the domino effect of moving one person into a new role in terms of impacts on other roles (e.g., is the succession plan robust—would we be willing to put person x into role y?), people (e.g., does anyone become a retention risk?), and overall human capital metrics (e.g., diversity, depth of capability sets).

There's little doubt that in the third edition of *Beyond Performance*, this section will be greatly expanded to incorporate many further advances in people analytics. The field remains in its infancy as only 8 percent of companies report that they are capable of predictive modeling when it comes to human capital. But it's advancing quickly: only a year earlier, the figure was 4 percent. It won't be long before organizations will be able to use sophisticated algorithms to anticipate and mitigate key talent departures, find otherwise "hidden" talent in the organization that is likely to be successful in key roles, and create development pipelines with dramatically increased precision. Consider that when the National Bureau of Economic Research pitted humans against an algorithm to hire candidates for more than 300,000 high-turnover jobs across 15 companies, human experience, instinct, and judgment were soundly defeated. Those picked by machines stayed longer and performed as well or better—a result that held whether picking frontline, middle management, or C-suite positions.[11]

Regardless of how sophisticated or digitally enabled, once you have information on JTBD and KSAEs for the top 50 value-creating roles (or more), an operationalized process typically involves revisiting the data monthly. This is typically done by the HR leadership team, who meet to identify trends across business units—for example, the lag in certifications of certain role-specific skill requirements, such as digital fluency. Working alongside leaders, the team might also assess changes in the performance of individuals in critical roles, asking questions such as, "Is this individual delivering the value expected? What interventions (for instance, coaching, training, or better-aligned incentives) can support this individual?" Or, conversely, "This individual has been flagged as an attrition risk, what's our save strategy?" Meanwhile, the question of, "Do we have the right people in the right roles?" is typically discussed and acted on quarterly by the most senior team.

The rewards of prioritizing roles by value, matching talent to those roles, and then turning it into "how we do things around here" going forward are significant. Based on our research, those companies that are characterized as "fast" talent reallocators are 2.2 times more likely to outperform their competitors on total returns to shareholders (TRS) than are slow talent reallocators.[12]

## Master Stroke: Ensure Fair Process

Celebrating the successful accomplishment of a change aspiration is a very special feeling. The feeling of achievement is coupled with a deep sense of belonging to a winning team—one that has accomplished far more than the sum of its parts. There is confidence for the road ahead and a humility gained from the many course-corrects made along the way, prompted by the numerous cycles of action and reflection. The significant skills built are linked to a new level of wisdom that can only come from experience.

Above all else, however, there is a new level of trust. We did what we said we'd do. We were transparent with one another. We learned from our mistakes along the way. We did what was authentically us—we didn't copy someone else. This base of trust is the ultimate foundation on which to drive continuous improvement in performance and health, and one that is exceedingly difficult for competitors to match.

Don't take it for granted! There's an old adage, "Trust arrives on foot and leaves on horseback." Of course, on many fronts you will have built the goodwill with employees such that they will generally give the organization the benefit of the doubt and seek information to clarify if things don't feel right. Two scenarios, however, cause the trust horse to bolt at champion thoroughbred speeds. The first scenario is obvious: steer clear of any violations of honesty and integrity. The second, however, can be easily violated unwittingly, as it comes from our "predictably irrational" relationship with fairness.

Take, for example, a bank that had gone through a major change program to increase revenues. It had rationalized its product portfolio, simplified its product set, strengthened the value proposition of those products that remained, revamped incentives, provided sales training, and so on. Once the revenue targets had been hit, the bank declared victory and pushed the responsibility for continuous improvement in sales to the channels and in pricing to marketing.

As the marketing department drove toward its continuous improvement targets, it created more sophisticated risk-adjusted rate-of-return models leveraging the improved skillsets, better data, and enhanced tools that had been put in place as a result of the change program. This modeling revealed that many of the banks' products were priced in a way that did not fully reflect the credit risk it was taking on. New pricing schedules were created and rolled out, and at the same time, sales incentives were adjusted to more appropriately reward customer profitability rather than volume. The result? Customers (profitable as well as unprofitable) deserted in droves. Price overrides soared, destroying a great deal of value.

So what had gone wrong? Looking at what's called an "ultimatum game" can offer us a clue. We give player A US\$10 and explain that the money has to be shared with player B. Player A has to propose how the money is split, and if player B accepts the offer, they both get the agreed shares. If B rejects the offer, though, no one gets any money. Studies show that if player A offers a US\$7.50/US\$2.50 split, player B will reject it more than 95 percent of the time, preferring to go home with nothing than see someone else get three times as much for no good reason. And that isn't because the absolute sums are so small: even when the money on offer is the equivalent of two weeks' pay, the results are similar.[13]

There's a clear message here for leaders. If employees are put in a position that violates their sense of justice and fair play, they will act *against their own self-interest* and therefore, even against whatever formal incentives are in force. This may seem irrational, but it's entirely predictable. This implication isn't just speculation from ultimatum games, either. In one of business school professor Sebastien Brion's experiments, for example, he not only found that bosses overestimate the strength of their bonds with subordinates, but also that subordinates of an unfair boss will form alliances against the boss, even when not in their financial interest to do so.[14]

Let's go back to the bank. When it raised its prices and adjusted its sales incentives, frontline staff thought it was being unfair to customers—a case of executives getting greedy and losing sight of customer service. Even though they were putting their own sales targets in jeopardy, many bankers bad-mouthed the new policies to customers, choosing to take their side rather than the bank's. They also used price overrides to show good faith to customers and take revenge on the organization.

Ironically, their perception of injustice was misdirected. Customers were, after all, only being asked to pay a price commensurate with the risk the bank was taking on. The whole sorry saga could have been avoided if the bank had only paid enough attention to employees' sense of fairness when it was developing the communications and training that accompanied the price changes.

Leaders are wise to keep in mind that during a Five Frames of Performance and Health change program, there is significant scaffolding in place to guard against violating employees' sense of fairness. There is a premium placed on employee involvement, explaining why, planning from the "receiver" view versus just from the "sender" view, and ensuring the big picture is constantly reinforced (recall the techniques discussed in Chapter 6 to overcome the "curse of knowledge"). When this scaffolding is pulled back, it's up to leadership to hold the sense of fairness sacred and keep it in place.

■ ■ ■

The Advance stage transitions your organization from the intense period of change (the steep part of the S-curve) into a period of continuous improvement (so that the top of the S-curve is gradually rising indefinitely). It does this by putting in place a learning infrastructure that embeds knowledge sharing, institutionalizes improvement processes, and facilitates continuous learning. It also involves getting leadership placement right by prioritizing roles by value, matching talent to priority roles, and operationalizing the process. Finally, it prompts leaders to guard against violating employees' perceived sense of fairness—doing so is a fast ticket to eroding the all-important trust base that has been developed in and across the organization during the course of the change program (Exhibit 7.1).

No doubt there will come a time when this ongoing adaptive approach to change will meet a challenge or see an opportunity that again calls for an intensive adjustment period in the form of a large-scale change program. This may be prompted by a change in the competitive landscape, technology innovations, shifts in customer needs, regulatory requirements, geopolitical events, or other shocks. When it does, you'll be ready—in a position of strength due to having a healthy organization to start with and knowing how to use the Five Frames of Performance and Health to make the needed change happen.

In the context of a never-ending journey, congratulations, you have arrived!

Exhibit 7.1

# A Proven Approach to Leading Large-Scale Change

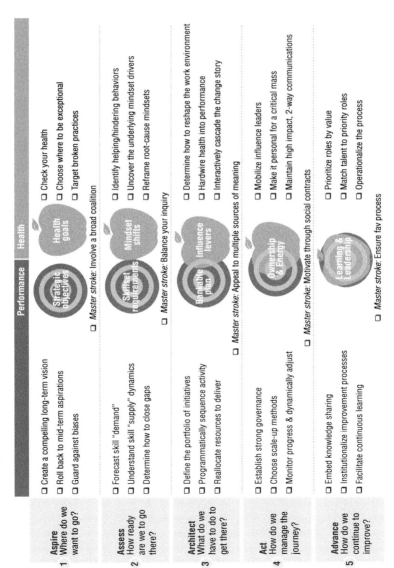

|  | Performance | Health |
|---|---|---|
| **Aspire** 1 Where do we want to go? | □ Create a compelling long-term vision <br> □ Roll back to mid-term aspirations <br> □ Guard against biases | **Strategic objectives** / **Health goals** <br> □ Check your health <br> □ Choose where to be exceptional <br> □ Target broken practices <br><br> □ *Master stroke:* Involve a broad coalition |
| **Assess** 2 How ready are we to go there? | □ Forecast skill "demand" <br> □ Understand skill "supply" dynamics <br> □ Determine how to close gaps | **Skillset requirements** / **Mindset shifts** <br> □ Identify helping/hindering behaviors <br> □ Uncover the underlying mindset drivers <br> □ Reframe root-cause mindsets <br><br> □ *Master stroke:* Balance your inquiry |
| **Architect** 3 What do we have to do to get there? | □ Define the portfolio of initiatives <br> □ Programmatically sequence activity <br> □ Reallocate resources to deliver | **Bankable plan** / **Influence levers** <br> □ Determine how to reshape the work environment <br> □ Hardwire health into performance <br> □ Interactively cascade the change story <br><br> □ *Master stroke:* Appeal to multiple sources of meaning |
| **Act** 4 How do we manage the journey? | □ Establish strong governance <br> □ Choose scale-up methods <br> □ Monitor progress & dynamically adjust | **Ownership & Energy** <br> □ Mobilize influence leaders <br> □ Make it personal for a critical mass <br> □ Maintain high impact, 2-way communications <br><br> □ *Master stroke:* Motivate through social contracts |
| **Advance** 5 How do we continue to improve? | □ Embed knowledge sharing <br> □ Institutionalize improvement processes <br> □ Facilitate continuous learning | **Learning & Leadership** <br> □ Prioritize roles by value <br> □ Match talent to priority roles <br> □ Operationalize the process <br><br> □ *Master stroke:* Ensure fav process |

# PART III

# Putting It All Together

# Chapter 8

# The Senior Leader's Role

## *Does Change Have to Start at the Top?*

By this point, we hope the Five Frames of Performance and Health approach to making change happen at scale has been laid out clearly. It's our firm belief that by following this path, almost any organization can make change happen successfully. What's more, the change you'll achieve will be both sustainable and continuously improved upon day after day, week after week, and month after month after the formal program concludes.

As we've seen again and again in the company examples we feature in this book, leadership and role modeling are central to the change journey. In some ways we were hoping our research would lead us to a counterintuitive insight that the role of senior leaders is far less important than we've all been led to believe by management literature. We found the opposite. Our research shows that transformations are 2.6 times more likely to succeed if they have strong involvement from the top of the organization.[1] John Mackey of Whole Foods Market explains why: "As the co-founder and CEO, I'm the most visible person in the company ... our team members are always studying me ... I'm always on stage."[2]

For this reason, we devote an entire chapter to the role of the senior leader in spearheading a transformation. Who exactly qualifies as the relevant "senior leader" will depend on the change challenge being taken on. Our work mostly revolves around enterprise-wide change programs, and the senior leader role in question is therefore the CEO of the corporation. In the public sector, the senior leader is typically the director of a government agency; in the social sector, it's the head of the nonprofit; and in family-owned businesses, it's often the matriarch or patriarch of the family. That said, in a change program taking place in the marketing department, the senior leader is likely the Chief Marketing Officer, in technology it's the Chief Technology Officer, and in the field the President of Sales, and so on.

199

Does that mean this chapter is for senior leaders only? Not at all. By learning what the senior leader's role in a transformation should be, readers at all levels of an organization—and would-be leaders, too—can help their own senior leader to fulfill the role they need to play. You can use this information to help them help you! If you're trying to change your organization, there's no doubt that the path will be easier and more direct if your most senior leader is on your side, supporting you and playing the role that only they can play to make the effort a success.

Don't forget that when you're trying to get your senior leader on board, you can draw on the influence model from Chapter 5. In doing so, you'll need to give some thought to their personal style and preferences. Whose opinions do they trust? What kind of change story will resonate with them and tap into their sources of meaning? Do they understand and accept the role they need to play? Will they need to build new skills to play it? And are there any processes that would help to make all this happen?

## What Only the Senior Leader Can Do

The senior leader's role is unique. The person at the top of the pyramid provides cues for everyone else in the organization as to what really matters around here. We often use what we refer to whimsically as the "gear reduction theory of management" to make the point more viscerally. Imagine a huge gear at the top of the system that is connected to progressively smaller ones. If the biggest gear does one click in a rotation, the next gear down will click five or six times, and the gear below that 10 or 12 times. Go down a few more gears in the system, and the little gears toward the bottom are spinning very fast indeed.

What happens if the biggest gear changes its mind, and decides to rotate one click in the opposite direction? This doesn't seem like a big deal to the big gear—it's a small redirection in the scheme of things at that level. Further down in the system of gears, however, it's a different story. The gear below screeches to a halt, and then starts moving in the opposite direction, as well. It's frictional, but the gear will survive and continue to click in the desired direction as needed. Down the line, all the other gears start to shear. Sparks fly and the poor little gear at the bottom screeches so much that it shears right off and out of the system. Such is the power of the senior leader!

Despite the importance of the role of the most senior leader, there's surprisingly little written about what a leader can and should do to best support a change program. Perhaps that's because there's no single recipe for success. The precise nature of the role will be influenced by the scale, urgency, and nature of the transformation, the organization's capabilities, and the senior leader's personal style. That said, our research and experience with scores of transformation efforts have enabled us to identify four key roles played by successful senior leaders:

- **Making the change meaningful.** The impact of the change story depends on the extent to which the senior leader makes it personal, openly engages others, and spotlights successes as they emerge.

- **Role modeling the ability to change.** Successful senior leaders typically embark on a change journey of their own. Through their actions, they show not only what good looks like in terms of outcomes, but also in terms of going through the process of improving oneself.

- **Building a strong and committed top team.** Tough decisions must be made about who has the capability and motivation to make the change journey, and time needs to be invested in aligning and building the team to drive the change.

- **Relentlessly pursuing impact.** For top priority initiatives—those with significant customer, financial, or symbolic value—there's no substitute for senior leaders rolling up their sleeves and getting personally involved. Further, across the entire "performance placemat," it's ultimately the role of the senior leader to hold people accountable.

In combination, these four roles help to ensure that the change effort wins what we call the "war for the middle." In most transformations we've seen, there's a small percentage of employees who are completely on board from the outset. At the other extreme, there's another small percentage who may never come on board and are likely to leave the organization if the changes come to pass (back to our influence model analogy from Chapter 5, once it's clear they are no longer in an opera house and are in a sports stadium, they choose to exit!). But the majority are in the middle, trying to work out whether this is just a passing fad, whether real change is possible, and whether it's worth the energy to get on board with the risk of being let down again. For this very large group, seeing the senior leader playing these roles goes a long way in persuading them to believe, get on board, and invest in turning the change aspiration into a reality.

## Make It Meaningful

Large-scale change programs call for extraordinary energy, as we've seen throughout this book, as leaders and employees are required to rethink and reshape the entire business while continuing to run it from day to day. A powerful transformation story helps employees to believe in the effort, in particular if it taps into all five sources of meaning and is re-inforced continuously through a great two-way communications program. Its full impact, however, ultimately depends on the senior leader do-ing three things: personalizing the story, openly engaging others, and spotlighting success.

## Personalize the Story

Senior leaders who take the time to personalize the transformation story unlock significantly more energy than those who dutifully present the con-tent that their working team has prepared for them. In practice this means that senior leaders need to think carefully about such questions as: "How does this relate to me and my role?"; "Why does it matter to me personally?"; "What hopes and fears do I personally have about my and our ability to pull this off successfully?" Then they need to share the answers with others. If the interactive story cascade that we described in Chapter 5 is used as part of the change program, this type of reflection and sharing is built into the process.

Effective leaders often talk about pivotal experiences and formative influ-ences in their own lives to underline their determination and demonstrate that obstacles can be overcome. Indra Nooyi, the former CEO of PepsiCo, is open about the struggles she had after setting off from India with a scholar-ship and not much else: "I had the immigrant feeling arriving in the U.S.... I had to do an extra-good job; if it didn't work out, where was I going to go?"[3] She used the story as a rallying cry to get her colleagues to work harder in the battle of the brands in the hope of one day getting to the very top.

Andy Grove, a former CEO of Intel, the world's largest maker of semi-conductor chips, conveyed the importance of courage and decisiveness by describing his escape from Hungary during the Russian occupation and his determination to make a new life in the United States. John Chambers, for-mer CEO of Cisco, describes growing up with a learning disability to illus-trate "how we can overcome anything that comes our way, and why it is so important to treat others as you would want to be treated."[4] David Roberts alluded to lessons from his hero Monty Roberts (the real-life horse whis-perer) when he talked about the transformation he led as CEO of Personal Financial Services at Barclays Bank.

David Novak, the former CEO of Yum! Brands, which owns franchises including KFC, Pizza Hut, and Taco Bell, neatly summarized how a personal approach helps employees feel connected to the collective effort: "They see their CEO and it makes a big company small." He points out that when employees get knowledge directly from their senior leader, they "care more about the company and [they're] more committed."[5]

## Openly Engage Others

Once the senior leader has crafted a clear transformation story, success comes from seizing every opportunity to talk about it with employees, explain what it means, draw out its relevance to different parts of the business, and prompt others to find a personal meaning of their own.

Leaders of successful change invest huge personal effort in taking their story out into the organization. While he was the CEO at IBM, Lou Gerstner flew more than a million miles to meet thousands of customers, employees, and business partners.[6] He famously had a sign in his office that declared, "A desk is a dangerous place from which to view the world," to act as a constant reminder of the importance of engaging with people inside and outside the organization.[7] As Intuit former CEO Steve Bennett explains, "A CEO can't make a series of changes by sending out e-mails. Change management has to happen face to face. It's a big commitment of time."[8] Bennett saw this approach pay off in his turnaround of Intuit from an underperforming tech start-up into a producer with double-digit revenues and four times the earnings it had when he took the helm. When Corrado Passera became CEO of Banca Intesa, he traveled the length and breadth of Italy to start spreading the change story to the bank's 60,000 employees: "It is a long process, but you have to put your face in front of the people if you want them to follow you."[9]

Sometimes leaders need to work especially hard to engage challenging stakeholder groups. Om Prakash Bhatt, former chairman of State Bank of India, invested a considerable amount of his time with trade unions: "I spent four days with 30 leaders from across the country ... [even though] some of my best advisers at the bank warned that the leaders weren't trustworthy and could be disruptive ... what hooked them was not only the quality of the discussions and the revelations but that the chairman was willing to spend so much time with them, eating and drinking, even singing and dancing."[10]

When engaging employees, it's important for senior leaders to also keep in mind the lessons we shared in Chapter 6 regarding two-way communications: use simple and memorable language, balance "telling" and "asking," and use multiple channels—both in person and electronic.

## Spotlight Success

As the change program progresses, an engaging way to reinforce the story is to spotlight where success is being achieved. This helps crystallize what the change means and gives people confidence that change really is happening. And when it comes personally from the senior leader, it's eminently more meaningful than a generic corporate communication.

Former Infosys chairman N. R. Narayana Murthy describes how he personally invited high-performing teams to make presentations to employees across the company "to show other people that we value such behavior."[11] Harry M. Jansen Kraemer Jr., former chairman and CEO of healthcare company Baxter International, forwarded his entire 55,000-strong workforce an e-mail from a woman thanking them for creating a product that had extended her father's life by 15 years. He told his employees, "This is what we do," and emphasized that changes being made would enable them to do more of it. Daniel R. DiMicco, former CEO of Nucor, one of the largest steel producers in the United States, personally shared the story of a shipping department supervisor to illustrate the importance of taking initiative. The supervisor asked for US$2,000 to study sister plants in other regions, and duly returned with ideas to save more than US$150,000 a year in his area alone. At Brazilian bank Itaú Unibanco, the chairman and top team take part in an awards night to acknowledge and celebrate people's efforts in driving desired changes. The event is followed up with extensive communications throughout the bank. When leaders spotlight successes in these ways, they are sending a strong message in line with Tom Peters' adage, "Celebrate what you'd like to see more of."

As a final thought, bear in mind that "success" doesn't necessarily mean getting things right. Failure—for the right reasons—can be equally worth celebrating when it provides valuable lessons for your organization. That's what happens at Google, as former CEO Eric Schmidt explains: "We celebrate our failures. This is a company where it's absolutely okay to try something that's very hard, have it not be successful, and take the learning from that."[12]

## Role Model Change

No matter how much employees *want* to believe in the change story, they won't unless the senior leader's actions back it up. "Every move you make, everything you say, is visible to all. Therefore, the best approach is to lead by example," advises Joseph M. Tucci, former CEO of EMC.[13]

The senior leader acts as the chief role model for the whole organization. The fullest embodiment of this involves undergoing personal change and taking symbolic actions.

### Undergo Personal Change

Earlier in the book, we discussed people's tendency to think they are better at certain things than they really are (see our discussion of the optimism bias in Chapter 3 and the self-serving bias in Chapter 6). Research shows that this phenomenon becomes more pronounced at the top of an organization. Kevin Roberts, former CEO of global advertising agency Saatchi and Saatchi, notes, "The further up the company you go the stupider you become ... you start believing your own stuff."[14]

His observation is backed by research. Take, for example, Jimmy Cayne, former CEO of Bear Stearns. On his last day, when leaving the ailing bank, he claimed there wasn't a dry eye in the house, and that heartbroken bankers sent him away with a standing ovation. According to research by author James Cohen in his book *House of Cards*, Cayne was so widely disliked that if he had stayed on for another year, there would have been a mass exodus of staff.

On reading Cayne's story, business school professor Sebastien Brion ran a series of tests to see how much leaders overestimate their subordinates' good opinion of them. The conclusion? Bosses set too much store by their strengths and habitually overestimate their ability to win respect and support from their employees. They also lose the aptitude to read subtle cues in others' behavior—so much so that Brion found that when a boss tells a joke to a subordinate, he loses the ability to distinguish between a real or fake smile.[15]

As a result of this phenomenon, we encourage the most senior leaders to eschew the advice that says, "Be the change you want to see in the world." Why? Because they probably think they already are! Instead, we suggest senior leaders heed the similar sounding but altogether different meaning advice of, "For things to change, first I must change." Senior leaders needn't just model the desired end state of the change (the "to" mindsets and behaviors), but also the *act* of changing oneself. After all, the change program is asking everyone else to change! It doesn't matter if the senior leader is already great (or thinks he is, anyway) at role modeling desired mindsets and behaviors; his job is to role model the abililty to become even better.

This level of *humility* is not easy for leaders who are literally at the top of their organizations, which is precisely why it's so powerful. As John Akehurst, the former CEO of Woodside Petroleum, reflects, "It took a lot of effort for me to recognize that I, as the chief executive, am entirely responsible for the culture of the organization ... When I took the time to really look at it, I had an amazing insight into how dysfunctional my behavior was, what an impact it had on other people, how much baggage we were all carrying around."[16]

Coupled with the humility to accept the challenge of personally learning and growing, it takes *courage* to step out of one's comfort zone to trial and adopt new ways of working. When N. R. Narayana Murthy decided to relinquish his authority as CEO to take on the novel role of "chief mentor" at Infosys, he had to reinvent himself: "You have to sacrifice yourself first for a big cause before you can ask others to do the same ... A good leader knows how to retreat into the background gracefully while encouraging his successor to become more and more successful in the job."[17] This type of change doesn't have to involve a lot of fanfare. When "Neutron Jack" Welch traded in the tough-guy image he'd acquired during the cost-cutting era at GE and adopted a "hard-headed, soft-hearted" persona instead, he didn't make a big deal about it. All the same, it signified a huge cultural change for both him and his organization.

Some leaders point out that if they knew what they could improve on, they'd already be doing it. After all, shame on them if they aren't already being the best they can be. To this end, we always ask them if they've formally gathered 360-degree feedback on how their perceived mindsets and behaviors tie in with the objectives of the broader change program. We also suggest they have their calendar analyzed to reveal how much time they actually spend on areas related to change priorities. Then we query whether the leader is open to being professionally coached, in response to the findings.

We're yet to find a leader who has done these things and not found areas to work on that have a profoundly positive role modeling impact on the rest of the organization. One senior leader, for example, was surprised to find that for every meeting he attended in the spirit of signaling the importance of the topic at hand, three more meetings would be created for others that otherwise wouldn't have taken place. As part of the change program related to combating bureaucracy, he was actually adding to it! Another leader was surprised to receive feedback that she didn't role model having a customer focus, which was an organizational health goal of the change being pursued. It was hard to escape the feedback, however, when the calendar analysis showed she hadn't spent a single minute with customers in the last month, and a word cloud of her last three company-wide addresses included the word "customer" a total of only three times.

Insights of this nature can be kept private and simply acted on, or they can be shared more broadly. Kevin Sharer, former CEO of Amgen, for example, asked each of his top 75, "What should I do differently?" and spoke candidly to them as a group about his development needs and commitment. In doing so, he inspired his team and others to do the same level of introspection and analysis about what personal change they could undergo in order to be even more effective in moving the organization forward.

## Take Symbolic Actions

For the most senior leader, the quickest way to send shockwaves through an organization is to perform one or two thoughtfully conceived symbolic acts that signal clearly, "Things will be different from now on."

When John Wilder, former CEO of the Texas energy utility TXU, gave a large bonus to a woman who had taken leadership of a key business initiative, he says, "It helped employees understand that rewards will be based on contributions, and that 'pay for performance' could actually be put into practice."[18] Daniel DiMicco of Nucor underscored his "focus on the frontline" by flying commercial airlines as opposed to private jets, forgoing an executive parking place, and making a fresh pot of coffee in the office if he happened to take the last cup.

Personal compensation is one area where simple steps by senior leaders can send powerful messages to everyone else in the organization. When times are hard, some leaders choose to draw a nominal salary and take their compensation in the form of stock options instead to show their commitment to creating value in the long term. John Mackey, CEO of Whole Foods Market, has gone a step further. He is so committed to his company's mission that he's decided not to take compensation of any kind: "I have reached a place in my life where I no longer want to work for money, but simply for the joy of the work itself and to better answer the call to service that I feel so clearly in my own heart."[19]

Going to work at the frontline can be another powerful symbolic act. To show the value he placed on creating a friendly and welcoming atmosphere for customers and colleagues, former Southwest Airlines CEO Herb Kelleher spent his holidays serving peanuts with flight attendants, loading baggage, and assisting ground crews. Michael Dell reinforces the need to stay focused on the customer by spending one day a month in Dell's call center working alongside the staff who deal with customer queries.

We'd like to end with a warning: important though it is for a senior leader to take action that supports organizational change aspirations, it's just as important to avoid behaving in a way that contradicts or undermines them. One packaged goods company was undergoing a change program to capture the value of collaboration. When problems that cut across businesses were brought to his attention, the hockey-loving CEO would dismiss them with, "I don't care how you do it. Crash 'em against the boards if you have to—just get it done." The result: things *didn't* get done, employees were dismayed at the mixed messages, resistance to change mounted, and cynicism prevailed.

## Build a Strong Team

The senior leader's team should be a valuable asset in driving a change program forward. Sharing a meaningful story and role modeling the desired mindsets and behaviors will increase the odds of getting the team on board. But it's vital to devote time and effort to building the team, as well. This involves getting the right people on the team, aligning them on a shared aspiration, and then building them into a high-performing team in how you pursue the aspiration.

## Get the Right People

The senior team of an organization undergoing a large-scale change often includes the same leaders that led it into the state from which it needs to change. In some cases, the need to change is driven by external factors, and as such, is not a reflection of the team. In other cases, however, the choices and actions of the leaders have landed the company in a challenged situation. *Regardless*, a senior leader should always ask whether the leaders are the right people in the right roles for the journey ahead.

Senior leaders should take time to assess the capabilities of the individual team members and then act swiftly on their findings. Some seek third-party input to create an objective basis on which to make their assessments. Many find just taking the time to map team members on a simple matrix of skill (versus what's required in their role going forward, e.g., technical competence, problem-solving capacity, emotional intelligence) and will (versus what's needed to make the change happen, e.g., felt need for change, grit, servant leadership) provides insight into what needs to be done. Some also find it clarifying to use methods such as forced rankings or forced distributions to help them think through where each person on the team stands in terms of capability and commitment.

Once a senior leader is equipped with all the relevant facts, it's not hard to know what to do with team members who are low in both skill and will—those who deliver poor results and exhibit unhelpful behavior. But what about individuals who are "high skill, low will"—those who deliver strong results but behave in unhelpful ways? The answer may lie in coaching and mentoring, redefining roles, and adjusting incentives. Beware, however, the organization will be watching closely to see how these people in particular are dealt with. Jack Welch was in no doubt: "If you get results without living our values, I'm coming for you."[20] Corrado Passera concurs: "If necessary, you have to get rid of those individuals—even the talented ones—who quarrel and cannot work together."[21] When we asked senior leaders to reflect on what they'd do differently on their change programs, 44 percent indicated they'd "move faster to neutralize people resistant to change."[22]

But how do senior leaders know *when* to act? The following questions, inspired by the influence model, offer a litmus test: does the team member know exactly what the expectations are of them in driving the change? Is it clear what the consequences are if he doesn't get on board? Has she been given a chance to build the skills and confidence needed? Is the team member surrounded by others (including oneself) who are role modeling the desired mindsets and behaviors? If the answer to all these questions is yes, then decisive action is justified.

When leaders make tough decisions like these, it shows that they mean business. Some leaders hesitate as they worry such actions might instill an unproductive fear in the organization. In our experience this is almost never the case. Instead, high-performing employees breathe a sigh of relief, grateful that the real issues are finally being dealt with from the top. Low performers begin to opt out, as they see the walls closing in. The majority in the middle get jolted out of their complacency, with many people becoming reinvigorated and choosing to raise their game.

## Align the Team

It falls to the most senior leader to ensure the team is aligned, that it spends time on the right things, and that the time spent is effective. To align the team, the most senior leader should head the "lottery ticket" lesson we introduced in Chapter 3 and have reiterated often since. Even if he or she feels they have the answer, it's important to let the team work through getting there (or to a better place) on their own. A powerful approach to creating shared conviction among a senior team on a performance and health aspiration and the plan to get from here to there is to conduct what we refer to as a "hold up the mirror" workshop.

These sessions start by enabling the team to jointly review the fact base, typically in a gallery walk-type format involving pairs reviewing and discussing posters with the relevant analyses so that they can self-pace their way through versus being marched through a presentation. Then areas of agreement and disagreement on the implications of the fact base are quickly identified, often using electronic polling technology. Real time is then spent on understanding and resolving areas of disagreement, facilitated in ways that ensure the fundamental assumptions come to the surface (an external facilitator is typically used given that the "from" mindsets and behaviors will otherwise very likely characterize the conversation, even though every participant won't feel they are complicit). Where consensus doesn't come, the most senior leader makes the call, and next steps are agreed upon.

Once the performance and health direction is set, the next order of business is for the team to discuss and align on what their collective role in driving the change forward will be—in other words, what can only be achieved by the team working together, as opposed to its individual members? What behaviors should they expect of themselves in order to collectively role model desired mindsets and behaviors? In the spirit of leadership not just being about what leaders do, but what they allow in their presence, what behaviors should they refuse to tolerate? More tactically, what topics and issues should the team spend team time on, and what shouldn't be discussed as a group? How often will the team meet? And where? These elements are often codified into what is referred to as a "team charter" that can then be used as a touchstone for how the team works together going forward.

## Achieve High Performance

Even with the right team in place sharing an aspiration, it takes work to ensure a group of smart, ambitious, and independent-minded individuals stay aligned and deliver on it. Consider the 1992 U.S. men's Olympic basketball team. The names read like a list of the greatest players in the history of the sport: Charles Barkley, Larry Bird, Patrick Ewing, Magic Johnson, Michael Jordan, Karl Malone, Scottie Pippen, and so on. Yet, even though the best players in the world were on the team, in the first month the team lost to a group of college players because, in the words of Pippen, "We didn't know how to play with each other."[23]

On the flipside, consider the 2016 German National football team (*soccer* for our American audience). They won the World Cup, as commentator Søren Frank on World Soccer Talk noted, due to "team effort and a collective approach ... no German player is a star ... the German team has been set up by Löw [the coach] to function as a team, to work like a team, to defend like a team, to attack like a team."[24] Michael Jordan reinforces this recipe for success when he says, "Talent wins games, but teamwork and intelligence wins championships."[25]

Once the team has an aligned direction, the team needs to spend time together on their priorities. The team charter should be formally revisited periodically so that the team can reflect on how it's working together, what's getting in the way of being even more high performing, and take steps to remove any interference. Corrado Passera brought his team together periodically to "share almost everything," "be clear to everyone who is doing what," and "keep the transformation initiatives, budgets, and financial targets knitted together."[26]

As a rule of thumb, 80 percent of the time the team spends together should be devoted to dialogue, and just 20 percent to presentations. Effective dialogue requires a well-structured agenda. Ideally, binding decisions on important topics shouldn't be made until the team has spent ample time on three separate activities: personal reflection, small group discussion, and large group dialogue.

Personal reflection time ensures that members form an independent point of view from the beginning of the conversation. This shouldn't be left to simple pre-reading unless it comes with pre-work that involves providing survey responses to the information. In the meeting, it can be effective to ask everyone to share their views one-by-one, although this approach risks significant biases distorting the conversation. A very efficient and effective way is to use electronic polling. Everyone essentially talks at once, and if everyone agrees, victory can be quickly declared, and the next topic moved to—thus avoiding people talking in "violent agreement." If there are diverse views, those can be surfaced and dealt with in a manner where all parties know the extent to which they may be outliers in the conversation.

Small group discussion typically happens in anywhere from pairs to groups of up to five team members. These discussions enable participants to refine their thinking by exploring assumptions at a deeper level than can be achieved as a full group, act as a way to create initial alignment so that a more focused set of possible solutions will be put forward in the larger group, and strengthens bonds between team members who have the opportunity to better get to know how each other think about the topic at hand. This sometimes isn't possible in video conference formats, though creativity can be used by having hubs where those on video conference convene, and each hub then acts as its own small group (or groups). Note that we don't mention conference calls for a reason. We agree with former Disney CEO Michael Eisner who ruefully noted, "The worst decisions I ever made were on conference calls. It is critical for successful alignment to get your team together and discuss eyeball to eyeball."[27]

Once there has been personal reflection and small group discussion, then a whole-team discussion is in order. If the first two steps have been taken, these conversations tend to be extremely targeted, efficient, and meaningful. Taken together, all three steps create a team experience that is wholly different than what we too often see—overpacked agendas where presentations dominate, the few questions that are asked lead to deep dives into minutiae while the rest of the team disengages, getting by with noncommittal head-nodding.

Building a high-performing team in the manner we've described is harder work than taking a more "dog and pony" show style approach, but it's always worth it. When Steve Luczo made teamwork the top priority in his turnaround of Seagate, for example, it had the desired effect. As his colleague, former CFO Charles Pope, noted, "People in the company now see us as a team. We get feedback that we are on the same wavelength. We are synced now. We respect one another. We've built the ability to align goals."[28]

## Relentlessly Pursue Impact

Former managing director of Time Life, C. D. Jackson, memorably observed that great ideas need landing gears as well as wings. Kicking off a large-scale change program is one thing; and sticking with it through the hard slog of execution is what really matters. There's no substitute for the senior leader channeling his/her personal energy into ensuring that the organization's change effort delivers impact.

## Roll Up Your Sleeves

In any large-scale change program there will be numerous initiatives on the "performance placemat" that we described in Chapter 5. A shortlist of those initiatives—those with the most significant customer, financial, and symbolic value—should have the most senior leader's direct and personal involvement to ensure maximum impact. By being in the flow of the priority initiatives, the senior leader signals their importance, understands the details enough to make decisions that accelerate impact, and provides wisdom and quality control to ensure value is maximized.

For some senior leaders, the need to roll up their sleeves may require them to rethink their priorities. Larry Bossidy, former chairman and CEO of AlliedSignal and former chairman of Honeywell, notes, "Many people regard execution as detail work that's beneath the dignity of a business leader. That's wrong ... it's a leader's most important job."[29] Mickey Drexler, known as the "merchant prince" due to his track record of turning around major retailers such as Gap, Inc., and Ann Taylor, affirms that in leading change, "You have to go, you have to see, you have to feel."[30]

Leaders who roll up their sleeves are willing to come down from the executive suite and help resolve issues. Peter Gossas, head of Sandvik Materials Technology, observes, "If there's a problem, it can be helpful if I come to the work floor, step up on a crate so that everyone can see me, and have a discussion with a shift unit that may be negative to change."[31]

Some senior leaders feel getting involved in initiatives is disempowering to the leaders they've tasked to deliver them. This is true if the senior leader doesn't listen and tries to take over without having a real understanding of what's happening. If, on the other hand, involvement comes from a place of conveying that the initiative is important, the senior leader won't let anything get in the way or slow it down that can be controlled, and they are there both to coach and learn in the process—that's generally viewed as nothing short of inspirational leadership.

## Hold Leaders Accountable

The most senior leader can't and shouldn't be involved in every initiative on the change placemat. However, they do have responsibilities across the full portfolio of initiatives: chairing reviews to assess progress against plans, celebrating successes, helping to solve problems in review meetings, and holding other leaders accountable for keeping the change on track.

Holding leaders accountable involves looking at both activities (Are people doing what they said they would?) and impact (Is it going to create the value we expected?). The most senior leader is also the one who sets the tone for whether equal time and energy in reviews will be spent on performance and health matters, ensuring that short-termism and an over-bias to financial measures doesn't overwhelm those that foreshadow the sustainability of such results.

In keeping with the fairness principle introduced at the end of Chapter 7, one of the roles of the most senior leader is to ensure that decisions are firmly rooted in facts. When Kevin Sharer kicked off the transformation of Amgen, he made it clear that where review meetings were concerned, "The days of winging it are over."[32]

Staying on top of a change program isn't easy. As Larry Bossidy comments, "This immense personal commitment is time-consuming and fraught with emotional wear and tear in giving feedback, conducting dialogues, and exposing your judgment to others."[33] Ultimately, holding people accountable is vital; however, as in the words of Stephen Covey, "Accountability breeds response-ability."[34]

∎ ∎ ∎

The role of the most senior leader is vitally important in making change happen at scale. It is up to this person to make the change meaningful by personalizing the change story, openly engaging others, and spotlighting success. The leader can role model change by undergoing personal change and taking thoughtful symbolic actions. Furthermore, this person ought to build a strong and committed top team by ensuring the right people are in the right roles, investing time in aspiration alignment, and building it into a high-performing team while driving the change forward. Lastly, the most senior leader should relentlessly pursue impact by rolling up her sleeves to support and enable key initiatives and holding leaders accountable to take the right actions and deliver the needed performance and health results.

We acknowledge that to many "type A" senior leaders, the role we've described includes too many soft elements. If you are one of these, we observe to you that research and experience are unequivocal in indicating that these elements matter, regardless if you see immediate value in them or not. We also observe that given your predisposition, getting them right will likely be very hard for you—which makes them ideal starting points for fulfilling your "undergoing personal change" mandate!

# Chapter 9

# The Change Leader's Role

## *What It Takes to Be a Great Change Leader*

You've volunteered, or been voluntold, to lead a large-scale change program on behalf of your organization—congratulations! It's no doubt a tribute to all you have accomplished in your career to date. If you're like most newly appointed heads of large-scale change programs, you'll be feeling a mix of excitement and anxiety about the challenges ahead. The excitement comes from the opportunity to make a difference on an even bigger stage, and to leave a legacy of forever having changed the trajectory of the organization (having "caterpillar to butterfly" impact!). The anxiety comes from the reality that expectations are extremely high, the spotlight will be intense, and the complexity of the job at hand is significant. What's more, you are aware that huge bodies of research indicate you are very unlikely to be successful.

We hope at this point in reading this book your excitement has been magnified and your anxiety diminished. You now know exactly what to *do* to beat the odds. You've got a clear, five-stage roadmap to help you stay focused on what matters for success on both the performance and health dimensions that you'll need to manage. Knowing what to do, however, doesn't necessarily mean you'll *be* a great change leader. Having spent the last eight chapters talking about what you will be "doing," we dedicate this chapter to how to "be" a great change leader. Before we dive in, let's get clearer on the difference between the two.

When you are in *doing* mode, by definition, the goal is to get things done. For example, in the Aspire stage, your thoughts and actions are focused on ensuring the long-term vision is crafted, rolled back to a mid-term aspiration, and that biases are guarded against in the process. You're also getting the organization's health checked, prompting the choice as to where to be exceptional and what broken practices need fixing. It's a lot to do! In this mode you are continually monitoring and evaluating the current situation against the standard of what's desired or required. When mismatches are found, your mind instructs you to take action to reduce the discrepancies.

The *doing* mode is extremely important to drive progress on all the task-related work involved in making change happen. It is decidedly not helpful when it comes to dealing with your own emotional state as a change leader. And your emotional state matters. After all, at the end of the day you are not a human doing, you are a human *being*. As we discussed in the "Master Stroke" at the end of Chapter 4, by endlessly and relentlessly think-ing about the problems, it's all too easy to become characterized by blame, fatigue, and frustration—in particular given that not all the variables related to change program success can be controlled by you. We've met many a change leader who started optimistic, excited, and determined, only to find themselves 12 months into driving change feeling jaded, resigned to "best efforts" progress, and increasingly impatient for their next role.

The *being* elements of change leadership are vital because they are what will keep you passionate about your work and satisfied with your life while leading the change. It enables you to avoid becoming narrowly preoccu-pied with closing the gap between what needs to be done and where things are today. Instead, it processes the current situation without losing the forest for the trees. You confidently tap into your intuition to avoid setbacks in complex situations. You see opportunities and learnings in the challenges that do emerge. You navigate ambiguity with creativity, and in turn create new possibilities for impact.

We realize some of you will read the previous paragraph, perhaps even twice over, and still be scratching your head wondering what we're getting at. We find the analogy to martial arts is instructive to make the distinction. Karate is what is known as a "hard" martial art—focused on blocking what your op-ponent is doing and punching and kicking back. It is based on resistance, and while helpful in some situations, it has the drawback of "what resists, persists."

Aikido, on the other hand, is a "soft" martial art. The goal is not to fight; the goal is to diffuse aggression by using the attacker's energy and flowing with it, redirecting it to where it does no harm. It requires intuitive, split-second discernment of the direction of an incoming attack. It then requires creative twisting and turning in accordance with the opponent's action to use the incoming momentum to off-balance and incapacitate the attacker as you remain fully centered.

As a martial artist in the field of leading change, if you've read this far you know what it means to be a blackbelt at Karate (the Five Frames). In this chapter, you will learn the most important Aikido moves—moves we collectively describe as the art of "centered leadership."

Exhibit 9.1

## The Elements of Centered Leadership

---

## *Being* a Centered Change Leader

Our research indicates there are five elements of "being" a centered change leader (Exhibit 9.1.)

When combined, these elements give change leaders the resilience and emotional capacity to lead the "doing" of the Five Frames of Performance and Health.

1. **Meaning:** knowing deep down why it is that what you're doing matters to you and enabling others to tap into their own sources of motivation and purpose.
2. **Framing:** discovering opportunities in adversity by viewing even the most difficult problems in ways that open up constructive and creative solutions.
3. **Connecting:** taking active steps to build a web of mutually beneficial internal and external sustaining relationships.
4. **Engaging:** generating the confidence and agility to successfully step up and act in the face of uncertainty and risk.

**5. Energizing:** investing systematically in fueling your physical, mental, emotional, and spiritual energy and creating the practices and norms to energize others.

Our research shows that these elements of centered leadership are mutually reinforcing.[1] Those who frequently practice all five feel passionate about their work, effective as leaders, and are satisfied with their lives (Exhibit 9.2.).

Knowing that the power of these elements lies in their combination, we'll now take a closer look at each one.

## Meaning

In the centered leadership model, "meaning" relates to a change leader's ability to motivate him or herself and others from within—grounded in a deep-seated belief that "what I/we are doing matters." Research by leading thinkers such as Danah Zohar and Richard Barrett illuminates where this motivation comes from. It's not about charisma and cheerleading—it's about engaging fully in

---

## Exhibit 9.2
## Multiplying the Benefits

Percent of respondents achieving high level of success in each outcome by number of dimensions practiced[1]

| Centered leadership Number of dimensions practiced frequently[1] | Passion for work | Leadership effectiveness | Life satisfaction |
|---|---|---|---|
| 0 out of 5 | 14 | 12 | 15 |
| 1 out of 5 | 15 | 18 | 18 |
| 2 out of 5 | 24 | 29 | 25 |
| 3 out of 5 | 42 | 45 | 47 |
| 4 out of 5 | 50 | 63 | 53 |
| 5 out of 5 | 100 | 100 | 100 |

1 Respondents answered a series of questions to assess how frequently they practice each dimension of centered leadership; "frequently" and "high level of success" both refer to the top 20 percent of respondents in each group.

one's own purpose and helping others connect with theirs.[2] When people act out of a connection to their source of authentic purpose, they become more compelling as role models and more inspiring as communicators. Of course, the opposite is equally true: when you can't help wondering, "Why am I doing this?" it's hard to find the motivation to drive hard for results, and people around you perceive your lack of conviction and find the same.

Change leaders who score high on meaning feel a deep personal commitment to the work they do and pursue their change goals with energy and enthusiasm. Of all the dimensions of centered leadership, meaning makes the greatest contribution to satisfaction with work and life. In fact, our research shows that its impact on overall life satisfaction is five times more powerful than that of any other dimension.[3] This is confirmed by thinkers in the field of positive psychology (the branch of psychology that focuses not on treating mental illness but on making normal life more fulfilling) who have determined that having meaning is the foremost ingredient in the recipe for happiness.[4] Psychologists Kennon Sheldon and Sonja Lyubomirsky, for example, show that meaningful work is the best way to increase overall happiness over the long term.[5]

The notion that leaders should be "meaning-makers" in the business lexicon is hardly news. Influential business thinker Gary Hamel urges modern managers to see themselves as "entrepreneurs of meaning."[6] Earlier in this book, we talked extensively about various techniques related to meaning-making. For example, tapping into the "lottery ticket effect" (increasing motivation for execution by involvement in crafting the solution that needs to be executed) and "five sources of meaning" (ensuring that your change narrative speaks to each). These, however, are all about the "doing" of meaning.

At the "being" level, there are three keys to mastering meaning. The first involves recognizing and using your unique *strengths*. As with the bowling team experiment in Chapter 4, when we are building on strengths we are more likely to be motivated to excel than if we are solely focused on addressing weaknesses.

Secondly, it involves having a strong sense of your leadership *purpose*. This isn't "hitting the targets" (that's the "doing" purpose); here we're talking about the impact you want who you are as a leader to have on others. To determine this, in addition to your strengths, consider your past—when in your life have you felt deeply happy and fulfilled? What have you learned from challenges you've faced? Also consider what is your essence. What core qualities have always been true about you? What would you love to contribute before you die? What is the biggest possibility for the impact you'll have as a human being? Then decide for yourself what you see the purpose is that sits beneath who you are as a leader in the workplace, regardless of role. What is the leadership legacy you want to leave when you retire (what do you aspire to characterizing the retirement speeches about you from colleagues, family, and friends)? And what does that mean for the leadership legacy you aspire to leave in the change leader role you are embarking on?

Thirdly, mastering meaning involves giving voice to your leadership *vision* by sharing it with others who will surround you with helpful challenge and support. With these three things in place, you'll find your actions and decisions are guided by a strong compass that keeps you grounded in what matters, whether in times of triumph or stress.

## Framing

In Chapter 4, we talked about the importance of "naming and reframing" underlying organizational mindsets to unlock improved organizational health and business performance. Similarly, as a change leader it's vital to become aware of the otherwise subconscious frames you personally see the world and process your experiences through. The frames you choose can make a huge difference to personal and professional outcomes alike. While the exploration of an individual's mindsets to uncover and shift performance-limiting or self-defeating viewpoints is intensely personal, there is one frame in particular that is of utmost importance to all change leaders: *optimism*.

It's easy to see how positive framing can improve change leadership capabilities. Pessimists tend to view negative situations as permanent, pervasive, and personal. This can limit their range of thinking, preventing them from seeing strategic options and rapidly draining energy in a downward spiral. Conversely, optimists view negative situations as temporary, specific, and externally caused. This helps them see the facts for what they are, identify new possibilities, and act swiftly.

Imagine you're giving a presentation to your bosses. They seem distracted, and halfway through, the most senior leader gets up and leaves the room. At the end of your presentation, you get a subdued response rather than the fanfare you'd secretly been hoping for. As you leave the room, what are the thoughts that run through your head? Do you wonder if your content or delivery were off the mark? Do you start to worry that management has lost confidence in you? Could your career be starting to spiral? If so, you have framed the situation through the lens of the pessimist. If you're not careful, you'll relentlessly dwell on the possible negatives to the extent that they ultimately paralyze your ability to take risks—something all change leaders must do to be effective.

If you are an optimist, your mind goes to altogether different places. You wonder if the team may be grappling with an urgent problem that's only just arisen? Perhaps your presentation came at a bad time, and yet they value you so much that they didn't want to cancel your slot? You might even have taken the opportunity to stop and ask, "Should I carry on with this, or do you need to be somewhere else right now? And is there anything I can do to be helpful?" These optimistic lenses create *resilience*: the ability to absorb shocks, assess their implications, and respond effectively. Inevitably things won't go according to plan in all cases, and when they go wrong, it's the optimists who recover gracefully.

Optimism correlates with success and much more: health and popularity, for starters. As former U.S. President Bill Clinton famously remarked, "No one in his right mind wants to be led by a pessimist." Author Roald Dahl captures the notion in saying, "Those who don't believe in magic will never find it."[7] Consider Thomas Edison's response when, at age 67, his laboratory was destroyed by fire. A perennial optimist, what was his response to seeing his life's work lay in ruins? "There's great value in disaster," he reflected, "All our mistakes are now burned and we can start anew." Three weeks later, he produced his first phonograph. Or how about Steve Jobs' view on getting fired from Apple in 1984, just eight years after he co-founded it? Instead of it being a career-ending blow as a pessimist would view it, he chose to believe, "Getting fired from Apple was the best thing that could have ever happened to me. The heaviness of being successful was replaced by the lightness of being a beginner again... it freed me to enter one of the most creative periods of my life."[8]

Of course, not everyone is a born optimist. Many of us aren't, and researchers say that as much as 50 percent of a person's outlook is genetically determined. However, in *Learned Optimism*, Martin Seligman argues that optimism can be acquired.[9] Pessimists can't change their basic personality, but they can learn to apply the tools that optimists habitually use, without even realizing it, to put events and situations into their proper context. The techniques to do so are the same self-awareness techniques as those described in the "Make it Personal" section of Chapter 6. It starts by working through your personal "iceberg" (looking into the mindset-related drivers of your behavior) to explore in what situations you default to optimistic or pessimistic frames. From there, you explore the root-cause needs you are fulfilling in doing so (hopes and fears related to failure, rejection, hurt, being judged, being found out, not having all the answers, and so on). With this *self-awareness*, you then explore possibilities for how these can be fulfilled through an optimistic lens instead.

To be clear, optimistic framing is very different than the optimism bias we discussed as something leaders should avoid in Chapter 3. This isn't about persisting in trying to resolve an intractable problem long after it's become time to move on. Nor is it the same as what people call "the power of positive thinking." Research shows that talking yourself into a positive outlook has at best a temporary effect. Genuine optimists, on the other hand, tend to be realists. Perhaps surprisingly, they are more able to face the brutal facts than pessimists are. This dynamic is vividly illustrated in the "Stockdale paradox," described by Jim Collins in his book *Good to Great*. Admiral Jim Stockdale was the highest-ranking U.S. military officer in the so-called "Hanoi Hilton" prisoner of war camp at the height of the Vietnam War. Imprisoned from 1965 to 1973, he was frequently tortured, and had no prisoners' rights, no release date, and no certainty that he would ever see his family again. How did he survive? "I never doubted not only that I would get out, but also that I would prevail in the end and turn the experience into the defining event of my life … [But] you must never confuse faith that you will prevail in the end—which you can never afford to lose—with the discipline to confront the most brutal facts of your current reality, whatever they might be."[10]

## Connecting

Another mark of the centered change leader is the ability to forge relationships with influential people from different stakeholder groups. Such leaders build complex networks that both amplify their personal influence and accelerate their personal development because of the diversity of ideas and experiences that they encounter through contact with others.

Psychology has long established that relationships are essential to our well-being. It turns out that they are just as important to our success. Research from Harvard professors Ronald Heifetz and Marty Linsky indicates that people who are thoughtful about personal relationships are more successful as change leaders.[11] Similarly, management scholar Ernest O'Boyle and colleagues showed that individuals' levels of *emotional intelligence* (EQ) has profound effects on performance, above and beyond those factors related to personality and IQ.[12] Studies at PepsiCo confirm these conclusions. In comparable bottling plants, teams with the highest EQ performed 20 percent above the norm, while those with the lowest rating performed 20 percent below.

Psychologist and science journalist Daniel Goleman popularized the concept of EQ in his book *Emotional Intelligence: Why it can matter more than IQ*. In it he reported his findings from analyzing the difference between "good" and "high" performers in thousands of positions in hundreds of companies. He found that 90 percent of the difference related to emotional intelligence—EQ, not IQ.[13] Perhaps more importantly, he showed that EQ is learnable. If leaders reflect on the right topics and questions, they can improve their ability to connect with others at an emotional level and so adopt the relational styles that will achieve the best results.

To be a great connector, our first suggestion to change leaders is that they invest time in building their EQ to best equip themselves for the role. Take the concept of trust, for example, which is fundamental to establishing strong relationships. If we asked you how trustworthy you are, it's likely you'd respond with "very." If we asked you the extent to which you embody the four elements of trust individually, however, you may gain some insight into how you can better connect with others. How reliable are you (you do what you say you'll do)? How accepting are you (listening to and respecting others' viewpoints empathetically and without personal judgement)? How open are you (giving and asking for input freely)? How congruent are you (saying and doing what you really feel and believe)? And if you were to answer these questions in the context of your behavior with your family versus at work, do the answers change? Why or why not, and does that synch up with the leadership legacy you want to leave that we discussed when talking about "meaning" a few sections earlier?

Our second suggestion to change leaders is to be strategic about the *networking* they need to maximize success in their role, and to invest methodically in building that network. In doing so, they should be aware of their gender and other biases in thinking about the network they need. Researchers have shown that whereas women prefer to build a small number of deep relationships (helping to get "let me tell you how it really is" type of advice), men tend to build broader but shallower networks (helpful in providing a wide range of resources to expand knowledge and opportunities).[14] Great change leaders have both kinds.

When we advocate building a network, we aren't just talking about one that consists of our peers or superiors in the organization hierarchy. We're also thinking beyond the influence leader-types we discussed in Chapter 6. We believe you should follow networking consultant Carole Kammen's advice to stress-test your network and ensure it provides a whole host of benefits: wisdom and experience, a sympathetic ear, challenges and shifts in perspective, help in navigating the social system, nonstop coaching, visionary inspiration, and sponsors who will pound the table for you. Sometimes these can take different forms than you'd expect. For example, when GE's Jack Welch was looking for mentoring on how to use the internet effectively, he hit on the idea of "reverse mentoring"—asking two people under the age of 30 at GE to help him get up to speed.[15]

Finally, we encourage change leaders to think through how to ensure there is *reciprocity* in the relationships in their network—equal give and take. Why? As social psychologist Jonathan Haidt notes, "Relationships persist to the degree that both people involved believe that what they are getting out of the relationship is proportionate to what they put in."[16]

## Engaging

Engaging is first about choosing to be fully *present* in all situations related to making the change happen. There's no question in anyone's mind that you're in it to win it. Second, it's about the willingness to be *bold* when needed. It's the change leader who recognizes, in the words of Irish footballer Jim Goodwin, that "the impossible is often the untried." Finally, it's about taking *accountability* for positively influencing their own, their organization's (team, peers, boss, employees), and their organization's stakeholders' experience of the change. This is the change leader who approaches work and life with the mindset of, "If it's to be, it's up to me."

On the other hand, people who are disengaged tend to be passive in their interactions, incremental in their actions, and feel that events are out of their control. Rather than trying to fix problems, they attribute blame. In our research on centered leadership, respondents who indicate they were poor at engaging—with risk, with fear, or even with opportunity—also lack confidence: only 13 percent thought they had the skills to lead change.[17]

Engagement differs from framing in that positive framing enables us to *see* an opportunity, while engagement gives us the courage to risk *capturing* it. Writing in 1951, the mountaineer and author W. H. Murray sums up one of the things that makes engaging so powerful: "Until one is committed, there is hesitancy, the chance to draw back, always ineffectiveness... the moment one definitely commits oneself, then providence moves, too." For him, engaging sets in motion a whole chain of events that "[raises] in one's favor all manner of unforeseen incidents, meetings, and material assistance which no man could have dreamt would have come his way."[18]

So how can we expand our level of engagement? It helps if we have an elementary grasp of how the physiology of the brain governs our instinctive responses. Put simply, the brain consists of three parts. The first is the brain stem, which deals with basic functions such as breathing. The second is the limbic system, which regulates emotions. The third is the neocortex, which governs logical reasoning and creativity.

Within the limbic system is an organ called the amygdala, whose function is to protect us from physical or emotional harm. As information about our surroundings enters our senses, the amygdala tests it on the way to the neocortex to determine whether we have time to think. If it detects a threat, it short-circuits our rational thought processes and prompts an immediate reaction. This process is often referred to as an "amygdala hijack"; we don't choose the response, it simply happens to us. When we're hijacked, our responses are quite primal—falling into the categories of fight, flight, or freeze.

Let's use some physical examples to bring these to life. Let's say it's April 1st, which in many Western cultures is known as April Fool's day—a day where playing harmless practical jokes and spreading hoaxes is celebrated. You are on your guard with your coworkers who tend to be pranksters even on "normal" days. As you walk into your office you are pleased to see everything appears to be in order. You proceed to sit down on your office chair, not realizing that an air horn has been rigged beneath it to go off as soon as it bears your weight. As 130 decibels of sound is blown, what is your response? You instinctively leap away from the chair with a panicked scream, landing with muscles tense and heart racing. It's only when you're safely off the chair and the sound has stopped that your brain takes the time to work out what's happened—and to notice your colleagues are laughing hysterically outside the glass walls of your office!

So what just happened? After all, it's very unlikely you are going to be in a life or death situation sitting on an office chair. Further, you were mentally on guard for a prank to happen today. Yet your amygdala was triggered, and your response was hijacked. There was nothing you could do about it. Thinking first and acting second could have ended in disaster, or so it seemed in the moment. You just experienced a *flight* response.

Now, let's say later that night you are home alone. As you walk through your dining room, you are startled by something you see in the corner of your eye, a movement of sorts. You find yourself instantly still and silent. You're experiencing a primal *freeze* response that attempts to keep a potential predator unaware of your presence by blending in. You then regain your composure and assess the situation, only to realize the effect was caused by the reflection of headlights from cars on the street outside reflecting off of the new vase of flowers your coworkers had purchased for you as an apology for the earlier scare! Even though there is no danger, you're now craving some company and decide to drive to a friend's house. En route, someone rudely cuts you off on the freeway. You feel a surge of adrenalin and let out a string of expletives, offering hand gestures to suit. Welcome to the *fight* response!

It's clear from the examples above that our amygdala assumes the worst. This is generally not a big problem in life when it comes to our responses to potential physical threats, but it does become problematic in the workplace and other social interactions. Why? Recall that our amygdala doesn't just protect us from physical pain, but also emotional hurt. For example, when a colleague says after a meeting, "I have some feedback for you," many people go into fight mode and listen defensively. Others go into flight mode and avoid having the conversation. Still others freeze and hear the feedback but aren't really listening. This can set off a downward spiral both internally (e.g., resentment, thoughts of revenge, writing people off) and externally (e.g., passive aggression, feigning agreement, an outright argument).

There is a different response available that is vitally important for change leaders to master. Instead of the "reactive response" that lets instinct take over, a leader can choose a "creative response," in which they take owner-ship of the situation, understand it more fully, and seek a win-win solution. Choosing the creative response starts with being aware of the physical cues that let you know a hijack is in process. These differ from individual to in-dividual, but typical examples include sweaty palms, increased heart rate, butterflies, flushing/turning red, clenched jaw, and so on. As soon as you feel these coming on, the next step is to activate your neocortex by asking yourself a question. The most helpful questions involve taking personal ac-countability for the situation. Examples include: "What is my role in creating this?"; "What can I learn from this?"; "How can we both win in this situa-tion?"; and "How can this situation bring us closer?". To give your rational mind time to regain control, it's often helpful to ask a question of the other party such as, "Tell me more" or "Help me understand further." The folk wis-dom of counting to 10 before reacting also applies, which effectively gives your neocortex a chance to process the situation at hand.

Consider the e-mail that you read at 2 a.m. while exhausted after a tough day trying to get one of your initiative teams staffed that says, "Not only do I think Jane is too valuable in what she's doing to go full time, but I'm also thinking we may want to revisit if the initiative is really necessary." The re-active response would dash off an immediate response copying the senior sponsor of the initiative along the lines of, "Really? We agreed … This type of backtracking is exactly why … If you don't … I'm copying … It's unac-ceptable that … I expect …" and so on. A more creative response would be, "Thanks for getting back to me. I'm keen to understand more here—let's get on the phone tomorrow," followed by getting some rest and strategizing with the executive sponsor in advance of the call regarding how to get the leader back on board with the program.

Change leaders can also take steps to eliminate unnecessary and un-helpful hijacks altogether. Doing so starts with taking time to understand one's triggers (e.g., criticism, feeling judged, integrity questioned, credibil-ity questioned, being interrupted, excessive details, unclear expectations). Once understood, exploring the root causes as to why these act as triggers can often reveal how formative experiences hardwired one's amygdala to have disproportionate responses. This puts leaders at the point of choice as to whether they want experiences from deep in their past to affect how they think and respond in the present and to let go of the often irrational fears that are driving them. In doing so, they are effectively reprogramming their amygdala.

Finally, there are also numerous tools from the field of mindfulness that are the equivalent of lifting weights for the muscle of managing one's amyg-dala. Mindfulness is the basic human ability to be present, aware of our in-the-moment thoughts, feelings, bodily sensations, and the surrounding environment, yet not overly reactive or overwhelmed by any of these things.

By being fully present, one isn't rehashing the past or worrying about the future. In this state, change leaders rarely get triggered, and when they do they are facile in ensuring it doesn't lead to unintended consequences.

There are numerous techniques to improve one's mindfulness through quality sleep practices, meditation, mindful movement and eating practices, among many others. As mindfulness increases, reactive response patterns decrease—gone are experiences of withdrawing, justifying, attacking, staying quiet, punishing, swearing, avoiding, and resignation. Enter instead more experiences of feeling of being in control, confidence to achieve high aspirations, and willingness to take bold actions.[19]

## Energizing

We've already discussed in Chapter 6 how, at the organizational level, change programs need to generate more energy than they consume. The same is true at the individual level, in particular for the change leader and his or her team. This means systemically restoring their own energy levels and creating the conditions for others to do likewise.

There are three ways we encourage change leaders to generate energy. The first is to heighten their *energy literacy* relating to what they personally find energy-generating and depleting. The second is to proactively *build recovery practices* into their daily routines. The third is to create the conditions for *flow* experiences to happen as often as possible.

Energy literacy enables change leaders to manage their energy with as much or more rigor than they manage their time. Doing so has out-sized benefits, as well. Time is finite, so managing it is like dividing up a pie. But if you manage energy well, you generate more, and so the whole pie gets bigger.[20] Life is full of things that generate and deplete our energy. Which is which, however, isn't always obvious. The same activity can have different effects on different people. Take driving home at the end of the day. For some, it can be calming and restorative—a buffer between work and home that provides a space to detach and recover from the events of the day. For others, the same drive in the same car in the same traffic can be stressful and draining. Or take folding laundry. Some enjoy the feeling of warm clothing just out of the dryer, find comfort in the order they are creating and the feeling of "getting something done" that is tangible. Others couldn't imagine a more mindless use of their time.

Practically speaking, what energy literacy enables you to do is identify what generates and depletes your personal stocks of four types of energy: mental, emotional, spiritual, and physical. Armed with this knowledge, you can then adjust your days and weeks so that you don't create energy troughs—long periods of time doing energy-depleting activities, after which you're ready to give up. Instead, you can sequence activities so that your baseline energy levels are more moderated, with generators interspersed with the depleters. You can also delegate as many energy-depleting activities to others as possible. As per our driving home and folding laundry examples, for many of these activities there will be someone who finds them energy-generating, thereby creating an energy "win-win." This can be done at work and at home.

The next tool for energizing is creating *recovery practices*. It's important to be aware that no one can stay in high-intensity work mode all the time. Consider a marathon runner. They don't run marathons every day, and after every race they take time to recover then build up appropriately for the next one. Or take driving: you can't just keep the pedal to the floor indefinitely or you're only going to move forward until your fuel tank runs empty or your engine overheats. By stopping to refuel and routinely maintain the engine, you can go whatever distance you need to—and ultimately in less time than if you tried to go all the way at top speed but broke down along the way.

The most successful change leaders formally structure time into their days, weeks, and months to restore and renew themselves in whatever ways work for them. This could be as simple as regularly going for a walk, spending time with friends, exercising, reading a book, meditating, getting enough sleep, stopping work to eat a nutritious meal, having technology-free time, or planning a vacation. Be warned: if you can't oscillate between intensity and recovery, you'll quickly find yourself moving from high-intensity positive emotion (peak performance) to high-intensity negative emotion (anger, frustration, impatience, stress). If you continue to ignore the advice to build in recovery time, be warned that it will be forced upon you in its negative form—burnout and depression.

The third tool for energizing is to look for what psychologist Mihály Csíkszentmihályi describes as *flow experiences*, when work becomes effortless and the concept of time seems to stand still.[21] Athletes describe this feeling as being "in the zone"; musicians call it "in the groove." Csíkszentmihályi studied thousands of subjects, from sculptors to factory workers, and asked them to record their feelings at intervals throughout the working day. When he correlated flow to performance, he found that individuals with frequent experiences of flow were more productive and derived greater satisfaction from their work. They also set themselves goals to increase their capabilities to meet greater challenges, thereby tapping into a seemingly limitless well of energy. In fact, their experience of flow was so pleasurable that they expressed a willingness to repeat flow-generating experiences, even if they were not being paid to do so!

Sounds great, but how do you get into flow? According to Csíkszentmihályi, it happens when we set meaningful goals that challenge us and require all our skills (related very much to what we covered above in our discussion on meaning), when we give an effort our full attention and focus (as we covered in our discussion on engaging) and when we receive regular feedback so that we can fine-tune our efforts for the greatest possible impact (something our networks can help us with). But what if we do every one of these things and still fail in achieving the outcomes we strive for? If that happens, and there are sure to be times when it does, our ability to pick ourselves up off the floor, use the experience to learn and grow, and continue to build toward a positive future (as discussed in the framing section) is key. As such, this is where all of the elements of centered leadership come together and enable us to tap into all of our energy sources in every moment we spend leading change!

■ ■ ■

We realize that it will feel clichéd to many readers for us to close this chapter with the well-known quote from Shakepeare's *Hamlet*, but it's obviously the right question for you as a change leader: "To be, or not to be?" "To be" is to act out of a deep sense of *meaning*. It's *framing* challenges as opportunities to learn and grow. It is *connecting* productively with a broad and deep network of important influencers. It's *engaging* creatively, confidently, and proactively in the face of adversity versus being "hijacked" into fight, flight, or freeze responses. It's systematically *energizing* yourself physically, mentally, emotionally and spiritually throughout the journey.

We hope that you can see the power and benefits of you "being" a great change leader, in addition to "doing" the right things to make change happen. We also encourage you to consider the power and benefits of all of the influence leaders also acting as centered leaders. And how about if 25 to 30 percent of the organization was characterized by centered change leadership? These aren't rhetorical questions. In fact, the Personal Insight Workshops (PIWs) mentioned in Chapter 6 are designed to do precisely that. They can be used to build your skills and confidence so that you become a powerful role model in all the areas we've described. As such, we recommend that you, your team, and a cadre of influence leaders become the pilot group for the PIWs. Once you've been through it (and made it better through your feedback), it can then roll out to a critical mass.

In practical terms, then, the work related to the "doing" and "being" aspects of change leadership are merged together in the Five Frames methodology—in very much the same way that performance and health become one in the process.

# Chapter 10

## Making It Happen
### *Do You Have What It Takes?*

In the 1999 film *The Matrix*, the protagonist, Neo, is offered a choice of two pills: one red, one blue. If he takes the red pill, it will show him that he's living in an illusion. He'll discover the painful truth that reality is far more complex and demands far more from him than he'd ever imagined. But if he chooses the blue pill, he'll go back to his old life, in blissful ignorance of the illusion. After a moment's thought, he takes the red pill—a choice that marks the beginning of an epic personal journey. In a series of heroic acts, Neo finally frees the human race from a prison: one it had created for itself through its dependence on intelligent machines that would ultimately turn against it.

We suspect that many leaders—perhaps you?—will be faced with a similar choice after reading this book. If you choose the red pill, you're committing yourself to adopting the approach to making change happen in the way that we've outlined here, an approach that is equally balanced between performance and health. The catch is that if you take this path, it will be more challenging than others you could follow and will make more demands of you as a leader both in terms of "doing" and "being." And despite the science that we've brought to bear, it's still a path that leads you into unknown territory as you likely haven't personally led or experienced the approach before—it's a leap of faith, if you will.

The alternative is the blue pill. Put the book down or hand it to a friend or colleague and go about managing and leading in the same way you've always done. Chances are it's served you reasonably well in the past, it keeps you within your comfort zone, and it fits in with what the people around you have come to expect. Maybe the change program you lead won't be as fully successful as it could otherwise be (the "butterfly"), but at least things will move forward ("a bigger, fuzzier caterpillar"). As long as things don't go south, you'll move to a new role soon enough and a stronger foundation will be there for the next leader to build on.

This chapter is for those of you who choose the red pill. It's for those who feel, as we do, that it's simply not good enough to apply traditional approaches that yield 30 percent success rates. In the spirit of Einstein's notion that, "Insanity is doing the same thing and expecting a different result," these leaders want a better way to change. They now see clearly that the balancing of human and mechanistic approaches that comes from applying the Five Frames of Performance and Health is proven to be that better way. It's also for those who want to deliver an impact that isn't just part of their job, it's part of their leadership legacy. Beyond the financial impact, they'll expand what's possible for individuals and the organization by building capability and reframing limiting mindsets. They'll delight not just shareholders, but also customers and other stakeholders who will see and experience the change as a beacon for "doing things the right way." They'll have built the organization's muscle for making change happen—leaving it more agile and able to shape a winning future in an ever-changing industry context.

In this chapter, we answer the top five most frequently asked questions we get from those who choose the red pill: What to do if you can't get your senior leader on board? What does the program of work look like for putting the Five Frames into practice? How can you catch up to address weaknesses or close gaps when your change program is already in mid-flight? How should you measure health improvements over time? In the context that we've covered an extraordinary amount of ground in a lot of detail in this book, what do we see are the most important takeaways for change leaders? We'll then close with a few parting thoughts to encourage you on your way!

## What If I Can't Get My Senior Leader on Board?

During the many Change Leader Forums we've held over the past few years, we've heard this question more often than any other. People say, "I have real conviction that putting an equal emphasis on performance and health and using Five Frames to do so is the way we should drive change, but my senior leader doesn't get it and won't support it—in particular, the health side of the equation. What can I do?" In response, we offer three pieces of advice.

First, a question for you: Have you applied the thinking behind the influence model to your boss? Let's start with fostering understanding and conviction: have you discussed using a balanced performance and health approach with them directly, or are you assuming he or she won't get it? Have you understood what your boss really cares about—the sources of meaning that motivate her or him (remember, contrary to what your logical mind might tell you, there's an 80 percent chance it's far more than just delivering the numbers)—and have you drawn on these passions to tell a compelling story about why this is the right way to approach the change?

Now let's move to role modeling. Have you identified who your leader looks to for advice, and got these individuals on your side? Have you put your leader in contact with other senior leaders or advisers who've gone through performance and health transformations of their own and can share their battle-hardened wisdom and experience?

Moving to the next influence lever related to building skills and confidence, have you shared this book (or a summary tailored to your specific situation) with him or her? Or have you had an expert on the approach join a conversation with him or her? Would she or he be willing to attend a Change Leaders Forum?

When it comes to the final lever of reinforcement using formal mechanisms—incentives, structures, processes, and systems—you may have little control over how these levers affect your boss. At the same time, running the OHI survey can give you a fact base specific to your organization on which to have the conversation about current and desired alignment on internal direction, quality of execution, and capacity for renewal. From there, the conversation about applying the Five Frames becomes a natural next step.

We're struck by how often the assumption that one's leader won't be comfortable with the idea of placing as much emphasis on health as on performance proves untrue. More often than not, it comes down to a misperception: it's not that leaders actually reject the idea of working on health with equal rigor and discipline, but rather that they're unaware of a scientific approach to do so that's both practical and reliable.

If using the influence model in the manner described here isn't enough to get your leader on board, our second piece of advice is to find a way to prove the power of the approach on a small scale. Along the same lines as our apple analogy in Chapter 6, talking about a successful change is different than providing a taste of its impact. If you can find a small-scale pilot in your organization that is less dependent on senior leader support to be successful, either because an appetite for change already exists (or can be developed quickly), or because your leader is willing to lend support on an experimental basis, then you have the opportunity for a "taste test." That should be enough to prove the benefits of making an apple a day part of the management menu, so to speak.

Our third piece of advice is this: if none of these suggestions pans out, ask for forgiveness instead of permission. All the evidence we've found shows that even if you can't adopt all our recommendations, every aspect of health that you pursue gives you a better chance of becoming and staying successful. It's a bit like your own health: even if your favorite meal is burgers and chips, going to the gym three times a week still pays dividends. So, although you'd undoubtedly do better to have your senior leader on board, you're not automatically doomed to failure if you don't; it's just that achieving the level of success you aspire to will be more difficult.

In everything we've said here, we've assumed that not having your senior leader on board simply means that she or he is unlikely to play the role we described in Chapter 8. That's one thing. But if for some reason your senior leader is actively opposed to your performance and health efforts, that's something else entirely. If you find yourself in this situation and even after following the steps described in this chapter, it remains, you'd be wise to consider investing your time and energy in another organization. Otherwise, research and experience are very clear that you'll be banging your head against a wall with very low probability of breaking it down. In other words, when you can't change your leader, it's time to change your leader (by moving to another part of the organization or leaving it altogether)!

## What Does It Look Like to Put the Five Frames into Practice?

In Part I of this book, we shared that when you put equal emphasis on performance and health, you'll increase your odds of successfully leading large-scale change from 30 percent to 79 percent. In Part II of this book, we shared the Five Frames of Performance and Health approach that described all of the steps required to achieve the right balance in every stage of the change program. This approach is summarized in Exhibit 10.1.

This is the overall roadmap and work plan. The work is directional in that you shouldn't move from one stage to the next until you've completed all of the needed steps. Bear in mind, however, that what you learn during one stage may prompt the need to refine decisions you've made in an earlier one—in that way, the process is iterative. Once you've addressed all of the elements in all of the stages, the odds are that your organization will be higher performing and healthier—able to continuously improve itself going forward.

One element that doesn't jump off the page in Exhibit 10.1 is how and when the senior team convenes as a team to make decisions together. This is in part because the answer to the question is very context-dependent, whereas everything included in the exhibit can be applied to almost every change challenge and opportunity, as the examples in this book demonstrate. You will recall, however, that we did address this topic in part in Chapter 8, as we discussed using the "hold up the mirror" session technique to align the team and then described techniques to enable it to become a high-performing team over time.

Exhibit 10.1

# A Proven Approach to Leading Large-Scale Change

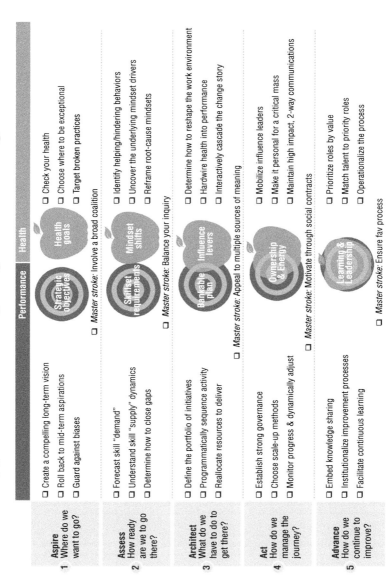

|  | Performance | Health |
|---|---|---|
| **Aspire** 1 Where do we want to go? | ☐ Create a compelling long-term vision<br>☐ Roll back to mid-term aspirations<br>☐ Guard against biases | **Strategic objectives** / **Health goals**<br>☐ Check your health<br>☐ Choose where to be exceptional<br>☐ Target broken practices<br>☐ *Master stroke:* Involve a broad coalition |
| **Assess** 2 How ready are we to go there? | ☐ Forecast skill "demand"<br>☐ Understand skill "supply" dynamics<br>☐ Determine how to close gaps | **Skillset requirements** / **Mindset shifts**<br>☐ Identify helping/hindering behaviors<br>☐ Uncover the underlying mindset drivers<br>☐ Reframe root-cause mindsets<br>☐ *Master stroke:* Balance your inquiry |
| **Architect** 3 What do we have to do to get there? | ☐ Define the portfolio of initiatives<br>☐ Programmatically sequence activity<br>☐ Reallocate resources to deliver | **Behavior plan** / **Influence levers**<br>☐ Determine how to reshape the work environment<br>☐ Hardwire health into performance<br>☐ Interactively cascade the change story<br>☐ *Master stroke:* Appeal to multiple sources of meaning |
| **Act** 4 How do we manage the journey? | ☐ Establish strong governance<br>☐ Choose scale-up methods<br>☐ Monitor progress & dynamically adjust | **Ownership & Energy**<br>☐ Mobilize influence leaders<br>☐ Make it personal for a critical mass<br>☐ Maintain high impact, 2-way communications<br>☐ *Master stroke:* Motivate through social contracts |
| **Advance** 5 How do we continue to improve? | ☐ Embed knowledge sharing<br>☐ Institutionalize improvement processes<br>☐ Facilitate continuous learning | **Learning & Leadership**<br>☐ Prioritize roles by value<br>☐ Match talent to priority roles<br>☐ Operationalize the process<br>☐ *Master stroke:* Ensure fav process |

235

That said, the pattern we observe most often is that the senior team convenes at the beginning of the effort to align on adopting the performance and health approach to making the change happen. This gives the team a common language and methodology to work with during the change process. They then convene again roughly halfway through each stage so as to generate hypotheses for the current stage based on an initial set of facts, and to make final decisions from the last stage having had their hypotheses road-tested by the working team. During the Act stage, which can often last for many months or even years, the senior team typically meets monthly in an Executive Steering Committee capacity to review progress on performance and health and adjust efforts as needed. Keep in mind that, all the while, as individuals, the team members will be involved in the work throughout the process—be it being interviewed in the Aspire and Assess stages, brainstormed with in the Architect stage, as initiative sponsors in the Act and Advance stages, and so on.

## How Can We Catch Up in Areas We've Neglected?

As management consultants, we often receive calls from leaders whose change programs have somehow gotten stuck. On inspection, we typically find that the reason they can't move forward is that they haven't paid sufficient attention to some aspect of health or performance at an earlier stage of their change efforts. The question is then how to get the program back on track. Can the organization make up for what it has neglected? Does it need to start all over again? Is it better off staying on the horse it's already riding? Or should it change horses midway through the race?

We find that the point of failure most often comes in the fourth stage of the change program—Act, when organizations find that plans don't get implemented as quickly as expected or achieve the desired impact. The reason is often hard to swallow: It's the result of a lack of discipline and rigor in tackling the health frames and applying the master strokes in the first three stages of the change program. When this is the case, most of the work already done related to performance is likely to stand, and the way forward is to invest time and resources in making good the missing health elements. In practical terms, this means completing the OHI, developing a health aspiration that targets a shortlist of management practices, digging into the mindsets that matter, and using the influence model levers to bring about any needed mindset shifts, taking care to build these actions into the implementation of the portfolio of performance initiatives in addition to other broad-based performance and health-related actions (e.g., interactively cascading the change story, mobilizing influence leaders, making it personal for a critical mass, and maintaining high-impact two-way communications).

More generally, the answer is to go back to the earliest moment of failure in the journey and start over at that point. For example, a company that didn't set clear medium-term "tough but doable" performance aspirations would do well to go back to the first performance frame ("strategic objectives") and start again, even if it has already gone a long way on its change journey. A company that's suffering from waning commitment and low energy levels but has laid a solid foundation in the first three stages may simply need to fine-tune the "ownership and energy" elements in the Act stage. And so on.

Most often it's health rather than performance factors that have been neglected. If that's the case, we'd emphasize that the right time to make a start—as would also be true in the personal health analogy—is always *right now*. Just as with personal health, every day you push forward on maximizing performance without tending to your health takes away from your longevity, so too with every day you push your change program forward with less than healthy practices, you are reducing the probability that your efforts will lead to sustainable impact.

## How Do We Measure Health Improvements Over Time?

We've talked about the OHI as the most robust diagnostic tool available to measure your health holistically. In Chapter 3, we likened it to the equivalent of getting a physical at the Mayo Clinic, widely regarded as one of the best hospitals in the world. Like a visit to the Mayo Clinic, however, it requires a meaningful investment of time. In the OHI's case, it's a 20-minute, 98-question survey. Given its intensity, most companies choose to use the full OHI annually, much like a human gets an annual physical.

In the interim, organizations typically employ a "pulse survey" approach to keep tabs on their health. This method asks a shortlist of questions related to the specific shifts being targeted. More specifically, a pulse survey typically consists of two questions per management practice priority, one being a question from the initial OHI survey so that the absolute change can be measured, and one that asks employees to say whether they feel they are seeing real progress on the topic. The survey then asks four questions related to the extent employees see positive role modeling, reinforcement mechanisms, storytelling, and an increase in their skills and confidence vis-à-vis the target mindset and behavior shifts. Two final, self-reflective questions are then typically asked: do the employees feel they are proactively leading the desired changes in their area? What interference is getting in the way of them doing even more? For an organization focused on three management practices, the pulse survey would be 12 questions in total

(6 covering the management practices, 4 related to the influence levers, and the 2 open-ended questions), and it would take only a minute or two to complete.

Pulse surveys have benefits beyond helping change leaders gauge progress. They also reinforce the importance of the health priorities in the minds of the respondents (in the spirit of John Doer's best-seller, *Measure What Matters*). It spotlights areas of best practice (and trouble areas) to be learned from. It can be deployed in targeted ways to test the efficacy of specific interventions (comparing the results of where an intervention has happened to the results of an area where it hasn't yet). It also reinforces personal accountability through the reflective questions at the end—and can be analyzed to create self-awareness where leaders have misconceptions of themselves. For example, if one's reports indicate they are experiencing tepid role modeling from their leaders, yet their leader feels they are a 10 on a 10 scale in proactively leading the desired changes, an insight to move a leader from being "unconsciously incompetent" to "consciously incompetent" awaits.

Another approach to monitoring health available to leaders that is becoming increasingly popular is what we call the OHI Live survey. OHI Live provides a reliable real-time read on health by asking employees just one randomized question a day on a rotating basis. Sampling is such that change leaders have a statistically valid read on organizational health on a daily basis—providing maximum visibility into what's working and where early intervention may be helpful.

## What Are the Most Important Takeaways for Change Leaders?

We have indeed covered a lot in this book, both in terms of breadth and depth. Beneath it all, we see three fundamental principles that sit behind everything you've read. They are right at the heart of our findings, and we'd encourage you to keep them in mind so that you stay grounded in the fundamentals of performance and health as you embark on and progress through your journey of leading change at scale.

The first principle is that *performance and health matter equally—and can be measured and managed with equal rigor.* As we've said previously, the most important word in the phrase *performance and health* is "and." In all the decisions you make and actions you take as a change leader, we encourage you to address both dimensions at once whenever you can. Bearing in mind that it's the health aspects that are most often neglected, we suggest you put extra emphasis on that side of the equation. We've seen time and time again that the more change leaders push themselves out of their comfort zone to address the health aspects, the further those zones expand such that, ultimately, they are equally comfortable with both sides of the equation. And we'd be remiss not to bring back a lesson we shared in Chapter 1: the better things are going on the performance-side of things, the more likely it is leaders will become complacent about organizational health. Change leaders need to guard against this tendency, and deal with it quickly should it arise.

The second principle is that *nothing changes unless people do*. In the end, improving an organization's performance and health comes down to getting people to do things in a different way. That requires us to understand why we behave the way we do both organizationally and individually (our underlying mindsets), and to take proactive steps to expand or outgrow any limiting beliefs that are present. We also need to accept and work with the "predictably irrational" inherent biases that are part of the human condition, no matter how silly they may seem in the cold light of logic. The approaches and tools we use should always be viewed through the lens of "How does this help us to understand and influence people in the organization to adopt the mindsets and behaviors we need to achieve our aspirations?" When our actions are guided by this principle, we are in the business of transforming human systems. Back to our analogy to the natural world, which we introduced in Chapter 4: by this we mean we're achieving the "can't go back" transformational effect of a caterpillar becoming a butterfly—not just creating a bigger, fatter, and fuzzier caterpillar.

The third principle we underscore is that *there is always choice*. As a change leader, we've done our best to equip you with insights and tools you need to influence employees to choose to change—both in terms of leading the proverbial horse to water (e.g., the influence model), as well as helping it become aware of its thirst (e.g., making it personal). At the end of the day, however, there can be no guarantees the horse will drink from the well. Even though it's not perfect, however, the approach we offer is certainly the best one out there as far as we're aware.

The concept of choice doesn't just apply to those you're looking to influence, but also to you as a change leader. This brings us back to the "red pill or blue pill" question. If we were having a conversation with you, we'd bet good money we could read what pill you'll choose by the language you use. We'll either hear the language of doubt such as, "I'd like to put what I've read into practice"; "I want to put it into practice"; or, "I will try to put it into practice." Or, we'll hear the language of mastery such as, "I will put what I've read into practice"; "I can be counted on to put it into practice"; or, "I am going to put it into practice."

The language of doubt comes from leaders who are very likely to become a statistic, reinforcing that 70 percent of change programs fail. Why?

Their language betrays their inner doubt. At the first sign of resistance they back down, reverting to the approaches they are comfortable with and that others won't challenge. The language of mastery, on the other hand, reveals an inner commitment and conviction that indicates they'll follow things through even in the face of initial resistance and expect to be judged on what they achieve.

So, where are you in relation to performance and health? Would you *like* to, do you *want* to, will you *try* to? Or *will* you, can you be *counted on* to, are you *going* to? In the spirit of a good Hollywood ending, we turn to another cinematic classic to offer you encouragement. To quote *Star Wars* Jedi Master Yoda, "Do or do not. There is no 'try.'"

■ ■ ■

David Whyte once wrote, "Work, paradoxically, does not ask enough of us, yet exhausts the narrow part of us we bring to the door."[1] The Five Frames approach addresses this paradox by tapping into our highest aspirations and deepest motivations at work. It does this by working directly with the human side of change with the same level of rigor and discipline as the technical side of change. When put into practice, it unleashes tremendous energy for change across large groups of people. Having witnessed the impact on many occasions, we can confidently say that leaders who use the Five Frames to pursue large-scale change will find that the work is among the most—if not *the* most—fulfilling of their careers. We look forward to profiling the success of your change program in our third edition!

# Notes

## Introduction

1. For a fuller treatment of the origin and evolution of research behind 30 percent success rates, please see Chapter 2. Regarding research in the time frame in which the first edition of *Beyond Performance* was published, some examples include: In 2008, John Kotter reasserted "the same appalling thirty-percent figure" in his book *A Sense of Urgency*; in 2008, Todd Senturia, Lori Flees, and Manny Maceda asserted, "70 percent of change initiatives still fail." Our 2008 and 2010 surveys of 3,199 and 2,314 executives respectively affirmed that one in three large-scale change programs are considered "very" or "extremely" successful; In 2012, John Ward and Axel Uhl reported, "We carried out 13 case studies of different types of business transformation... Of these, 30 percent were successful."

2. David Jacquemont, Dana Maor, and Angelika Reich, "How to Beat the Transformation Odds," *McKinsey Quarterly* survey, April 2015. In this survey, 7 percent of the sample followed the full Five Frames of Performance and Health approach that was published in the first edition of *Beyond Performance* (116 of the total data set of 1,669 responses. Note that the difference between this total data set and the 1,713 overall sample size is explained by removal of 44 "don't know" responses). Of those 116 responses, 84 (72 percent) were reported to be fully successful (success being defined as achieving performance objectives and preparing for long-term sustainability of these improvements). In the same survey, we also tested approaches developed since the first edition of *Beyond Performance* was published, which have been included in this revised edition. Companies that also employed these approaches reported success rates of 79 percent, as reported by Jacquemont, Maor, and Reich.

3. Gary Hamel, "Foreword," in *Beyond Performance*, by Scott Keller and Colin Price (Hoboken, NJ: John Wiley & Sons, 2011), ix–xii.

4. William C. Taylor, *Practically Radical* (New York: William Morrow, 2011).
5. Malcolm Gladwell, *Outliers: The Story of Success* (New York: Little, Brown and Company, 2008).
6. Data from multiple McKinsey-conducted longitudinal studies conducted from 1999–2005. These are explained further, and the data set shared, in Chapter 2.
7. Results from December 2016 OHI survey.
8. Personal interview.
9. Gary Hamel, "Foreword," in *Beyond Performance*, by Scott Keller and Colin Price (Hoboken, NJ: John Wiley & Sons, 2011), ix–xii.
10. Innosight, "Creative Destruction Whips Through Corporate America," Winter 2012.
11. M. W. Johnson, *Reinvent Your Business Model: How to Seize the White Space for Transformative Growth* (Boston: Harvard Business Review Press, 2018).
12. Based on analysis in Stuart Crainer and Des Dealove, "Excellence Revisited," *Business Strategy Review*, March 2002, updated to 2006.
13. Chris Bradley, Martin Hirt, and Sven Smit, *Strategy Beyond the Hockey Stick: People, Probabilities, and Big Moves to Beat the Odds* (Hoboken, NJ: John Wiley & Sons, 2018).
14. Emma Margolin, "'Make America great again'—who said it," *NBC News*, September 2016.
15. Information from Yasmeen Serhan, "François Hollande's Legacy," *The Atlantic*, December 2016; and Julian Birkinshaw and Gwen Delhumeau, "French Lessons: How Emmanuel Macron Is Turning the Tide on Populism," *Forbes*, June 2017.
16. Laignee Barron, "Malaysia's Longest-Serving Prime Minister Returns to Power Promising a Tide of Change," *Time*, May 2018.
17. Jesselyn Cook, "Justin Trudeau Promised 'Real Change.' Here's What He Accomplished in His First Year," *Huffington Post*, November 2016.
18. "'This Will Be a Government of Change,' Jacinda Arden Tells Caucus," *NZ Herald*, October 20, 2017.
19. "How Andres Manuel Lopez Obrador Will Remake Mexico," *The Economist*, June 2018.
20. Based on Annissa Alusi, Sergey Kiselev, Jukka Maksimainen, Gauri Nagraj, and Maksim Varshavvskiy, "Global Trends Influencing Economies Throughout 2050," *McKinsey Perspective*, November 2013; and Richard Dobbs, James Manyika, and Jonathan Woetzel, *No Ordinary Disruption: The Four Global Forces Breaking All Trends* (New York: Public Affairs, 2016).
21. Jon Clifton and Ben Ryan, "Only 1.3 Billion Worldwide Employed Full-Time for Employer," *Gallup World News*, August 2014.

22. Annissa Alusi, Sergey Kiselev, Jukka Maksimainen, Gauri Nagraj, and Maksim Varshavvskiy, "Global Trends Influencing Economies Throughout 2050," *McKinsey Perspective*, November 2013.

## Chapter 1 Performance and Health

1. Neville Isdell, David Beasley, *Inside Coca-Cola: A CEO's Life Story of Building the World's Most Popular Brand*, St. Martin's Press, New York, 2011.
2. Ibid.
3. Dean Foust, "Gone Flat," *Business Week*, December 20, 2004.
4. Adrienne Fox, "Refreshing a Beverage Company's Culture," *HR Magazine*, November 1, 2007.
5. Ibid.
6. Personal interview.
7. Larry Bossidy, *Execution: The Discipline of Getting Things Done* (New York: Crown Business, 2002).
8. Personal interview.
9. Josselyn Simpson, "Transforming a Nation's Education System: An Interview with the Chief Executive of Bahrain's Economic Development Board," *Voices on Transformation*, McKinsey & Company, 2010.
10. Results from December 2016 OHI survey.
11. Mel Cowan, "Pixar Co-Founder Mulls Meaning of Success," USC News Bulletin, University of Southern California, December 10, 2009.
12. Ed Catmull, "How Pixar Fosters Collective Creativity," *Harvard Business Review,* September 2008.
13. "Gulf of Mexico Oil Leak 'Worst US Environment Disaster,'" BBC News, May 30, 2010.
14. Sarah Boseley, "Mid-Staffordshire NHS Trust Left Patient Humiliated and in Pain," *Guardian*, February 24, 2010.
15. "VW Admits Emissions Scandal Was Caused by 'Whole Chain' of Failures," *Guardian*, December 10, 2015.
16. Quoted in Steve Kovach, "Samsung's Culture Needs to Change to Survive," *Business Insider*, November 5, 2016. Also see Yoolim Lee and Min Jeong Lee, "Rush to Take Advantage of a Dull iPhone Started Samsung's Battery Crisis," *Bloomberg*, September 18, 2016; Miyoung Kim, "Samsung's Crisis Culture: A Driver and a Drawback," *Business News*, September 2, 2012.
17. Ken Sweet, "Wells Fargo Board Faults Aggressive Culture in Sales Scandal," *The Mercury News*, April 10, 2017.
18. Sheelah Kolhatkar, "At Uber, A New CEO Shifts Gears," *The New Yorker*, April 2018.

19. Marco della Cava, "Uber Has Lost Market Share to Lyft During Crisis," *USA Today*, June 2017.

20. Rick Tetzeli, "Mary Barra Is Remaking GM's Culture—and the Company Itself," *Fast Company*, October 17, 2016.

21. Ibid.

22. Louis Lavelle, "Eight Isn't Enough," *Bloomberg Businessweek*, February 28, 2005.

23. Kurt Lewin, "Frontiers in Group Dynamics: Concept, Method and Reality in Social Science; Social Equilibria and Social Change," *Human Relations* 1, no. 1 (1947): 5–41.

24. George Johnson, *Strange Beauty: Murray Gell-Mann and the Revolution in Twentieth-Century Physics* (Vintage: New York, 1999).

25. Personal interview.

26. Personal interview.

27. See www.ted.com/talks/dan_ariely_asks_are_we_in_control_of_our_own_decisions.html.

28. In Stratford Sherman, "How Tomorrow's Leaders Are Learning Their Stuff," *Fortune*, November 27, 1995.

## Chapter 2 The Science of Change

1. John P. Kotter, *Leading Change* (Harvard Business School Press, 1996).

2. Michael Hammer and James Champy, *Reengineering the Corporation: A Manifesto for Business Revolution* (New York: Harper Business, 1993).

3. Martin E. Smith, "Success Rates for Different Types of Organizational Change," *Performance Improvement* 41, no. 1 (2002): 26–33.

4. With hindsight, we now know that their views were often influenced by their company's choice of recipe—a subject we explore in Chapter 3.

5. In terms of geographic reach, 35 percent of respondents are in North America, 29 percent in Europe, 26 percent in China, India, and other developed economies in Asia, and the rest in other regions. Half of the panel comes from privately held companies, 39 percent from publicly held companies, and the rest from government and nonprofit organizations.

6. The technical requirement for journals was a top 50 impact factor or immediacy score as calculated in the 2007 Journal Citation Reports—Social Science Data for Business Journals.

7. "Organizing for Change Management," *McKinsey Quarterly* survey, 2006.

8. See "Creating Organizational Transformations," *McKinsey Quarterly* survey, July 2008; and "What Successful Transformations Share," *McKinsey Quarterly* survey, January 2010.

9. Ian Davis, "How to Escape the Short-Term Trap," *McKinsey Quarterly,* April 2005.

10. Analysis based on Michael Beer and Nitin Nohria, editors, *Breaking the Code of Change* (Boston: Harvard Business School Press, 2000); Kim S. Cameron and Robert E. Quinn, *Diagnosing and Changing Organizational Culture: Based on the Competing Values Framework* (Reading, MA: Addison-Wesley, 1999); Bruce Caldwell, "Missteps, Miscues: Business Re-Engineering Failures Have Cost Corporations Billions and Spending Is Still on the Rise," *InformationWeek,* June 20, 1994; "State of Re-Engineering Report (North America and Europe)," *CSC Index,* 1994; Tracy Goss, Richard Tanner Pascale, and Anthony G. Athos, "The Reinvention Roller Coaster: Risking the Present for a Powerful Future," *Harvard Business Review,* November 1, 1993; John P. Kotter and James L. Heskett, *Corporate Culture and Performance* (New York: Free Press, 1992).

11. "What Successful Transformations Share," *McKinsey Quarterly* survey, January 2010.

12. Ibid.

13. C. K. Bart, N. Bontis, and S. Taggar, "A Model of the Impact of Mission Statements on Firm Performance," *Management Decision* 39, no. 1 (2001): 19–35.

14. J. C. Collins and J. I. Porras, *Built to Last: Successful Habits of Visionary Companies* (New York: Random House, 2005).

15. S. Lieberson and J. F. O'Conner, "Leadership and Organizational Performance: A Study of Large Corporations," *American Sociological Review* 37, no. 2 (1972): 117–30.

16. C. A. Hartnell, A. J. Kinicki, L. S. Lambert, M. Fugate, and P. Doyle Corner, "Do Similarities or Differences between CEO Leadership and Organizational Culture Have a More Positive Effect on Firm Performance? A Test of Competing Predictions," *Journal of Applied Psychology* 101, no. 6 (2016): 846.

17. J. P. Kotter and J. L. Heskett, *Corporate Culture and Performance* (New York: Free Press, 1992).

18. J. B. Sorenson, "The Strength of Corporate Culture and the Reliability of Firm Performance," *Administrative Science Quarterly* 47, no. 1 (2002): 70–91.

19. S. H. Wagner, C. P. Parker, and N. D. Christiansen, "Employees That Think and Act Like Owners: Effects of Ownership Beliefs and Behaviors on Organizational Effectiveness," *Personnel Psychology,* no. 56 (2003): 847–871.

20. G. Brown, J. L. Pierce, and C. Crossley, "Toward an Understanding of the Development of Ownership Feelings," *Journal of Organizational Behavior* 35 (2014): 318–338.

21. S. Davis and T. Albright, "An Investigation of the Effect of Balanced Scorecard Implementation on Financial Performance," *Management Accounting Research*, no. 15 (2004): 135–153.

22. J. Gittell, "Coordinating Mechanisms in Care-Provider Groups: Relational Coordination as a Mediator and Input Uncertainty as a Moderator of Performance Effects," *Management Science* 48, no. 11 (2002): 1408–1426.

23. A. M. McGahan and M. E. Porter, "How Much Does Industry Matter Really?" *Strategic Management Journal* 8, no. 4 (1997): 15–30.

24. T. R. Crook, S. Y. Todd, J. G. Combs, D. J. Woehr, and D. J. Ketchen, "Does Human Capital Matter? A Meta-Analysis of the Relationship Between Human Capital and Firm Performance," *Journal of Applied Psychology* 96, no. 3 (2011): 443–456.

25. J. Krueger and E. Killham, "Feeling Good Matters," *Gallup Management Journal*, December 8, 2005.

26. C. P. Cerasoli, J. M. Nicklin, and M. T. Ford, "Intrinsic Motivation and Extrinsic Incentives Jointly Predict Performance: A 40-year Meta-Analysis," *Psychological Bulletin* 140, no. 4 (2014): 980–1009.

27. S. F. Slater and J. F. Narver, "Does Competitive Environment Moderate the Market Orientation-Performance Relationship?" *Journal of Marketing* 58 (1994): 46–55.

28. C. Cano, F. Carrillat, and F. Jaramillo, "A Meta-Analysis of the Relationship between Market Orientation and Business Performance: Evidence from Five Continents," *International Journal of Research in Marketing*, no. 21 (2004): 179–200.

29. S. Zahra and J. Covin, "The Financial Implications of Fit between Competitive Strategy and Innovation Types and Sources," *Journal of High Technology Management Research*, no. 5 (1994): 183–211.

30. Paladino, "Investigating the Drivers of Innovation and New Product Success: A Comparison of Strategic Orientations," *Journal of Product Innovation Management*, no. 24 (2007): 534–553.

31. N. Schmitt, "Uses and Abuses of Coefficient Alpha," *Psychological Assessment* 8, no. 4 (1996): 350.

## Chapter 3 Aspire

1. "Creating Organizational Transformations," *McKinsey Quarterly* survey, July 2008.

2. *McKinsey Quarterly* transformational change survey, 2010.

3. *McKinsey Quarterly* transformational change survey, January 2012.

4. "Tesco Chief Sir Terry Leahy to Retire," BBC News, June 8, 2010; Marcus Leroux, "Sir Terry Leahy Checks Out at Tesco After 14 Years," *The Times*, June 9, 2010.

5. Eugene Kim, "Microsoft Has a Strange New Mission Statement," *Business Insider,* June 25, 2015.
6. Howard Schultz, *Onward: How Starbucks Fought for Its Life Without Losing Its Soul* (New York: Rodale, 2011).
7. At a press conference in July 1993.
8. Rajat Gupta and Jim Wendler, "Leading Change: An Interview with the CEO of P&G," *McKinsey Quarterly,* July 2005.
9. "What Successful Transformations Share," *McKinsey Quarterly* survey, January 2010.
10. "'Goals Gone Wild': How Goal-setting Can Lead to Disaster," *Knowledge@Wharton,* February 18, 2009.
11. Gautam Kumra, "Leading Change: An Interview with the Managing Director of Tata Motors," *McKinsey Quarterly,* January 2007.
12. In an annual survey conducted by Brand Finance and *Economic Times.*
13. Howard Schultz, *Onward: How Starbucks Fought for Its Life Without Losing Its Soul* (New York: Rodale, 2011).
14. Ben Rossi, "Kodak Presses the Digital Switch," *Information Age,* February 2006.
15. Chris Bradley, "Hockey-stick Dreams, Hairy-back Reality," *The McKinsey Strategy Corporate Finance Blog,* January 2017.
16. "Dan Ariely on Irrationality in the Workplace," *McKinsey Quarterly,* February 2011.
17. See, for example, Sheen S. Levine and David Stark, "Diversity Makes You Brighter," *New York Times,* December 9, 2015; "Better Decisions Through Diversity," *KelloggInsight,* October 1, 2010; Bill Synder, "Deborah Gruenfeld: Diverse Teams Produce Better Decisions," *Insights by Stanford Business,* April 1, 2004.
18. At a McKinsey leadership retreat for senior executives in February 2010.
19. *McKinsey Quarterly* transformational change survey, 2010.
20. John Roberts, *The Modern Firm* (Oxford: Oxford University Press, 2004).
21. Recipes were identified by performing a comprehensive cluster analysis of the OHI database.
22. Adam Morgan, *The Pirate Inside* (Hoboken, NJ: John Wiley & Sons, 2004).
23. Peter Burrows, "Welcome to Planet Apple," *BusinessWeek,* June 28, 2007.
24. Ibid.
25. Analysis of McKinsey's OHI database.
26. Chris Gagnon, Elizabeth John, and Rob Theunissen, "Organizational Health: A Fast Track to Performance Improvement," *McKinsey Quarterly,* 2017.
27. Bryan Burwell, "Tossing Off Pebble Costs the Cardinals Mountain of Bucks," *St. Louis Post-Dispatch,* Sports Section (NewsBank Access World News), November 23, 2003, F1.

28. Bureau of Labor Statistics (2016), "Nonfatal Occupational Injuries and Illnesses Requiring Days Away from Work, 2015." Retrieved from www.bls.gov/news.release/osh2.nr0.htm.

29. All insights drawn from OHI database.

30. William Schutz, *Profound Simplicity* (Los Angeles: Learning Concepts, 1979).

31. Taken from Alex Bellos, *Here's Looking at Euclid: A Surprising Excursion through the Astonishing World of Math* (New York: Free Press, 2010).

32. See "Creating Organizational Transformations," *McKinsey Quarterly* survey, July 2008.

33. For more on Coca-Cola's transformation under Isdell, see the beginning of Chapter 1.

34. Examples from Arne Gast and Michael Zanini, "The Social Side of Strategy," *McKinsey Quarterly*, May 2012.

35. Alex Dichter, Fredrik Lind, and Seelan Singham, "Turning Around a Struggling Airline: An Interview with the CEO of Malaysian Airlines," *McKinsey Quarterly*, November 2008.

36. Quoted in Bronwyn Fryer and Thomas A. Stewart, "Cisco Sees the Future: An Interview with John Chambers," *Harvard Business Review*, November 2008.

37. Personal interview.

## Chapter 4 Assess

1. "Chad Holiday," *Reference for Business*, 2019.

2. "E.I. du Pont de Nemours and Company Information Business, Information, Profile, and History," Company History JRank Article, 2019.

3. *McKinsey Quarterly* transformational change survey, January 2010.

4. Daniel Gross, *Forbes Greatest Business Stories of All Time* (New York: John Wiley & Sons, 1997).

5. Erin E. Arvelund, "McDonald's Commands a Real Estate Empire," *New York Times*, March 17, 2005.

6. *McKinsey Quarterly* transformational change survey, January 2010.

7. Tom Vander Ark, "Hit Refresh: How a Growth Mindset Culture Tripled Microsoft's Value," *Forbes*, April 18, 2018.

8. This story comes from Alan Deitschman, "Change or Die," *Fast Company*, May 1, 2005.

9. Quoted on Tim Gallwey's website www.theinnergame.com.

10. Roger Bannister, *The Four-Minute Mile* (Guilford, CT: Lyons Press, 1981).

11. University of Wisconsin research as cited in Bernard J. Mohr and Jane Magruder Watkins, *The Essentials of Appreciative Inquiry* (Arcadia, CA: Pegasus, 2002).

12. *McKinsey Quarterly* transformational change survey, January 2010.
13. Quoted in David L. Cooperrider, Diana Whitney, and Jacqueline M. Stavros, *The Appreciative Inquiry Handbook for Leaders of Change* (San Francisco, CA: Berrett-Koehlerz, 2008).
14. Personal interview.

# Chapter 5 Architect

1. Ram Charan, Dominic Barton, and Dennis Carey, "How Volvo Reinvented Itself Through Hiring," *Harvard Business Review*, March 12, 2018.
2. *McKinsey Quarterly* transformational change survey, January 2010.
3. Ibid.
4. Ibid.
5. *McKinsey Quarterly* transformational change survey, 2014.
6. Ibid.
7. *McKinsey Quarterly* transformational change survey, January 2010.
8. Stephen Hall, Dan Lovallo, and Reiner Musters, "How to Put Your Money Where Your Strategy Is," *McKinsey Quarterly*, March 2012.
9. Rajat Gupta and Jim Wendler, "Leading Change: An Interview with the CEO of P&G," *McKinsey Quarterly*, July 2005.
10. John Greathouse, "Steve Jobs: Five (More) Motivational Business Tips," Forbes.com, May 18, 2013.
11. Debbie Weil, "Three Things on Jim Collins' Stop-Doing List," *Inc.*, September 2008.
12. Rajiv Chandran, Hortense de la Boutetière, and Carolyn Dewar, "Ascending to the C-suite," *McKinsey Quarterly*, April 2015.
13. *McKinsey Quarterly* transformational change survey, 2010.
14. Leon Festinger, *A Theory of Cognitive Dissonance* (Stanford, CA: Stanford University Press, 1962).
15. *McKinsey Quarterly* transformational change survey, 2014.
16. Ibid.
17. Giancarlo Ghislanzoni and Julie Shearn, "Leading Change: An Interview with the CEO of Banca Intesa," *McKinsey Quarterly*, August 2005.
18. See, for example, B.F. Skinner, "Operant Behavior," *American Psychologist* 18, no. 8 (1963): 503.
19. Richard Pascale, Jerry Sternin, and Monique Sternin, *The Power of Positive Deviance: How Unlikely Innovators Solve the World's Toughest Problems* (Boston: Harvard Business Press, 2010).
20. Quoted in Robert Howard, "The CEO as Organizational Architect: An Interview with Xerox's Paul Allaire," *Harvard Business Review*, September 1992.
21. *McKinsey Quarterly* transformational change survey, 2010.

22. Felix Brück and Jack Welch, "Leading Change: An Interview with the CEO of EMC," *McKinsey Quarterly*, August 2005.
23. Quoted in James Dunn, interview with Jack Welch, *Leadership Victoria*, Spring 2003.
24. *McKinsey Quarterly* transformational change survey, 2010.
25. IBM research; John Whitmore, *Coaching for Performance: Growing People, Performance and Purpose*, 3rd ed. (London: Nicholas Brealey, 2002).
26. *McKinsey Quarterly* transformational change survey, 2010.
27. Ibid.
28. Victor H. Vroom and Kenneth R. MacCrimmon, "Toward a Stochastic Model of Managerial Careers," *Administrative Science Quarterly*, June 1968.
29. Quoted in Jon Ashworth, "Time to Move on for Chief Who Is Best 'Being Me,'" *The Times*, June 21, 2004.
30. Albert Bandura, "Social Learning Theory of Aggression," *Journal of Communication* 28, no. 3 (1978): 12–29.
31. Karl Lorenz, *King Solomon's Ring* (New York: Crowell, 1952).
32. *McKinsey Quarterly* transformational change survey, 2014.
33. Interview by Gautam Kumra and Jim Wendler, "The Creative Art of Influence: Making Change Personal," *Voices on Transformation* 1, McKinsey & Company, 2005.
34. *McKinsey Quarterly* transformational change survey, January 2012.
35. *McKinsey Quarterly* transformational change survey, July 2008.
36. *McKinsey Quarterly* transformational change survey, January 2012.
37. *McKinsey Quarterly* transformational change survey, 2014.
38. *McKinsey Quarterly* transformational change survey, 2010.
39. Robert B. Cialdini, *Influence: The Psychology of Persuasion* (New York: William & Morrow Inc., 1984, 1993).
40. *McKinsey Quarterly* transformational change survey, 2014.
41. Natalie J. Allen and John P. Meyer, "The Measurement and Antecedents of Affective, Continuance and Normative Commitment to the Organization," *Journal of Occupational Psychology* 63, no. 1 (1990): 1–18.
42. Robert H. Miles, "Beyond the Age of Dilbert: Accelerating Corporate Transformations by Rapidly Engaging All Employees," *Organizational Dynamics* 29, no. 4 (Spring 2001).
43. Lawrence M. Fisher, "Symantec's Strategy-Based Transformation," *Strategy + Business*, no. 30 (Spring 2003).
44. Noel M. Tichy, *The Cycle of Leadership: How Great Leaders Teach Their Companies to Win* (New York: HarperCollins, 2002, 2004).
45. See, for instance, Danah Zohar, *Spiritual Intelligence* (London: Bloomsbury, 1999); Don Beck and Christopher Cowen, *Spiral Dynamics* (Oxford: Blackwell, 1996); and Richard Barrett, *Liberating the Corporate Soul* (Oxford: Butterworth-Heinemann, 1998).

46. Susie Cranston and Scott Keller, "Increasing the 'Meaning Quotient' of Work," *McKinsey Quarterly*, January 2013.
47. John Mackey, "Creating a High-Trust Organization," *Huffington Post*, March 14, 2010.
48. Rajat Gupta and Jim Wendler, "Leading Change: An Interview with the CEO of P&G," *McKinsey Quarterly*, July 2005.

## Chapter 6 Act

1. Personal interview.
2. *McKinsey Quarterly* transformational change survey, 2010.
3. We look at the CEO's personal role in leading the transformation later, in Chapter 8.
4. *McKinsey Quarterly* transformational change survey, 2014.
5. *McKinsey Quarterly* transformational change survey, 2010.
6. Quoted in Peter de Wit, "Scaling Up a Transformation: An Interview with Eureko's Jeroen van Breda Vriesman," *Voices on Transformation* 4, McKinsey & Company, 2010.
7. Darrell K. Rigby, Jeff Sutherland, and Andy Noble, "Agile at Scale," *Harvard Business Review*, May–June 2018.
8. Rita Gunther McGrath, "How the Growth Outliers Do It," *Harvard Business Review*, January–February 2012.
9. *McKinsey Quarterly* transformational change survey, 2010.
10. Josep Isern and Julie Shearn, "Leading Change: An Interview with the Executive Chairman of Telefónica de España," *McKinsey Quarterly*, August 2005.
11. Data from 2012 McKinsey Survey.
12. Quoted in Carolyn Aiken and Scott Keller, "The CEO's Role in Leading Transformation," *McKinsey Quarterly*, February 2007.
13. All WAVE data comes from M. Bucy, T. Fagan, B. Maraite, and C. Piaia, "Keeping Transformations on Target," *McKinsey Quarterly*, March 2017.
14. Based on P. David Elrodd II and Donald D. Tippett, "The 'Death Valley' of Change," *Journal of Organizational Change Management* 15, no. 3 (2002); and an adaptation of the model proposed by Elisabeth Kübler-Ross, *On Death and Dying* (New York: Scribner, 1969).
15. *McKinsey Quarterly* transformational change survey, 2010.
16. Aaron De Smet, Martin Dewhurst, and Leigh Weiss, "Tapping the Power of Hidden Influencers," *McKinsey Quarterly*, January 2014.
17. Ola Svenson, "Are We All Less Risky and More Skillful than Our Fellow Drivers?" *Acta Psychologica* 47, no. 2 (February 1981).
18. Mark D. Alicke and Olesya Govorun, "The Better-Than-Average Effect," in Mark D. Alicke, David A. Dunning, and Joachim I. Krueger, editors,

*The Self in Social Judgment: Studies in Self and Identity* (New York: Psychology Press, 2005).

19. Michael Ross and Fiore Sicoly, "Egocentric Biases in Availability and Attribution," *Journal of Personality and Social Psychology* 37, no. 3 (1979): 322.

20. *McKinsey Quarterly* transformational change survey, 2014.

21. For example, see Damon Centola, Joshua Becker, Devon Brackbill, and Andrea Baronchelli, "Experimental Evidence for Tipping Points in Social Convention," *Science* 360, no. 6393 (2018): 1116–1119.

22. Speaking at the HR Vision Amsterdam, June 2014. See https://www.youtube.com/watch?v=NRFWYwB0tNQ.

23. *McKinsey Quarterly* transformational change survey, 2010.

24. Cited by Chip Heath and Dan Heath, "The Curse of Knowledge," *Harvard Business Review*, December 2006.

25. Quoted in Carolyn Aiken and Scott Keller, "The CEO's Role in Leading Transformation," *McKinsey Quarterly*, February 2007.

26. Giancarlo Ghislanzoni, "Leading Change: An Interview with the CEO of Eni," *McKinsey Quarterly*, August 2006.

27. Personal interview.

28. Giancarlo Ghislanzoni and Julie Shearn, "Leading Change: An Interview with the CEO of Banca Intesa," *McKinsey Quarterly*, August 2005.

29. Upton Sinclair, *I, Candidate for Governor, and How I Got Licked* (New York: Farrar & Rinehart, 1935).

30. D. Kahneman and A. Deaton, "High Income Improves Evaluation of Life but not Emotional Well-being," *PNAS* 38 (2010): 16489–16493.

31. Example borrowed from Dan Ariely, *Predictable Irrationality: The Hidden Forces that Shape Our Decisions* (New York: HarperCollins, 2008).

32. Example borrowed from Stephen Dubner and Stephen Levitt, *Freakonomics: A Rogue Economist Explores the Hidden Side of Everything* (New York: Doubleday, 2005).

33. Sam Walton, *Sam Walton: Made in America* (New York: Bantam, 1993).

## Chapter 7 Advance

1. Mark Westfield, "Lame Duck Bank Is Flying," *The Australian*, April 27, 2001.

2. Quoted in Ron Krueger, "A Cultural Transformation Journey," NSW Business Chamber, retrieved from www.nswbusinesschamber.com.au/?content=/channels/Building_and_sustaining_business/Sustainability/Sustainable_ business/culturaltransformationjourney.xml.

3. Mark Westfield, "Lame Duck Bank Is Flying," *The Australian*, April 27, 2001.

4. *McKinsey Quarterly* transformational change survey, 2014.
5. Quoted in ANZ's 2002 annual report.
6. Bill Gates, *The Road Ahead* (New York: Viking, 1995).
7. *McKinsey Quarterly* transformational change survey, 2014.
8. Joseph A. De Feo and William W. Barnard, *Juran Institute's Six Sigma Breakthrough and Beyond: Quality Performance Breakthrough Methods* (New York: McGraw-Hill, 2004).
9. Examples drawn from Susanne Hauschild, Thomas Licht, and Wolfram Stein, "Creating a Knowledge Culture," *McKinsey Quarterly*, February 2001.
10. See "What Successful Transformations Share," *McKinsey Quarterly* survey, January 2010.
11. Nathan R. Kuncel, Deniz S. Ones, and David M. Klieger, "In Hiring, Algorithms Beat Instinct," *Harvard Business Review*, May 2014.
12. S. Andrianova, D. Maor, and B. Schaninger, "Winning Your Talent Management Strategy," *McKinsey Insights*, August 2018.
13. Lisa Cameron, "Raising the Stakes in the Ultimate Game: Experimental Evidence from Indonesia," *Economic Inquiry* 37, no. 1 (1999); and E. Hoffman, K. McCabe, and Vernon Smith, "On Expectations and the Monetary Stakes in Ultimate Games," *International Journal of Game Theory*, no. 25 (1996).
14. "Who's Behind Me? The Powerful Overestimate the Support of Underlings," *The Economist*, June 2013.

## Chapter 8 The Senior Leader's Role

1. "What Successful Transformations Share," *McKinsey Quarterly* survey, January 2010. Subsequent references to research or surveys in this chapter refer to this source.
2. John Mackey, "Creating a High-Trust Organization," *Huffington Post*, March 14, 2010.
3. "Women at the Top: Indra Nooyi," *Financial Times* supplement, November 16, 2010, retrieved from http://womenatthetop.ft.com/articles/women-top/ca66b59e-ed92-11df-9085-00144feab49a.
4. Bronwyn Fryer and Thomas A. Stewart, "Cisco Sees the Future: An Interview with John Chambers," *Harvard Business Review*, November 2008.
5. Jia Lynn Yang, "A Recipe for Consistency," *Fortune*, October 29, 2007.
6. Lou Gerstner, *Who Says Elephants Can't Dance? Inside IBM's Historic Turnaround* (New York: HarperCollins, 2002).
7. Rupert Cornwell, "The Iconoclast at IBM," *Independent*, August 1, 1993.
8. William A. Sahlman and Alison Berkley Wagonfeld, "Intuit's New CEO: Steve Bennett," Harvard Business School case, May 24, 2004.

9. Giancarlo Ghislanzoni and Julie Shearn, "Leading Change: An Interview with the CEO of Banca Intesa," *McKinsey Quarterly*, August 2005.

10. Roger Malone, "Remaking a Government-Owned Giant: An Interview with the Chairman of the State Bank of India," *McKinsey Quarterly*, April 2009.

11. Quoted in Carolyn Aiken and Scott Keller, "The CEO's Role in Leading Transformation," *McKinsey Quarterly*, February 2007.

12. Speaking at a Techonomy conference, August 4, 2010.

13. Felix Brück and Jack Welch, "Leading Change: An Interview with the CEO of EMC," *McKinsey Quarterly*, August 2005.

14. Quoted in "Expert Business Advice: Want Great Business Ideas? Leave Your Office!" press release, August 4, 2004, retrieved from pressbox. co.uk.

15. "Who's Behind Me? The Powerful Overestimate the Support of Underlings," *The Economist*, June 2013.

16. Personal interview.

17. Quoted in Carolyn Aiken and Scott Keller, "The CEO's Role in Leading Transformation," *McKinsey Quarterly*, February 2007.

18. Warren L. Strickland, "Leading Change: An Interview with TXU's CEO," *McKinsey Quarterly*, February 2007.

19. John Mackey, "Creating a High-Trust Organization," *Huffington Post*, March 14, 2010.

20. Quoted in James Dunn, interview with Jack Welch, *Leadership Victoria*, Spring 2003.

21. Giancarlo Ghislanzoni and Julie Shearn, "Leading Change: An Interview with the CEO of Banca Intesa," *McKinsey Quarterly*, August 2005.

22. *McKinsey Quarterly* transformational change survey, 2014.

23. Todd Johnson, "'Dream Team' Documentary's Five Most Intriguing Moments," *The Grio*, June 2012.

24. Søren Frank, "Why Germany Won the World Cup and Why They May Not Be Perfect," *World Soccer Talk*, July 2014.

25. Dave Kerpen, "15 Quotes to Inspire Great Teamwork," *Inc.com*, https://www.inc.com/dave-kerpen/15-quotes-to-inspire-great-team-work.html.

26. Quoted in Carolyn Aiken and Scott Keller, "The CEO's Role in Leading Transformation," *McKinsey Quarterly*, February 2007.

27. Quoted in Suzy Wetlaufer, "Common Sense and Conflict: An Interview with Disney's Michael Eisner," *Harvard Business Review*, January 2000.

28. Quoted in Rosabeth Moss Kanter, Douglas Raymond, and Lyn Baranowski, "Driving Change at Seagate," Harvard Business School case, September 30, 2003.

29. Larry Bossidy, *Execution: The Discipline of Getting Things Done* (New York: Crown Business, 2002).

30. Nick Paumgarten, "The Merchant," *New Yorker*, September 20, 2010.

31. Johan Ahlberg and Tomas Nauclér, "Leading Change: An Interview with Sandvik's Peter Gossas," *McKinsey Quarterly*, January 2007.

32. Carolyn Aiken and Scott Keller, "The Irrational Side of Change Management," *McKinsey Quarterly*, April 2009.

33. Larry Bossidy, *Execution: The Discipline of Getting Things Done* (New York: Crown Business, 2002).

34. Stephen R. Covey, *Principle-Centered Leadership* (New York: Free Press, 1990, 1991).

## Chapter 9 The Change Leader's Role

1. *McKinsey Quarterly* survey of 1,147 executives in financial services, July–October 2009. See Joanna Barsh and Aaron De Smet, "Centered Leadership through the Crisis: McKinsey Survey Results," *McKinsey Quarterly*, October 2009.

2. See, for instance, Danah Zohar, *Spiritual Intelligence* (London: Bloomsbury, 1999); Don Beck and Christopher Cowen, *Spiral Dynamics* (Oxford: Blackwell, 1996); and Richard Barrett, *Liberating the Corporate Soul* (Oxford: Butterworth-Heinemann, 1998).

3. Joanna Barsh, Josephine Mogelof, and Caroline Webb, "How Centered Leaders Achieve Extraordinary Results," *McKinsey Quarterly*, October 2010.

4. See, for instance, William C. Compton, *An Introduction to Positive Psychology* (Stamford, CO: Thomson Wadsworth, 2005); Tal Ben-Shahar, *Happier: Learn the Secrets to Daily Joy and Lasting Fulfillment* (New York: McGraw-Hill, 2007); and Martin E. P. Seligman, *Authentic Happiness: Using the New Positive Psychology to Realize Your Psychology for Lasting Fulfillment* (New York: Free Press, 2004).

5. Kennon M. Sheldon and Sonja Lyubomirsky, "Achieving Sustainable Gains in Happiness: Change Your Actions, Not Your Circumstances," *Journal of Happiness Studies* 7, no. 1 (2006).

6. Gary Hamel, "Moon Shots for Management," *Harvard Business Review*, February 2009.

7. Roald Dahl, *The Minpins* (London: Penguin Group, 1991.)

8. In a commencement address at Stanford University in 2005.

9. Martin Seligman, *Learned Optimism: How to Change Your Mind and Your Life* (New York: Vintage, 2006).

10. Quoted in Jim Collins, *Good to Great: Why Some Companies Make the Leap … and Others Don't* (New York: Random House, 2001).

11. Ronald A. Heifetz and Marty Linsky, *Leadership on the Line* (Cambridge, MA: Harvard Business School Press, 2002).

12. E. H. O'Boyle, R. H. Humphrey, J. M. Pollack, T. H. Hawver, and P. A. Story, "The Relation between Emotional Intelligence and Job Performance: A Meta-analysis," *Journal of Organizational Behavior* 32 (2011): 788–818.

13. See, for instance, Daniel Goleman, *Emotional Intelligence: Why It Can Matter More Than Iq* (London: Bloomsbury, 1996).

14. See, for instance, Roy F. Baumeister, "Is There Anything Good about Men?," address to the American Psychological Association, 2007; Shelley E. Taylor, *The Tending Instinct: Women, Men, and the Biology of Our Relationships* (New York: Holt, 2003).

15. Jack Welch, *Jack: Straight from the Gut* (New York: Warner Books, 2001).

16. Jonathan Haidt, *The Happiness Hypothesis: Finding Modern Truth in Ancient Wisdom* (New York: Basic Books, 2006).

17. Joanna Barsh, Josephine Mogelof, and Caroline Webb, "How Centered Leaders Achieve Extraordinary Results," *McKinsey Quarterly*, October 2010.

18. W. H. Murray, The Scottish Himalayan Expedition (London: Dent, 1951).

19. Y. H. Kee and C. K. J. Wang, "Relationships between Mindfulness, Flow Dispositions and Mental Skills Adoption: A Cluster Analytic Approach," *Psychology of Sport and Exercise* 9, no. 4 (2008): 393–411.

20. Tony Schwartz and Catherine McCarthy, "Manage Your Energy, Not Your Time," *Harvard Business Review*, October 2007.

21. See, for instance, Mihály Csíkszentmihályi, *Flow: The Psychology of Optimal Experience* (New York: Harper & Row, 1990).

## Chapter 10 Making It Happen

1. David Whyte, *The Heart Aroused: Poetry and the Preservation of the Soul in Corporate America* (New York: Doubleday Currency, 1996).

# Recommended Reading

Ariely, Dan. *Predictably Irrational: The Hidden Forces that Shape Our Decisions*. New York: HarperCollins, 2009.

Barsh, Joanna, and Johanne Lavoie. *Centered Leadership: Leading with Purpose, Clarity, and Impact*. New York: Crown Business, 2014.

Beer, Michael, and Nitin Nohria. *Breaking the Code of Change*. Boston: Harvard Business School Press, 2000.

Boyatzis, Richard, and Annie McKee. *Resonant Leadership: Renewing Yourself and Connecting through Mindfulness, Hope, and Compassion*. Boston: Harvard Business School Press, 2005.

Charan, Ram, Dominic Barton, and Dennis Carey. *Talent Wins: The New Playbook for Putting People First*. Boston: Harvard Business School Press, 2018.

Collins, James C., and Jerry I. Porras. *Built to Last*. New York: HarperCollins, 1994.

Fifty Lessons Limited. *Managing Change: Lessons Learned—Straight Talk from the World's Top Business Leaders*. Boston: Harvard Business School Press, 2007.

Gallwey, Timothy W. *The Inner Game of Work: Overcoming Mental Obstacles for Maximum Performance*. London: Texere, 2003.

Goleman, Daniel. *Emotional Intelligence: Why It Can Matter More than IQ*. London: Bloomsbury, 1996.

Grant, Adam. *Give and Take: Why Helping Others Drives Our Success*. New York: Penguin Books, 2013.

Hamel, Gary. *What Matters Now: How to Win in a World of Relentless Change, Ferocious Competition, and Unstoppable Innovation*. San Francisco: Jossey-Bass, 2012.

*Harvard Business Review on Change: The Definitive Resource for Professionals*. Boston: Harvard Business School Press, 1998.

Heath, Chip, and Dan Heath. *Switch: How to Change Things When Change Is Hard*. New York: Random House, 2010.

Kegan, Robert, and Lisa Laskow Lahey. *How the Way We Talk Can Change the Way We Work: Seven Languages for Transformation*. New York: Jossey-Bass, 2003.

Keller, Scott, and Mary Meaney. *Leading Organizations: Ten Timeless Truths*. London: Bloomsbury, 2017.

Kofman, Fred. *Conscious Business: How to Build Value through Values*. Louisville, CO: Sounds True, 2007.

Kotter, John P. *Leading Change*. Boston: Harvard Business School Press, 1996.

Mourkogiannis, Nikos. *Purpose: The Starting Point of Great Companies*. Basingstoke, UK: Palgrave Macmillan, 2008.

Peters, Thomas J., and Robert H. Waterman Jr. *In Search of Excellence*. New York: Harper & Row, 1982.

Pettigrew, Andrew, and Richard Whipp. *Managing Change for Competitive Success*. Oxford: Blackwell, 1993.

Pink, Daniel H. *Drive: The Surprising Truth About What Motivates Us*. New York: Penguin Group, 2009.

Schein, Edgar H. *Humble Inquiry: The Gentle Art of Asking Instead of Telling*. San Francisco: Berrett-Koehler, 2013.

Senge, Peter M. *The Fifth Discipline: The Art and Practice of the Learning Organization*. New York: Random House, 1993.

Sutton, Robert I., and Huggy Rao. *Scaling Up Excellence: Getting More Without Settling for Less*. New York: Crown Publishing, 2014.

Ulrich, David, and Wendy Ulrich. *The Why of Work: How Great Leaders Build Abundant Organizations That Win*. New York: McGraw-Hill, 2010.

# Acknowledgments

Make a difference. Most humans are wired to want to do so. We've been thrilled to see how our first edition of *Beyond Performance* made a difference to many leaders and organizations who had the courage to take the red pill! Our hope is that this fully revised version makes an even bigger difference. Whether that happens or not is out of our hands. We are in control, however, of ensuring that those who have made a massive difference to us in helping shape the thinking that you hold in your hands are acknowledged and thanked.

The lineage of McKinsey & Company's thought leadership in the area of organizational excellence can be traced back to 1982, when Tom Peters and Robert Waterman wrote *In Search of Excellence*, one of the bestselling and most influential management books of all time. We owe them our thanks for the groundbreaking work on which we are building. Although we haven't been so bold as to entitle our book *Excellence Found*, our goal has been to provide leaders with new tools and fresh insights that meaningfully build on their work.

Credit for many of these tools and insights goes to a host of people who are passionate about helping leaders make successful change happen, who have taken time to share their facts, stories, and wisdom with us. It is our privilege to be able to pass on what we have learned from them. Among those we'd like to acknowledge by name are the 30 senior leaders from around the world who graciously spent significant time with us during our initial research:

- John Akehurst, former CEO of Woodside Petroleum, who in seven years transformed it into a top-decile performer, creating AU$7 billion of new shareholder value on a base of AU$3 billion.

- Don Argus, retired chairman of BHP, who oversaw the merger that created the world's largest diversified resources company, with a market capitalization of US$190 billion.

- Alejandro Baillères, CEO of Grupo Nacional Provincial, who restored Mexico's largest insurance company to its former glory.

- Saad Al-Barrak, former CEO of Zain, who led the transformation of the Kuwait-based telco into a regional presence serving 56 million people in the Middle East and Africa.

- Om Prakash Bhatt, chairman of State Bank of India, who transformed the former monolith into a Fortune Global 500 company.

- Pierre Beaudoin, president and CEO of Bombardier, who led its aerospace division through some of the most tumultuous times the airline industry has ever known.

- Sir William Castell, chairman of the Wellcome Trust, who led the UK's largest charity to expand its vision to challenges such as climate change and population control.

- Fulvio Conti, CEO of Enel, who masterminded the transformation of the monopolistic Italian energy player into an international force.

- Adam Crozier, CEO of ITV, who led one of the biggest corporate turnarounds in the UK in his former role as CEO of Royal Mail.

- Tom Glocer, CEO of Reuters and subsequently Thomson Reuters, who led his company to become a world leader in information services, with more than US$12 billion in revenue.

- John Hammergren, chairman, president, and CEO of McKesson, who led the company as it doubled its revenues to US$108.7 billion and rose to fourteenth place in the Fortune 500.

- E. Neville Isdell, former chairman and CEO of The Coca-Cola Company, who reinvigorated the beleaguered company, reinvigorating the brand and increasing the capital value of the company by $30 billion.

- Idris Jala, former CEO and managing director of Malaysian Airlines, who led the state-controlled carrier from the brink of bankruptcy to record-breaking profits in less than two years.

- Ravi Kant, vice-chairman and former managing director of Tata Motors, who helped it transform from a leading commercial vehicles manufacturer to India's largest carmaker, with a strong international presence.

- Leo Kiely, CEO of MillerCoors, who guided the company's growth through a succession of mergers and acquisitions that produced the third-largest brewer in the United States.

- Alan G. Lafley, retired CEO of Procter & Gamble, who led a change effort that doubled the company's sales, quadrupled its profits, and increased its market value by more than US$100 billion.

- Julio Linares, managing director and COO of Telefónica de España, who led its transformation from a loss-making domestic incumbent telco into a global player delivering double-digit revenue growth.

- N. R. Narayana Murthy, chairman and chief mentor of Infosys Technologies, who helped build a company started with US$250 in seed capital into a leader in consulting and information technology.

- Richard Parsons, who as chairman and CEO turned around Time Warner and subsequently became chairman of Citigroup.

- Corrado Passera, managing director and CEO of Banca Intesa, where he led a major turnaround, and former managing director at Poste Italiane, where he led the restructuring that produced the company's first operating profit in 50 years.

- Alessandro Profumo, former CEO of UniCredit, who led the bank through a series of well-orchestrated mergers that saw its market capitalization increase from €1.5 billion (US$2.2 billion) to €37 billion (US$53.4 billion).

- Michael Sabia, president and CEO of the Caisse de dépôt et placement du Québec, and former CEO of Bell Canada, the country's largest phone company, where he led a turnaround.

- Paolo Scaroni, CEO of multinational oil and gas company Eni, who previously led corporate turnarounds at Enel, Italy's leading electric utility, and UK glassmaker Pilkington.

- Roberto Setubal, CEO and vice-chairman of Itaú Unibanco, who led the merger of Itaú and Unibanco to form one of the world's top 20 banks by market capitalization.

- Jim Sutcliffe, former CEO of Old Mutual, who expanded the insurer's international operations in Asia, Europe, the United States, and South America before becoming chair of the U.K.'s Board for Actuarial Standards.

- Joseph M. Tucci, chairman, president, and CEO of EMC, who rebuilt the company after its share value fell by 90 percent in nine months at the end of the dot-com boom, and restored it to double-digit annual earnings growth.

- John Varley, former group CEO of Barclays Bank, who grew it into the world's tenth largest banking and financial services group, and the twenty-first largest company overall.

- Daniel Vasella, chairman and former CEO of Novartis, who led the successful merger between Ciba-Geigy and Sandoz, and holds the record as the longest-serving CEO in the pharmaceutical industry.

- Willie Walsh, CEO of British Airways, who within three years led the near-bankrupt Aer Lingus to become a profitable low-cost carrier, before leading a transformation at his current company.

- C. John Wilder, former chairman and CEO at TXU, who oversaw its financial and operational turnaround before leading it in one of the largest leveraged buyouts in the world.

All of their stories are full of human drama, high-stakes decision-making, battles won and lost, lessons learned, and wisdom gained. We've done our best to do justice to their extraordinary work.

Our experiences with senior executives helped inform our view of what works and what doesn't work. To understand *why*, however, we looked to academia. Why do leaders who follow their natural instincts to solve a problem themselves often unintentionally sabotage their ability to make change stick? How is it that hard-working, well-meaning, and capable people can find themselves working together in ways that prevent everyone from performing to their best ability? Why don't changes to incentive plans create substantively different levels of motivation? It was in the process of exploring questions like these that we were greatly assisted by academic colleagues:

- Heike Bruch, Professor of Strategic Leadership and Director of the Institute for Leadership and Human Resources Management, Universität St Gallen

- Douglas T. Hall, Morton H. and Charlotte Friedman Professor of Management, Boston University School of Management

- Andrew Pettigrew OBE, Professor of Strategy and Organization, Saïd Business School, University of Oxford

- Michael Tushman, Paul R. Lawrence MBA Class of 1942 Professor of Business Administration, Harvard Business School

- D. Sunshine Hillygus, Professor of Political Science, Duke University Sanford School of Public Policy, and specialist in survey research

We didn't stop at senior executives and academics, though. The reliability of our prescriptions—whether or not they yield the same results in different environments—has been directly tested by many change leaders: typically, people one or two levels below the senior leader who are responsible for activating change in their organization. As we mentioned in the introduction, for over 15 years, we have brought together groups of people around the world playing this role in a series of two-day peer-learning events known as the Change Leaders Forum. There is now a community of more than 3,000 alumni who have acted as a source of inspiration, a sounding board, and a test bed for the insights in this book. As they have often been the first to implement new ideas and approaches, they have had to endure the inevitable "Uh-oh" moments that happen whenever thinking is pushed beyond proven boundaries. They've done it so you don't have to! We can't thank them enough.

We also want to thank our colleagues at McKinsey who've worked side-by-side with us to develop the thinking and prove the approaches herein.

Starting with those who have spearheaded the design and delivery of the aforementioned Change Leaders Forums around the world, we thank Simon Blackburn, Arne Gast, and John Parsons. On the big idea of organizational health, we want to thank Aaron De Smet, Colin Price, Mark Loch, Chris Gagnon, Matt Guthridge, Richard Elder, Lili Duan, Brooke Weddle, Carla Arellano, and Lisa Seem for their pioneering work. Without these people and the others who support them, the Organizational Health Index and its database would never have existed, and neither would this book. Their contribution was not limited to the data whose breadth and depth provides us with such a distinctive research base; we also derived a huge benefit from their extraordinary ability to draw practical insights from this rich source.

Next up, there's Josep Isern, Mary Meaney (Scott's co-author of *Leading Organizations: Ten Timeless Truths*), Giancarlo Ghislanzoni, and Felix Brück, who all played important roles in the evolution of our thinking on how organizations can make large-scale change happen successfully and sustainably. This group laid the foundation for how to think in an integrated way about the performance and health aspects of a change program.

Then there's Michael Rennie, Carolyn Dewar (Scott's co-authors for *The Performance Culture Imperative*), Tom Saar, Gita Bellin, and Mike Carson, who have brought real innovation to the practice of influencing shifts in mindsets and behavior. In a context where managing the "hard stuff" is seen as table stakes, they have gone above and beyond the call of duty to bring insight, rigor, and discipline to managing the "soft stuff."

Further, we thank our colleague Lowell Bryan—the accomplished author of books such as *Race for the World*, *Market Unbound*, and *Mobilizing Minds*—from whom we've taken the concept of strategy as a portfolio of initiatives. Finally, we thank Joanna Barsh and Susie Cranston (co-authors of *How Remarkable Women Lead*), Johanne Lavoie (co-author with Joanna Barsh of *Centered Leadership*), and Caroline Webb (author of *How to Have a Good Day*) for their cutting-edge research into what it means to be a centered leader.

Special thanks also go to colleagues who have led the charge in relation to the all-important on-the-ground research, project management, and expert advisory of this effort, as well as the first edition. Svetlana Andrianova, Alice Breeden, Natasha Bergeron, Seham Husain, Taylor Lauricella, and Rodgers Palmer toiled tirelessly to ensure that what you hold in your hands reflects our latest and best thinking. Throughout the writing process, we've worked closely with Louise Tucker, our editor, who has made this book eminently more readable and understandable than it otherwise would have been. We also thank Rik Kirkland, who made the publishing process as pain-free as possible and in so doing put his editorial stamp on the content. Similarly, we are grateful to Bill Falloon, executive editor at

John Wiley & Sons, whose feedback and encouragement to create a revised edition has been invaluable.

And when it comes to making a difference, we also owe a deep debt to our families for their patience, sacrifices, and support for us in the writing process, in our careers, and in our lives in general. When writing this book, we didn't ask how many working days we had before the next deadline, but rather how many weekends. A heartfelt thank-you goes from Scott to his superhero wife, Fiona, and their three boys: Lachlan (also a published author!), Jackson (a special-needs teenager whose miraculous story will no doubt be published someday), and Camden (an avid reader when not pursuing his passion for water polo). Bill would like to thank his "life wife" and partner, Becky Keptner, for her unending commitment to him, their partnership, and their blended family—the Surrey Five. The kids—Will, Anna, and Vaughn—continue to be an ongoing source of laughter, motivation, and inspiration.

Finally, we want to thank you, our readers, for your interest in this book. We are thrilled that the core of the thinking from our first edition has stood the test of time and proven helpful. At the same time, we are pleased to share some new truths, better methods, and improved explanations in this fully revised version. We continue to want to improve ourselves and the impact of this work and, in this spirit, we welcome any feedback you are willing to share. You can reach us at scott.keller@mckinsey.com and bill .schaninger@mckinsey.com.

# About the Authors

**S**cott Keller is a senior partner in the Southern California office of McKinsey & Company. He joined the firm in 1995. He co-leads McKinsey's global CEO and Board Excellence service line, which is part of the Firm's Strategy and Corporate Finance practice. He is also a leader in the Firm's Organization Practice. He spends the vast majority of his time serving Fortune 100 CEOs and top teams in leading enterprise-wide, multiyear change programs, often also playing a direct coaching role to CEOs and senior teams.

He is the co-founder and a lead faculty member of McKinsey's Change Leaders Forums and Executive Transitions Masterclasses, and a featured speaker at multiple senior executive roundtable events, including at the World Economic Forum. He is also a guest lecturer at the University of Southern California's Marshall School of Business, University of Dublin's Trinity Business School, and St. Mary's College of California's Executive MBA program.

Scott has written multiple books on organization effectiveness, including *Leading Organizations: Ten Timeless Truths* (2017), *Organization Answers: A Practical Guide to Creating a High-Performing Organization* (2015), *Breaking New Ground: Making a Successful Transition into Your New Executive Role* (2013), *Beyond Performance: How Great Organizations Build Ultimate Competitive Advantage* (2011), *Performance and Health: An Evidence-based Approach to Transforming Your Organization* (2010), and *The Performance Culture Imperative: A Hard-nosed Approach to the Soft Stuff* (2007). Among his many articles are three of the most read *McKinsey Quarterly* articles of all time, "The CEO's Role in Leading Transformation," "The Irrational Side of Change Management," and "Increasing the Meaning Quotient at Work." Scott is also a featured writer on HBR.com.

Outside McKinsey, Scott is a co-founder of Digital Divide Data, an award-winning social enterprise that utilizes a sustainable IT-service model to benefit some of the world's most disadvantaged people. He is also the founder and leader of a global affinity group for parents of special-needs children.

An avid traveler, Scott has been to 194 of the world's 196 countries. His favorite place, however, is his home in Seal Beach, California, where he, his wife, and three boys enjoy the surf, sun, sand, and skydiving. He also plays lead guitar in a local heavy metal band.

Scott holds an MBA and a BS in mechanical engineering from the University of Notre Dame and has also worked as a manufacturing manager with Procter & Gamble and a photovoltaic engineer for the U.S. Department of Energy.

**Bill Schaninger**, PhD, joined McKinsey's London office in 2000. Bill was part of the team that created the Organizational Health Index (OHI) and the Influence Model. Over the course of his time at McKinsey, Bill has developed and led the Organizational Diagnostics team, the North America Transformational Change service line, and the Global Talent Management service line. He has also been the Global Knowledge Leader for the Organization Practice.

Bill now focuses his energy on helping CEOs, CHROs, government leaders, and other executives across a broad range of organizational topics. He brings strong experience in large-scale change, strategic human resources, organizational redesign, and culture.

Bill holds a BA and MBA from Moravian College. He also has an MS and PhD from Auburn University. Bill has been published in academic and professional journals and is a frequent speaker at conferences globally.

In his continued commitment to his community, Bill holds a seat on both the Board of Directors for United Way of the Greater Lehigh Valley and the Advisory Board for the Harbert College of Business at Auburn University, and he is a trustee for Moravian College.

# Index